Maker Innovations Series

Jump start your path to discovery with the Apress Maker Innovations series! From the basics of electricity and components through to the most advanced options in robotics, Machine Learning, and even the metaverse, you'll forge a path to building ingenious hardware and controlling it with cutting-edge software. All while gaining new skills and experience with common toolsets you can take to new projects or even into a whole new career.

The Apress Maker Innovations series offers project-based learning with a strong foundation in theory and best practices. So you get hands-on experience while also learning the key concepts, terminology, and creative processes that professionals such as entrepreneurs, inventors, and engineers, use when developing and executing hardware projects. You can learn to design circuits, program AI, create IoT systems for your home or even city, or build immersive environments for the Metaverse. Each book provides the building blocks to bring your ideas to life, and so much more!

Whether you're a beginning hobbyist or a seasoned entrepreneur working out of your basement or garage, you'll scale up your skillset to become a hardware design and engineering pro. And often using low-cost and open-source software such as Raspberry Pi, Arduino, PIC microcontroller, and Robot Operating System (ROS). Programmers and software engineers will also find opportunities to expand their skills, as many projects use popular languages and operating systems like Python and Linux.

If you want to build a robot, set up a smart home, assemble a weather-ready meteorology system, create a brand-new circuit using breadboards and design software, or even build anything with LEGO, this series has all that and more! Written by creative and seasoned Makers, every book tackles both tested and leading-edge approaches and technologies, for bringing your visions and projects to life.

More information about this series at https://link.springer.com/bookseries/17311.

Robotic Vehicles Design

A Coding Approach with the New ArduPilot Libraries

Julio Alberto Mendoza-Mendoza
Orlando Garcia-Perez
Jorge Fonseca-Campos
Juan Luis Mata-Machuca

Apress®

Robotic Vehicles Design: A Coding Approach with the New ArduPilot Libraries

Julio Alberto Mendoza-Mendoza
Mechatronics Department,
Interdisciplinary Professional Unit in Advanced
Engineering and Technologies (UPIITA) and
Network of Experts in Robotics and Mechatronics,
Instituto Politécnico Nacional (National
Polytechnic Institute),
Mexico City, Mexico

Orlando Garcia-Perez
Independent researcher,
Hidalgo, Mexico

Jorge Fonseca-Campos
Basic Sciences Department,
Interdisciplinary Professional Unit in Advanced
Engineering and Technologies (UPIITA),
Instituto Politécnico Nacional (National
Polytechnic Institute), Mexico City, Mexico

Juan Luis Mata-Machuca
Mechatronics Department,
Interdisciplinary Professional Unit in Advanced
Engineering and Technologies (UPIITA) and
Network of Experts in Robotics and Mechatronics,
Instituto Politécnico Nacional (National
Polytechnic Institute),
Mexico City, Mexico

ISBN-13 (pbk): 979-8-8688-1750-2
https://doi.org/10.1007/979-8-8688-1751-9

ISBN-13 (electronic): 979-8-8688-1751-9

Copyright © 2025 by Julio Alberto Mendoza-Mendoza, Orlando Garcia-Perez, Jorge Fonseca-Campos, Juan Luis Mata-Machuca

This work is subject to copyright. All rights are reserved by the Publisher, whether the whole or part of the material is concerned, specifically the rights of translation, reprinting, reuse of illustrations, recitation, broadcasting, reproduction on microfilms or in any other physical way, and transmission or information storage and retrieval, electronic adaptation, computer software, or by similar or dissimilar methodology now known or hereafter developed.

Trademarked names, logos, and images may appear in this book. Rather than use a trademark symbol with every occurrence of a trademarked name, logo, or image we use the names, logos, and images only in an editorial fashion and to the benefit of the trademark owner, with no intention of infringement of the trademark.

The use in this publication of trade names, trademarks, service marks, and similar terms, even if they are not identified as such, is not to be taken as an expression of opinion as to whether or not they are subject to proprietary rights.

While the advice and information in this book are believed to be true and accurate at the date of publication, neither the authors nor the editors nor the publisher can accept any legal responsibility for any errors or omissions that may be made. The publisher makes no warranty, express or implied, with respect to the material contained herein.

    Managing Director, Apress Media LLC: Welmoed Spahr
    Acquisitions Editor: Miriam Haidara
    Project Manager: Jessica Vakili

Cover image by eStudioCalamar

Distributed to the book trade worldwide by Springer Science+Business Media New York, 1 New York Plaza, New York, NY 10004. Phone 1-800-SPRINGER, fax (201) 348-4505, e-mail orders-ny@springer-sbm.com, or visit www.springeronline.com. Apress Media, LLC is a Delaware LLC and the sole member (owner) is Springer Science + Business Media Finance Inc (SSBM Finance Inc). SSBM Finance Inc is a **Delaware** corporation.

For information on translations, please e-mail booktranslations@springernature.com; for reprint, paperback, or audio rights, please e-mail bookpermissions@springernature.com.

Apress titles may be purchased in bulk for academic, corporate, or promotional use. eBook versions and licenses are also available for most titles. For more information, reference our Print and eBook Bulk Sales web page at http://www.apress.com/bulk-sales.

Any source code or other supplementary material referenced by the author in this book is available to readers on the Github repository: https://github.com/Apress/Robotic-Vehicles-Design. For more detailed information, please visit http://www.apress.com/source-code.

If disposing of this product, please recycle the paper

Table of Contents

Preamble xi

About the Authors xiii

About the Technical Reviewer xvii

Acknowledgments xix

Prior Knowledge and Target Audience xxi

Very Important Note xxiii

Disclaimer xxv

General Precautions xxvii

Relationship with Predecessor Books xxix

Part I: Introduction 1

Chapter 1: Introduction and Prerequisites 3
    Introduction to ArduPilot Libraries 4
    Advantages and Disadvantages of ArduPilot Libraries 9
    Differences Between Old and Current ArduPilot Libraries 10
    Introduction to OOP Work Format 12
    Description of Main Files to Modify Simultaneously in the New ArduPilot Libraries 29
    About Design and Its Scope 32
    Suggested Extensive Mechatronic Methodology 36

v

TABLE OF CONTENTS

Summary of Mechatronic Components of Prototypes in This Book 39

Linkage and Uses with Mission Planner 41

Chapter Summary 59

Part II: Installation and Description of Commands and Mechatronics of Generic Components Used in This Book 61

Chapter 2: Installation and Command Description 63

Basic Setup on Windows and Code Upload to Autopilot 64

Extended "Hello World" 93

Comparison of Commands and Features of Current and Old ArduPilot Libraries 96

Chapter Summary 105

Chapter 3: Mechatronic Description of Generic Components Used in This Book 107

Mechanics 110

    Shafts 110

    Couplings 111

    Bearings 114

    Pillow Blocks 116

    Carbon Fiber or Engineering Plastics 118

    Structural Profiles 119

    Supports 120

    Specialized Fasteners 121

    Clamping Elements 123

    Propellers 124

Electronics 125

    Brushless Motors 125

    Coaxial Contrarotating Brushless Motors 127

TABLE OF CONTENTS

    ESCs (Electronic Speed Controllers) 128
    Insulation and Connectors 131
    Batteries and/or Power Supplies 132
    Battery Chargers 133
    Brushed DC Motors 134
    Motor Drivers for Brushed DC Motors 135
    Remote Control 136

Control 137
    Logical and Analytical Control 137
    Logical Control and State Machines 138
    PD-Type Analytical Control 142
    Robustness vs. Adaptability 145
    Differential Robot Concept 148
    Explanation of the Difference Between Logical and Arithmetic
    Control Based on the Differential Wheeled Robot 151
    Closed-Loop and Open-Loop Control 154
    Gravity Compensation or Bias 154
    Direct and Indirect Control 155
    Dirty Derivative 157

Programming 159
    Hardware: Autopilots 159
    Software: Generic Modification Codes for All Book Projects 162
    Software: PseudoSetup 169
    Software: ArduPilot Time Management 170
    Software: Signal Filtering 171

Safety Requirements for the Aeropendulum and Quadcopters 172
    Verification of the Desired Operation of the Aeropendulum Without
    Propellers 173

TABLE OF CONTENTS

    Verification of the Desired Operation of the Quadcopter Mounted on a Test Stand and the Free Flight Quadcopter Without Propellers 175

    Chapter Summary 179

Part III: Extensive Examples 181

Chapter 4: Aeropendulum 183

    Description and Applications of the Aeropendulum 183

    List of Materials and Minimum Knowledge Required to Build an Aeropendulum 190

    Assembly and Component Details 193

    Electrical and Electronic Analysis 200

    About Connectors and Analog, Serial, and Real-Time Tests 204

    Restoring the Autopilot to Its Factory Settings 231

    Mechanical Analysis 232

    Control Analysis 238

    Code Analysis Illustrated with the Arduino Version 240

    Assembly and Testing with ArduPilot 244

    Chapter Summary 270

Chapter 5: Quadcopter Mounted on a Test Stand 271

    Description and Applications of the Quadcopter Mounted on a Test Stand 271

    List of Materials and Minimum Knowledge Required to Build a Quadcopter Mounted on a Test Stand 274

    Previous Designs 277

    Some Assembly Details 278

    Electrical and Electronic Analysis 279

    Mechanical Analysis 279

    Control Analysis 282

Code Analysis Illustrated with Old ArduPilot Libraries for Comparison 284

Redesign and Results with the New ArduPilot Libraries 292

Chapter Summary 312

Chapter 6: Free Flight Quadcopter, Altitude, Planar Position, and Orientation Control 313

Description and Applications of the Free Flight Quadcopter 314

List of Materials and Minimum Knowledge Required to Operate a Free-Flight Quadcopter 316

Electrical and Electronic Analysis 318

Mechanical Analysis 318

Control Analysis 320

Code Analysis 320

Assembly and Testing of the Free Flight Quadcopter Using the New ArduPilot Libraries 322

Chapter Summary 350

References: Selected References **351**

Appendices **363**

Glossary **397**

Index **399**

Preamble

The purpose of this book arose from the need to give continuity to my first book on the ArduPilot libraries. Although it may seem exaggerated, it only took a few years for the programming style to undergo radical changes. Thus, and although the first book is not entirely obsolete and we will even reference it throughout this reading, it is really necessary to provide an equally radical update.

This book, initially and due to the success of its predecessor (which was even translated into Korean and Chinese), was proposed as a second edition. However, considering the many changes in the use and coding of the libraries, we preferred to give it a new approach and present it as a mostly independent book with its own examples and discourse. Although, again, we decided to give it an extensive practical and didactic approach, noting that, due to our background, the text presents an orientation toward mechatronics and computer sciences.

We hope that this reading will be enjoyable and useful for you, just as it has been in years of teaching for our colleagues and students.

Julio, Orlando, Jorge, and Juan
Mexico 2024

"Tetikayotl amo uala tlen ipan se itlakayo uala tle ipan tochikanejneuil."

"Strength comes not from physical ability, but from indomitable will."

About the Authors

Julio Alberto Mendoza-Mendoza is currently a professor and researcher affiliated with the IPN at UPIITA, where he teaches subjects in Mechatronics, Energy, Bionics, Automotive Systems, and Telematics, and at UPIICSA, where he is part of the master's program in Informatics.

He is a member of the IPN's robotics and mechatronics expert network and an SNII1 researcher in Mexico's National System of Researchers.

He holds a postdoctoral degree from FI UNAM, a Ph.D. in Computer Science from CIC IPN, a master's degree in Advanced Technology from UPIITA IPN, and a degree in Mechatronics Engineering also from UPIITA. He was awarded the National Prize for Mexican Inventors by IMPI and Mexico's Ministry of Economy in 2020. He has authored two books published by Apress-Springer, with translations in South Korea and China.

His areas of expertise and interest include robotics in general, intelligent and analytical control, mechatronics, programming, electronics, intellectual property, and augmented reality applications, on which he has published JCR papers, has been granted patents, and spoken in international conferences.

ABOUT THE AUTHORS

Orlando Garcia-Perez, originally from Veracruz, Mexico, holds a master's and a Ph.D. degree in Autonomous Navigation Systems for Aerial and Underwater Vehicles from the Center for Research and Advanced Studies of the National Polytechnic Institute. He is currently a professor-researcher at the Autonomous University of the State of Hidalgo. His research interests include autonomous multirotor vehicle control, embedded systems, and optimal control.

His passion lies in mobile robotics, with ongoing projects focused on autonomous navigation using multirotors for tasks such as crop monitoring, terrain mapping, and disease identification through computer vision and drone technology. With a background in Computer Systems Engineering, he enjoys programming, particularly object-oriented programming for embedded systems like Pixhawk using ArduPilot libraries.

Jorge Fonseca-Campos was born in Mexico City, Mexico, in 1973. He received a B.S. degree in engineering physics from Universidad Autónoma Metropolitana in 1997 and an M.S. degree in optical physics from Centro de Investigación Científica y de Educación Superior de Ensenada, Baja California, Mexico, in 2021. He is currently pursuing a Ph.D. degree in the Department of Biotechnology and Bioengineering at Centro de Investigación y de Estudios Avanzados del

ABOUT THE AUTHORS

IPN (CINVESTAV). Since 2001, he has been a professor at UPIITA-IPN. His research interests include optics, data acquisition systems, solar energy, electronic instrumentation, data analysis, water quality monitoring, biotechnology, and unmanned aerial vehicles.

Juan Luis Mata-Machuca is a full-time professor and researcher in the Department of Advanced Technologies at UPIITA-IPN, Mexico, where he teaches mechatronics engineering courses. He earned his master's and Ph.D. degrees in Automatic Control from CINVESTAV-IPN in 2009 and 2013, respectively. He is a member of the National System of Researchers (Level 1) since 2015 and a member of the IPN's institutional expert network in robotics and mechatronics since 2018. He has authored and co-authored three books and over 40 papers in international journals and conferences with proceedings. He has supervised and co-supervised over 40 degree projects in mechatronics engineering and one degree project in telematics engineering. His research interests include chaos synchronization, nonlinear dynamical systems control and monitoring, nonlinear observers, fault diagnosis, feedback control, and fractional-order systems.

xv

About the Technical Reviewer

Gustavo Mandujano Rojas is a Mechatronics Engineer with a strong passion for technology, robotics, and artificial intelligence. From the beginning of his career, he has been involved in the design and development of autonomous systems, both in academic and professional settings. His experience ranges from creating immersive 3D, VR, and AR video games—including projects such as *Día de Muertos VR* and *La Planchada VR*—to actively participating in research projects on autonomous land, aerial, and underwater vehicles at CINVESTAV-IPN.

He is currently pursuing a Master of Science in Computer Engineering at the Center for Computing Research of the IPN (CIC-IPN), specializing in computer vision and deep learning for autonomous drone navigation. He holds certifications in machine learning and deep learning from institutions such as Stanford University and DeepLearning.AI and has complemented his training with studies in agile project management.

Among his notable achievements are the development of an early detection system for sugarcane diseases at the "El Potrero" sugar mill and multiple awards in national robotics competitions, including first place in the 120 lb category at the "Guerra de Robots" in 2016 and 2017.

Gustavo is driven by the motivation to apply technology to real-world problems, contributing to the creation of solutions that generate a positive societal impact. He firmly believes in multidisciplinary collaboration and lifelong learning as essential engines of technological progress. At

ABOUT THE TECHNICAL REVIEWER

Robotti3D, he has led initiatives focused on additive manufacturing, drone design, and rapid prototyping, consolidating a comprehensive vision of modern engineering.

Acknowledgments

I want to express my gratitude to my grandmother Guille, my pillar of support and formation, and to the people of Mexico.

Also I want to thank to the people who have shaped me and are my best friends and mentors including Tornillos Irator.

And last but not least to the National Polytechnic Institute (IPN Mexico), UPIITA and UPIICSA, and the IPN's robotics and mechatronics expert network, for funding the prototypes.

To SECIHTI and the National System of Researchers, for the economic stimulus granted.

—Julio

I would like to express my deepest gratitude to my friends from my master's and doctoral studies, whose support and camaraderie made the journey unforgettable. To my students, from whom I have learned as much as I have taught, your curiosity and dedication continue to inspire me.

To my professors, whose guidance and knowledge have shaped my path, and to my parents, whose unwavering support and encouragement have been my greatest strength.

Thank you all for being part of this journey.

—Orlando

I want to express my gratitude to my wife and children, who have always been patient with me and for the time that I have been unable to share with them. I also wish to thank my parents, my brother, my friends, and my colleagues, who have always supported me in my activities. I also thank

ACKNOWLEDGMENTS

Dr. Julio Alberto Mendoza-Mendoza, who invited me to participate in this project. Finally, I express my gratitude to the National Polytechnic Institute for the opportunity to pursue my passions: teaching and research.

—Jorge

I want to dedicate this book to my family, students, and colleagues.

I want to acknowledge to the Secretariat of Research and Postgraduate Studies of the National Polytechnic Institute for the research project grant SIP20250976.

Finally I want to acknowledge to SECIHTI for the research scholarship by the National System of Researchers.

—Juan

Prior Knowledge and Target Audience

The reader is expected to have basic knowledge in the following areas:

Mathematics:
- Differential and integral calculus of one variable
- Solving elementary matrix equation systems

Mechanics:
- Basic physics (statics and dynamics)
- Mass-spring-damper system
- Free body diagrams and resultant forces and moments

Electricity and Electronics:
- Basic electrical and electronic components
- Operation of DC and BLDC motors

Programming:
- Intermediate programming in Arduino (serial ports, motor control, etc.)
- Intermediate notions of object-oriented programming (OOP)

Control:
- Mass-spring-damper system

PRIOR KNOWLEDGE AND TARGET AUDIENCE

Language:

- Intermediate proficiency in English, as many important resources are available in this language

Finances:

- It is expected that the reader is aware that in a large number of countries, the components used here (especially hardware components) involve medium to high distribution or manufacturing costs and times, in addition to paying taxes and shipping fees, which must be carefully considered when developing their own prototypes.

Very Important Note

Unlike the older ArduPilot libraries, i.e., those from four or even three years before this work, modern ArduPilot libraries take object-oriented programming (OOP) modularity very seriously. Therefore, this book, unlike the title *Advanced Robotic Vehicles Programming* by Mendoza-Mendoza et al. published by Apress in 2020, no longer uses OOP superficially. It should be noted that in those versions, a single main file called Copter was modified, using it as an adaptable template where knowing OOP was more of a nod to its existence. This time, multiple files are modified through the concepts of modularity, encapsulation, methods, and attributes, so the reader MUST HAVE AT LEAST INTERMEDIATE KNOWLEDGE OF OOP.

Given the above, the audience is anyone interested in robotic vehicle programming, ranging from high school students to researchers, but with standardized knowledge of object-oriented programming. Since the purpose of this work is not to be a text on this computational paradigm, we will only highlight the topics that we consider necessary for the proper flow of reading.

For the audience that prefers other programming standards different from OOP, we want to mention that we would also prefer and love to use those paradigms, but since we are only users of the ArduPilot libraries and not their developers, we are limited to their predefined and standard use for the development of this book.

Disclaimer

Neither the authors, the publisher, nor the developers of the hardware and software used throughout this book are responsible in any way for the improper use that the reader or end-user could make of the prototypes and codes presented in this book. These are simply for educational and demonstrative purposes, so any damage or injury to the readers themselves, to third parties, or to objects or animals is the responsibility of each reader's understanding and care. The codes were tested and documented in the indicated software and hardware, but this is no guarantee that they will work directly on the end-user's systems and prototypes due to a variety of situations regarding versions of libraries, autopilots, compilation systems, etc. The reader should remember that "free" hardware and software change radically and volatilely.

The word "free" is quoted due to the final scope of the type of license, and it is the reader's responsibility to see these scopes on the official pages of the autopilot and ArduPilot libraries.

Neither the authors, the publisher, nor the developers of the hardware and software used throughout this book, under any argument or urgency, will answer questions related to individual or group projects of any reader. It is recommended to read this book properly or consult forums.
Neither the authors nor the publisher are responsible for changes or updates to the hardware and software used with this book, understanding that they are entities that evolve or conclude over time and such evolution or conclusion is entirely at the disposal of their developers.

General Precautions

Some or many of the hardware and software components used here may be subject to legally restricted use in some countries or operating zones, especially those concerning the free operation of unmanned vehicles and radio communication systems.

It is recommended that the reader be aware of local laws and regulations and put them into practice before conducting operations in public or private areas.

The operation of aircraft is particularly hazardous, so it is also recommended to have a suitable location for operating the devices described, using safety measures such as impact-resistant goggles, and having emergency stops in place whenever possible.
Never use propellers unless you are very sure of the correct operation of a system, including its mounting and control.

Relationship with Predecessor Books

The book *Advanced Robotic Vehicles Programming*, which is the first book in this "series" (if we can call it that, given that each text can be used entirely independently of the other), has material that tends to become more obsolete every year in terms of code, but also has a series of algorithms and useful descriptions for understanding this text, especially on topics related to data transmission, using motors other than BLDC; commented references; and above all, it allows the reader to make a proper comparison between old and recent ArduPilot programming styles.

On the other hand, our other book *Drones to Go* offers extensive details on modeling, control, and simulation of quadcopters, which complements in great detail the extensive projects in this book regarding free and mounted quadcopters.

Thus, among the three texts, a study plan or a branch of robotics or mechatronics concerning robotic vehicles design could be established, with the order indicated in Figure 1:

> *Drones to Go*—For the basics of drone modeling and control, specifically the case of quadcopters.
>
> *Advanced Robotic Vehicles Programming*—For the basics of general programming of robotic vehicles.
>
> This book—As a detailed practice book with a mechatronics focus, and also with an update on the new ArduPilot libraries.

RELATIONSHIP WITH PREDECESSOR BOOKS

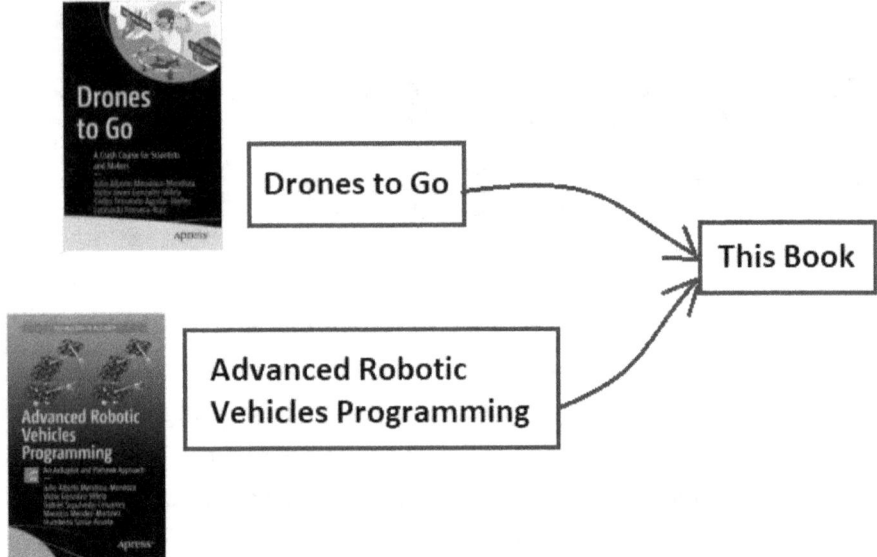

Figure 1. *Relation of this book to our previous works*

PART I

Introduction

CHAPTER 1

Introduction and Prerequisites

This first chapter aims to familiarize you with the ArduPilot libraries and the mechatronic design mode to be used throughout the book.

It presents a contextual introduction to the ArduPilot libraries, their history, main features, alternate modes of use, and differences between the old 2018 versions and the current 2023 versions. A couple of comparative examples between sequential programming modes and OOP are provided, highlighting the modularity feature based on the Arduino platform for better understanding (it is assumed that the reader has at least intermediate knowledge of OOP, as this book is not an extensive treatise on the subject).

A detailed description of the main modular files to be modified in the ArduPilot libraries in their 2023 version is also presented (currently, the libraries have evolved through at least four versions, but this version is precisely the one we started and finished writing this book with).

Finally, a section is added on the interaction between the ArduPilot libraries and their companion project, Mission Planner.

CHAPTER 1   INTRODUCTION AND PREREQUISITES

Introduction to ArduPilot Libraries

The ArduPilot libraries originated in the late 2000s, specifically around 2007, when Chris Anderson and Jordi Muñoz, the original founders of the renowned drone company 3DRobotics, began their development.

Initially, ArduPilot referred to both a series of development libraries and an autopilot system (i.e., both software and hardware specialized in designing autonomous or semi-autonomous unmanned vehicles, primarily aerial). However, the maintenance and documentation of the software libraries have endured and gained popularity among developers and users worldwide.

This is due to the fact that the ArduPilot software project was designed from its inception to be relatively simple to use, with a complexity similar to Arduino libraries (as reflected in part of its name).

Over the years, the project has become more complex but also more powerful. Currently, it is not only useful for UAV flight but also for terrestrial, aquatic, and even amphibious vehicles.

A couple of notable examples among many are the bird deterrent project in a contaminated lake in Montana (WaterDog) and a company of colleagues in Mexico dedicated to industrial robotic projects using ArduPilot.

> Meet The Man Who Shoots At Birds All Day To Keep Them Off A Toxic Pit, Business Insider

```
https://www.youtube.com/watch?v=qtlPTE-UmY4
CRBT
https://www.robotsmoviles.com.mx/
```

CHAPTER 1   INTRODUCTION AND PREREQUISITES

Currently ArduPilot has different programming modes as indicated in Table 1-1; some of the most notable ones are

- Matlab Simulink: Useful for the scientific community; this is currently the most widely used language by this group.

- ROS: A growing alternative used by the scientific and technological community, especially those related to robotic vehicles development.

- LUA Scripts: These allow modifying the behavior of pre-defined vehicles by the ArduPilot team in a relatively fast way and without altering the core flight code, using the syntax of a programming language called LUA, somewhat similar to PYTHON in ease but with more direct machine interaction.

- Superficially from the GUI called Mission Planner: This is one of the most widely used modes, especially by users who don't want to spend too much time on code and just want to operate an unmanned vehicle by simply defining desired route values and some actions like servo or camera activation without delving into deep modeling, programming, communications, and control (with many limitations, especially regarding available pre-defined vehicles).

- Directly from the base code using C++: This is directly relevant to this book and is considered the most complex mode but also offers the greatest development and customization possibilities, as it allows modifying the core flight code in depth and detail.

CHAPTER 1 INTRODUCTION AND PREREQUISITES

Table 1-1. ArduPilot programming modes

ArduPilot programming mode	Required software knowledge	Who could make the most of it	Scopes	Additional comments
Matlab Simulink	Matlab Simulink	A scientist or researcher who wants to use libraries without wasting time	Up to this point, it only supported predefined robotic platforms, not custom ones	Given its reliance on Matlab and Simulink, this option doesn't guarantee real-time performance or fast process execution due to its non-embedded nature
ROS	Python or C++, Linux	Same as the previous case, but to interface with specific hardware like cameras or sensor systems more quickly.	It's currently the second most powerful way to utilize ArduPilot libraries, enabling control of nearly the entire hardware and software ecosystem, albeit with some ROS-related limitations.	An even more powerful alternative to ROS is using ArduPilot libraries directly to generate custom DLLs for specific hardware or software, though ROS was created to simplify the process and avoid such low-level details.

Mission Planner	It simply requires using the interface, which is fast, albeit non-trivial, and doesn't require any programming knowledge	Anyone more interested in rapid application development than in learning about drones, robotics, or control systems	This mode is limited to predefined robotic platforms and is only useful for parameter tuning or basic action programming. The vehicle is modeled as a particle with XYZ motion and heading angle, without detailed control or individual motor programming	This mode is popular among rapid prototypers and makers. A recommended read on this topic is by Ty Audronis.

(continued)

Table 1-1. (*continued*)

ArduPilot programming mode	Required software knowledge	Who could make the most of it	Scopes	Additional comments
LUA scripts	This mode enhances the previous one by adding internal customization capabilities via LUA scripting, which is similar to Python in syntax and usage	It's perfect for customizing actions based on events or state machines, like triggering sensors or lights at specific locations or intervals.	It builds on Mission Planner's capabilities with added scripting flexibility for customizing certain actions.	This mode is becoming more widely used.
Direct implementation in C++	This mode offers the highest level of control, leveraging object-oriented C++ programming	Users who want to design and modify every aspect of the code, from control to sensors	This mode offers total control, allowing users to define a custom robotic platform from scratch, beyond pre-built templates	Requires advanced engineering and programming skills

> **Tip** To learn more about the programming modes described, consult
>
> The official ArduPilot project page: https://ardupilot.org
>
> My previous book available on Springer: *Advanced Robotic Vehicles Programming*
>
> The book by Ty Audronis: *Designing Purpose-Built Drones for ArduPilot Pixhawk 2.1*

Advantages and Disadvantages of ArduPilot Libraries

The advantages typically surpass the disadvantages in terms of application and utility. Key benefits include

- A large global user community and forums.
- Regular updates.
- Open source flexibility. This allows for total customization, from vehicle setup and individual motor control to communication system design and control programming.
- Annual conferences, showcase updates and activities, with live streams on social media.
- Compatibility with various hardware and software platforms.
- They are free and largely open for use (Don't forget to check the license limitations).

CHAPTER 1   INTRODUCTION AND PREREQUISITES

- They are pioneers in their field.
- They offer versatility across fixed robotic platforms and diverse vehicle types.

However, there are some drawbacks:

- ArduPilot libraries are becoming increasingly complex, requiring advanced programming knowledge.
- Library installation is notoriously difficult and volatile.
- Rapid updates can make previous knowledge obsolete, with significant changes in syntax and use between versions.
- While changes may seem subtle, they can have a profound impact on functionality.
- The forums and official documentation can be overwhelming and hard to navigate.
- ArduPilot remains as a unique and powerful tool. This could potentially lead to a technological monopoly.

Differences Between Old and Current ArduPilot Libraries

The key points are outlined in Table 1-2 and further detailed in the book.

Table 1-2. *Difference between old and current ArduPilot libraries in terms of OOP features*

Feature	Older libraries	Current libraries
OOP	For illustrative purposes only	Mandatory mode
Hardware compatibility across various autopilot systems	Medium	Very high
Cross-platform compatibility and diverse programming options	Medium	Highly flexible with multiple options: ROS Simulink LUA Python Scripts C++ Mission planner
Mission Planner integration	Medium	Extensive, particularly for setting up variables, commands, sensors, radio control, and serial data interfaces
Required configuration files to edit	One, usable as a template	Several for modularity; although it's an already clarified advantage of OOP, it also represents the disadvantage of not directly knowing which file and function affect others.
Base platform	nuttix	chibios
Ease of use	Very high	Mid-range; on the other hand, allows many more functionalities and code-order

(*continued*)

Table 1-2. (*continued*)

Feature	Older libraries	Current libraries
Documentation	Medium	Extended
Basic commands	They are as easy as using Arduino	Notable changes, some commands were kept and others changed or coding and syntax alternatives were created

Introduction to OOP Work Format

The ArduPilot libraries have used a HAL (Hardware Abstraction Layer) format based on OOP (Object-Oriented Programming) since their creation. Until my first book on this topic, it wasn't necessary to deeply understand this concept; it was enough to modify the base file called Copter. However, the most recent versions visibly exploit the modularity feature of this programming paradigm, not limiting themselves to editing a single file but several of them.

In this way, we consider it useful for the reader to teach them how this modularity feature works (the rest of the OOP properties are not as essential for understanding this book).

Tip Although at first it may seem like a quite rough and even questionable way of programming (especially if very short coding tasks are performed), the use of OOP in ArduPilot facilitates the location, modification, and coding of specific tasks without altering the entire main program. Another much more evident and more important reason to use OOP is that it was designed this way by the original programmers of ArduPilot along with all its existing software. Sorry to the functional programmers, we also wish to program like that, haha; remember, when in Rome, do as the Romans do ;).

CHAPTER 1 INTRODUCTION AND PREREQUISITES

For the rest of the OOP properties and their general understanding, we recommend

> Books on C++ by Joyanes, courses on the topic by Jean Cedric Chappelier, and some Apress books described in the reference section of this book.
>
> Also the SOLID principles of OOP
>
> https://www.digitalocean.com/community/conceptual-articles/s-o-l-i-d-the-first-five-principles-of-object-oriented-design

Next, we will explain and use the concept of modularity seen from the Arduino platform:

Let's start with a simple task performed in a single file called LED. ino as shown in Figure 1-1, whose objective is to turn on a couple of LEDs intermittently as indicated in Listing 1-1.

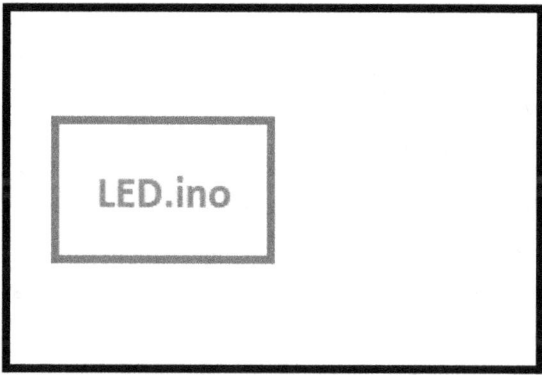

Figure 1-1. *A working folder for turning on a couple of LEDs with a single file without modularity*

CHAPTER 1 INTRODUCTION AND PREREQUISITES

Listing 1-1. Blinking a couple of LEDs without OOP nor modularity

```
// Define the pins associated with each LED
int led1=5;
int led2=6;
// The setup is defined below, which sets the previously
indicated pins as outputs
void setup()
{
  pinMode(led1, OUTPUT);
  pinMode(led2, OUTPUT);
}
// Now the main program that runs continuously while the
Arduino is powered.
void loop() {
  // LED 1 is turned on and the program pauses;
  // after the pause, LED 1 is turned off.

  digitalWrite(led1,HIGH);
  delay(1000);
  digitalWrite(led1,LOW);
```

// Next, LED 2 is turned on, the program pauses, and after the pause, LED 2 is turned off, repeating the process of turning on LED 1 and LED 2 in a two-light traffic light sequence.

```
  digitalWrite(led2,HIGH);
  delay(2000);
  digitalWrite(led2,LOW);
}
```

CHAPTER 1   INTRODUCTION AND PREREQUISITES

Let's rewrite this code using OOP, splitting it into two files as illustrated in Figure 1-2: one to define the initialization and lighting functions, and another for the main execution.

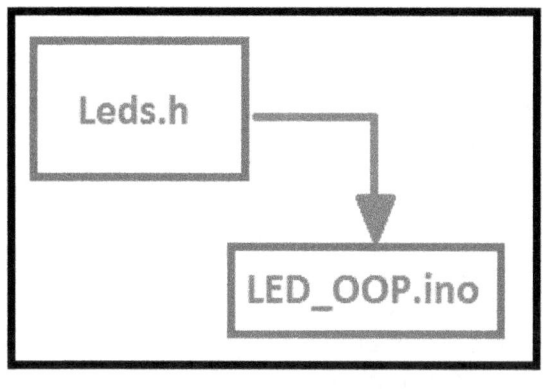

Working folder

Figure 1-2. *Working folder to turn on an LED with more than one file using OOP modularity*

The file containing the initialization and lighting functions, called Leds.h, is described in Listing 1-2 as follows. Note that the HIGH and LOW constants are native to the Arduino environment; otherwise, they must be defined:

Listing 1-2. Blinking a couple of LEDs with OOP and modularity Leds.h file

```
// Class name
class Led
{
// Attributes or variables, in this case, pin number and time
duration in milliseconds
  private:
  int pin, tiempoms;
```

15

CHAPTER 1   INTRODUCTION AND PREREQUISITES

// Methods or functions, in this case, the necessary class constructor and the turn-on, turn-off, and initialization functions

```
  public:
  Led(int pin, int tiempoms);
  void Encender(); // turn on function
  void Apagar(); // turn off function
  void init();
};
// End of the class
```

// Definition of the constructor function
```
Led::Led(int pin, int tiempoms)
{
  this->pin=pin;
  this->tiempoms=tiempoms;
}
```

// Definition of the initialization function to be used in the Arduino-style setup in the main code LED_OOP.ino

```
void Led::init()
{
  pinMode(pin,OUTPUT);
}
```

// Definition of the turn on function in this case it uses the turn off function inside

```
void Led::Encender()
{
  digitalWrite(pin,HIGH);
  delay(tiempoms);
  Apagar();  // turn off inside
}
// Definition of the turn off function
void Led::Apagar()
{
  digitalWrite(pin,LOW);
}
```

Next is the main file LED_OOP.ino described in Listing 1-3, which uses the previous file:

Listing 1-3. Blinking a couple of LEDs with OOP and modularity LED_OOP.ino file

```
// The first line calls the file where the classes, methods,
// and attributes were defined, so they must be in the same folder
// or provide the address of that file, although it's most common
// for them to share the same folder.
#include "Leds.h"

// Objects of type LED are created, one associated with pin 5
// and the other with pin 6, as well as the times they should be
// turn-on and turn-off.

Led led1(5,1000);
Led led2(6,2000);

// In the setup, the init methods are invoked for each LED.
```

CHAPTER 1 INTRODUCTION AND PREREQUISITES

```
void setup()
{
  led1.init();
  led2.init();
}

void loop()
{
```

// And now, the turn-on and turn-off methods. Note from the .h file that the turn-on method contains the turn-off method, but you can modify them according to your needs.

```
  led1.Encender();
  led2.Encender();
}
```

Let's repeat the process for a slightly more complex task: a basic line-follower robot.

Figure 1-3 describes the task to be performed. First, our line follower consists of two motorized wheels, right and left. It also has two sensors that detect the color black, left and right. It has a pair of non-motorized support wheels, a path to follow, and a goal (both black in this case), and the background of our scenario is considered white.

CHAPTER 1 INTRODUCTION AND PREREQUISITES

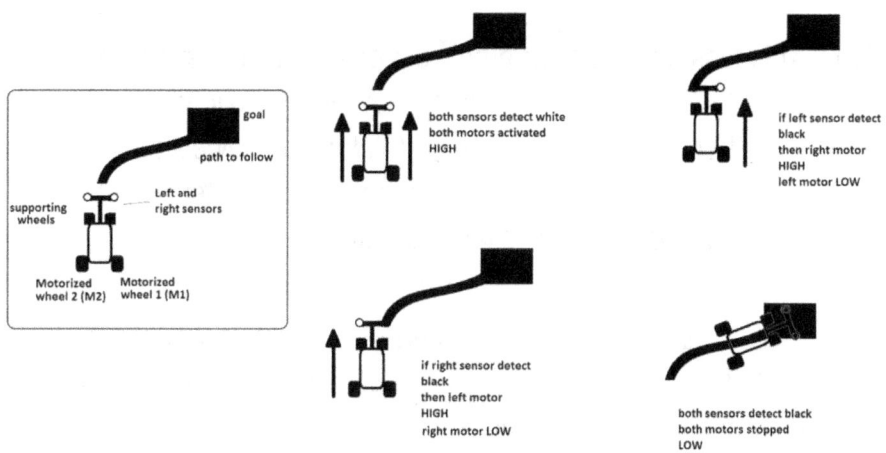

Figure 1-3. *A line-follower's basic tasks*

Once the system is described, the task consists of four basic scenarios:

- When both sensors do not detect the color black, in this case, both motors turn on.

- When the right sensor detects the path in black, the robot will try to rotate to stay roughly in the middle of the path by activating the left motor and turning off the right motor.

- If the sensor that detects the path is the left one, the right motor should turn on and the left motor should turn off.

- Finally, when both sensors detect the color black, it means they have reached the goal; in this case, both motors turn off.

19

CHAPTER 1 INTRODUCTION AND PREREQUISITES

Tip This task has been extremely simplified; it's the simplest way to perform the task, and it can cause slow, jerky movements with a lot of chattering, and even false goal detection. However, for our coding purposes, it's adequate. For smoother and faster algorithms, there's plenty of information available online.

Once said that, the non-modular and non-OOP Arduino code is illustrated in Listing 1-4 to be executed in a single file as indicated in Figure 1-4—in this case, Follower.ino.

Working folder

Figure 1-4. *Working folder for a line follower with a single file without using modularity*

Listing 1-4. Line follower code without OOP nor modularity

```
// Define the two pins for sensors and the two for motors, in this case, assuming continuous photoresistor sensors (analog light sensors with a range of 0-1024 or white-black)
const int left_sensor =A0;
```

CHAPTER 1   INTRODUCTION AND PREREQUISITES

```
const int right_sensor=A1;
const int left_motor=5;
const int right_motor=6;
```

// Everything above the threshold value of 400 is black and everything below or equal is white

```
const int umbral=400;
```

// Now we configure the input and output ports for sensors and actuators

```
void setup()
{
  pinMode(left_sensor,INPUT);
  pinMode(right_sensor,INPUT);
  pinMode(left_motor,OUTPUT);
  pinMode(right_motor,OUTPUT);
}
```

// And now the main loop, which runs indefinitely while the robot is powered

```
void loop()

{

// Read the two sensors

  int lectura_l_sensor=analogRead(left_sensor);
  int lectura_r_sensor=analogRead(right_sensor);
```

// First case, if both sensors detect white, then both motors activate

CHAPTER 1   INTRODUCTION AND PREREQUISITES

```
  if(lectura_l_sensor<umbral && lectura_r_sensor< umbral)
  {
   digitalWrite(left_motor,HIGH);
   digitalWrite(right_motor,HIGH);
  }
// Second case, if both sensors detect black, the car is at the
goal and both motors stop
  else if(lectura_l_sensor>umbral && lectura_r_sensor> umbral)
  {
   digitalWrite(left_motor,LOW);
   digitalWrite(right_motor,LOW);
  }
// Third case, if the left sensor detects black, the right
motor activates and the left motor turns off
  else if(lectura_l_sensor>umbral)
  {
   digitalWrite(left_motor,LOW);
   digitalWrite(right_motor,HIGH);
  }
// Fourth case, if the right sensor detects black, the left
motor activates and the right motor turns off
  else if(lectura_r_sensor>umbral)
  {
   digitalWrite(left_motor,HIGH);
   digitalWrite(right_motor,LOW);
  }
// A small pause to allow the motors and actuators to react;
later, we'll see that real-time management is preferable to
pauses, but for this introductory code, it's not important.
```

After the pause, the sequence of reading sensors and motor actions repeats.

```
  delay(10);
}
```

Now the Modular OOP version, this version consists of three files as presented in Figure 1-5.

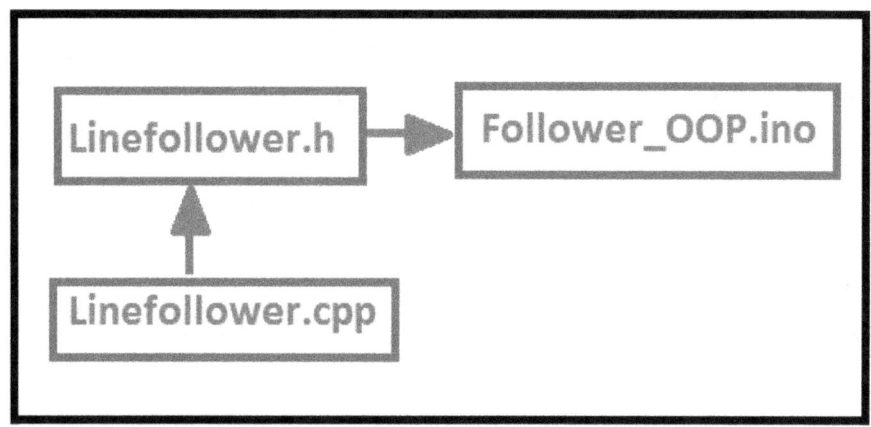

Working folder

Figure 1-5. Working folder for a line follower with multiple files using OOP modularity and the relationship among those files

Similar to the style used in programming (including ArduPilot libraries), the definition of the class methods has been separated into a .cpp file from its declaration now exclusively in the .h file (in the first example, both the definition and declaration were in the same file with a .h extension). However, the .h file remains the link between the classes to be used and the main program as follows:

Now, in Listing 1-5, you have the Linefollower.h file, which contains exclusively the declaration of functions or methods and attributes or variables of the class.

CHAPTER 1   INTRODUCTION AND PREREQUISITES

Listing 1-5. Line follower code with OOP and modularity
Linefollower.h file

```
class Seguidor   //the follower class
{
// its attributes
private:
int left_sensor,left_motor,rigth_sensor, rigth_motor;
```

// its methods, including the constructor, its move forward
task, the stop task, the left and right turns of the car
through its motors, as well as reading left and right sensors,
and finally the initialization that will be used in the setup
of the main program

```
public:
Seguidor(int left_sensor, int rigth_sensor, int left_motor, int
rigth_motor); // the class constructor
void avanzar(); //move forward
void detener(); //stop
void vuelta_derecha(); //turn right
void vuelta_izquierda(); //turn left
int leer_Sizquierdo(); //read left sensor
int leer_Sderecho();   // read right sensor
void init();
};
```

And here, in Listing 1-6, is the Linefollower.cpp file, which contains the definition of the methods from the previous file.

Listing 1-6. Line follower code with OOP and modularity
Linefollower.cpp file

```
// Include both the Arduino.h library for using its commands
and the Linefollower.h file that contains its prototypes or
declarations

#include "Linefollower.h"
#include "Arduino.h"

// The constructor
Seguidor::Seguidor(int left_sensor, int rigth_sensor, int left_
motor, int rigth_motor)
{
  this->left_motor=left_motor;
  this->left_sensor=left_sensor;
  this->rigth_motor=rigth_motor;
  this->rigth_sensor=rigth_sensor;
}

// The initializer
void Seguidor::init()
{
  pinMode(this->left_motor,OUTPUT);
  pinMode(this->rigth_motor,OUTPUT);
  pinMode(this->left_sensor,INPUT);
  pinMode(this->rigth_sensor,INPUT);
}
// The car's forward movement with both motors
void Seguidor::avanzar()
{
  digitalWrite(this->rigth_motor,HIGH);
```

CHAPTER 1   INTRODUCTION AND PREREQUISITES

```cpp
  digitalWrite(this->left_motor,HIGH);
}

// The braking of both motors
void Seguidor::detener()
{
  digitalWrite(this->rigth_motor,LOW);
  digitalWrite(this->left_motor,LOW);
}

// The right turn
void Seguidor::vuelta_derecha()
{
  digitalWrite(this->rigth_motor,LOW);
  digitalWrite(this->left_motor,HIGH);
}

// The left turn
void Seguidor::vuelta_izquierda()
{
  digitalWrite(this->rigth_motor,HIGH);
  digitalWrite(this->left_motor,LOW);
}

// Reading the right sensor
int Seguidor::leer_Sderecho()

{
  return analogRead(this->rigth_sensor);
}

// Reading the left sensor
int Seguidor::leer_Sizquierdo()
{
```

CHAPTER 1 INTRODUCTION AND PREREQUISITES

```
    return analogRead(this->left_sensor);
}
```

Finally, the Follower_OOP.ino file is shown in Listing 1-7, which uses the two previous files.

Listing 1-7. Line follower code with OOP and modularity Follower_OOP.ino file

```
// Include the library that contains the definition of the
class to be used

#include "Linefollower.h"

// Create the Follower object called seguidor composed of (left
sensor, right sensor, left motor, right motor)

Seguidor seguidor(A0,A1,5,6);

// Any value greater than the threshold of 400 is black, and
anything less than or equal is white

const int umbral=400;

// The initialization part invoking the initializer
method inside
void setup()
{
  seguidor.init();
}
// The main loop with the same logic as the non-modular
program, but now invoking the methods of the Follower class

void loop()
{
```

CHAPTER 1 INTRODUCTION AND PREREQUISITES

```
// First case, if both sensors detect white, then both motors activate
if(seguidor.leer_Sderecho()<=umbral && seguidor.leer_Sizquierdo()<=umbral)
{
  seguidor.avanzar();
}
// Second case, if both sensors detect black, the car is at the goal and both motors stop
else if(seguidor.leer_Sderecho()>umbral && seguidor.leer_Sizquierdo()>umbral)
{
  seguidor.detener();
}
// Third case, if the right sensor detects black, the left motor activates and the right motor turns off
else if(seguidor.leer_Sderecho()>=umbral)
{
  seguidor.vuelta_derecha();
}
// Fourth case, if the left sensor detects black, the right motor activates and the left motor turns off
else if(seguidor.leer_Sizquierdo()>=umbral)
{
  seguidor.vuelta_izquierda();
}
}
```

Tip Now that the concept of modularity has been illustrated, keep in mind the following analogy: the previous book in this series, *Advanced Robotic Vehicles Programming*, corresponds to the single-file mode, while this book corresponds to the modular mode with multiple files. The description of the ArduPilot library files and how they should be modified will be done soon.

Description of Main Files to Modify Simultaneously in the New ArduPilot Libraries

We remind the readers that in older libraries, it was recommended to modify the main file as a template; in our case, we used the ArduCopter.pde file directly.

Currently, although the users can modify all the files they deem necessary or add other ones, in our experience, the main files are

Frequently modified files:
mode_rolquad.cpp
In this file, we define our custom code or class methods.
Note that this is not a file included with the original libraries; you create it, so the name of this file is free to choose.

mode.h
In this file, we declare our custom code (our class and its methods).

UserCode.cpp
This file is modified in specific lines to include the previous customized methods (tasks) in order to be executed at certain specific frequencies.

CHAPTER 1　INTRODUCTION AND PREREQUISITES

UserVariables.h

This file is modified to declare certain variables for changing our flight modes.

Those variables will be used in the UserCode.cpp file, where faster and slower tasks are declared.

Log.cpp

This file contains all the information that is saved to the SD card, whether it's predefined or what we need.

APM_config.h

In this case, it's where the modes defined in the config.h file are disabled (try to avoid this functionality) and also the tasks and loops of different frequencies (slow, fast, etc.) are used (be free to use this functionality).

Files with unusual but relevant modifications:

Copter.cpp

This is our main file, which calls all other files, data, and functions, including those described and used in our custom code.

It also allows us to disable some unnecessary tasks for our custom code.

config.h

This file, among other things, allows us to declare our own mode of operation or disable those that we don't need, such as LOG writing modes.

Copter.h

Here, we declare the variables that we need to define in our custom program and, redundantly, our custom flight mode already made in config and apm config.

mode.cpp

This file allows us to add our flight mode to the state machine of the existing flight modes.

Files with a not desirable or recommended modification:

In extreme cases, if global variables are needed, which is not recommended because it overloads the autopilot's memory and breaks one of the principles of OOP based on the use of methods and attributes, the following three files are used.

Parameters.h

UserParameters.h

Parameters.cpp

Files with practically no modification:
ALL OTHER FILES

Their dependency is described in Figure 1-6 (note that it's much more complex in its interconnection than the previous Arduino examples):

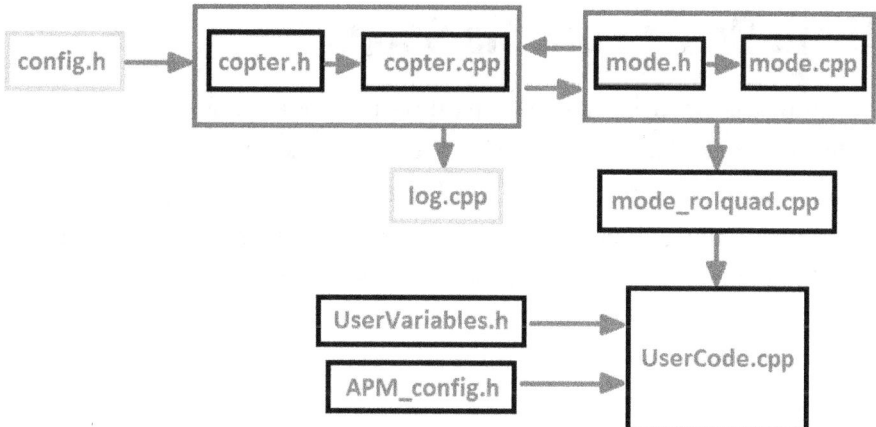

Figure 1-6. *Approximate relationship between the various modular files of the ArduPilot libraries (limited to those most used in this book)*

Note that, of the above, the main one is still the copter file, but the concept of modularity is used to modify the dependencies that are useful to each designer that are available in other files. In this case, the user generates customized code in UserCode, which simply uses information from sensors or actuators already available in copter.

Tip Although we frequently use the copter file, there is no impediment to using any of the other main projects, such as the rover or airplane. However, this should not affect the designer's performance, since we use the customizable programming and control capabilities of motors, sensors, communications, etc., rather than the pre-configured vehicle. This way, adapting it to platforms that are not even available should be a relatively direct task, although not necessarily simple.

About Design and Its Scope

Indicating the word "design" in the title of the book is risky, as it may exhibit a degree of ambiguity, so it's necessary to know the scope of it. Design can range from a simple hand-drawn sketch and be purely artistic to indicating, through calculations and extensive simulations, even the selection of the smallest screw used as exemplified in Figure 1-7.

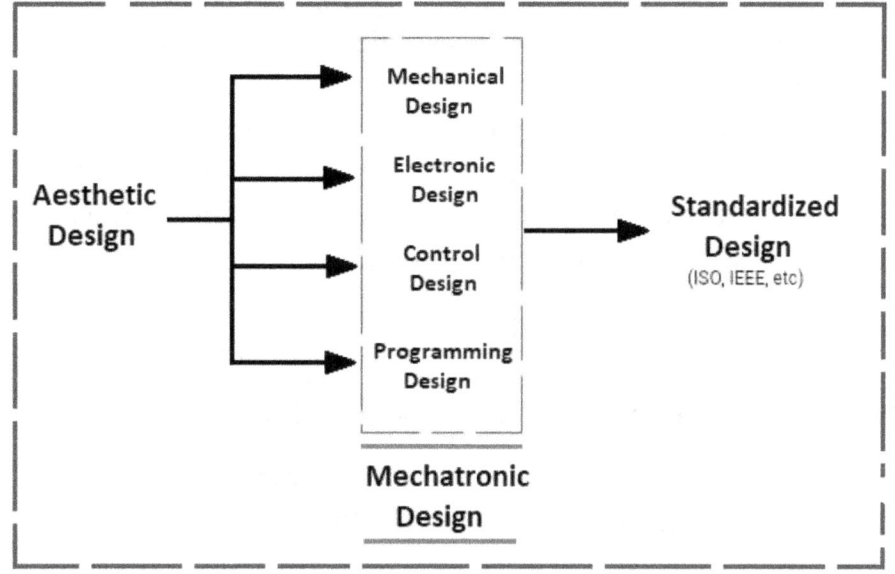

Figure 1-7. Scope of design

So, in a robotics book, design can vary from sketching, mechanical design, mechatronic design, physical and mathematical design, technical design focused on assembly and machining, etc.

Due to page limitations, but also to respond to or facilitate the reader's knowledge, the purpose of this book is to focus on a central axis of programming aimed at ArduPilot libraries, around which modules of mechatronic design with a medium-depth and somewhat technical scope orbit. Except for certain cases that the authors, due to their relevance, decide to extend to facilitate understanding. If more extensive details are required, the authors provide a section with more complete references for each project.

It should be clear that the prototypes presented here, Table 1-3, are a functional basis for replication, but they are not a strict mold. We present them to our own students, and they develop their own variants, which in some cases end up being superior to our designs.

Table 1-3. *Types of robots described in this book and their scope*

Type of robot	Detailed description	Book section	Project type
Aeropendulum	Yes, with code and experimental tests	Aeropendulum chapter	Basic
Quadcopter mounted on a test stand	Yes, with code and experimental tests	Quadcopter mounted on a test stand chapter	Derived from the aeropendulum
Free flight quadcopter	Yes, with code and experimental tests	Free flight quadcopter chapter	Derived from the quadcopter mounted on a test stand
Zeppelin	Yes, but without code or experimental tests, which is left as an exercise for the readers	Appendix about the zeppelin	Basic

(*continued*)

Table 1-3. (*continued*)

Type of robot	Detailed description	Book section	Project type
Propeller-driven car	No, only mentioned as a predecessor to the zeppelin, but its construction is direct and much more than the zeppelin itself	Appendix about the zeppelin	Predecessor to the zeppelin
Hovercraft	No, only mentioned as a predecessor to the zeppelin, but its construction is direct and much more than the zeppelin itself	Appendix about the zeppelin	Predecessor to the zeppelin
Boat	No, only mentioned as a derivative work of the zeppelin, but its construction is direct	Appendix about the zeppelin	Derived from the zeppelin
Submarine	No, only mentioned as a derivative work of the zeppelin, but its construction is not direct or trivial	Appendix about the zeppelin	Derived from the zeppelin or quadcopter
Differential car with rotary motors and wheels	Yes, but without code or experimental tests, which is left as an exercise for the readers	Appendix about the differential car	Basic

(*continued*)

CHAPTER 1 INTRODUCTION AND PREREQUISITES

Table 1-3. (*continued*)

Type of robot	Detailed description	Book section	Project type
Robotic arm	Briefly, but without code or experimental tests, which is left as an exercise for the readers	Appendix about the differential car	Basic, complementary to the robotic vehicles described in this book
Robotic arm on a mobile platform	No, only mentioned as a derivative work of the differential car, and its construction can be very simple or complicated and non-trivial depending on the target task and actuators used	Appendix about the differential car	Derived from the robotic arm and differential car

Suggested Extensive Mechatronic Methodology

As a suggestion to the reader, a more or less common way to carry out mechatronic projects is indicated, based on the scientific method, and which we have used in an abbreviated form due to the extension and purposes of this book.

CHAPTER 1   INTRODUCTION AND PREREQUISITES

INTRODUCTION

Observation

System sketch (drawing, even if it's hand-drawn, indicating all parts)

Quick description of the system

Research

State of the art (current, at least three of the following)

Local

National

International

Non-academic

Background (what was done years ago, at least three of the following)

Local

National

International

Non-academic

Hypothesis

Mechanics

Proposed structure or chassis (materials and approximate measurements)

Proposed construction (how the structure will be made)

Extensive description based on simulations and equations (finite element, free body diagrams)

Electronics

Description of the functioning of electronic or electrical components to be used (sensors, actuators, etc.)

Extensive description based on simulations and equations (analog, digital, power electronics, etc.)

CHAPTER 1   INTRODUCTION AND PREREQUISITES

Electrical diagrams

Protoboard diagrams (if applicable)

Programming

Von Neumann diagrams

Hardware

What computing unit will be used and its abbreviated technical specifications in a table

Software

What commands will be used?

Proposed algorithm (this goes hand-in-hand with control)

State machines

Control

Proposal for extensive logical controls (intelligent controls)

Proposal for extensive analytical controls (classic ones, based on ODEs)

List of materials and preliminary costs

DEVELOPMENT

Description of experiments

Component testing

Sensor testing

Actuator testing

Communication testing

Independent mechanism testing

Preliminary operation testing

For example, testing a very basic line follower in slow mode

For example, testing a line follower with gaps in the trajectory and in slow mode

Full system testing

> For example, testing a line follower with gaps at high speed

Analysis of results or validations

> **HERE THE PREVIOUS EXPERIMENTS ARE TABULATED, PERFORMANCE GRAPHS ARE MADE, STATICS ARE SHOWN, ETC., ESPECIALLY FOR THE FINAL EXPERIMENTS**
>
> **OUTCOME**

Conclusions

> **Conclusions: Objective verbs; we demonstrated, we did, we built, we verified**
>
> **Discussions: Subjective verbs; we think, we believe, we opine**
>
> **Future work: Proposals for improvements**

Appendices

> **References**
>
> **Datasheets**

Summary of Mechatronic Components of Prototypes in This Book

In Table 1-4, there is a sneak peek at the three main projects of this book.

Table 1-4. *A glimpse of the main projects described or mentioned in this book*

Project	Mechanics	Electronics	Control	Programming
Aeropendulum	Design restricted to a pendulum with control over the main pendulum mass using a single motor and its propeller and a free pivot.	Power (ESC) Motor Control interface (Pixhawk) Sensors (Pixhawk) Embedded automatic control	Automatic PD control	ArduPilot
Quadcopter mounted on a test stand	A 4-motor aerial vehicle with fully restricted cartesian movement through a ball joint, allowing only 3D rotational movements.	Power (ESC) Motor Control interface (Pixhawk) Sensors (Pixhawk) Embedded semi-automatic control with remote external control	The user commands orientation via remote control, which is automatically executed by the Pixhawk in PD mode	ArduPilot

(*continued*)

Table 1-4. (*continued*)

Project	Mechanics	Electronics	Control	Programming
Free flight quadcopter	A 4-motor aerial vehicle without restriction	Power (ESC) Motor Control interface (Pixhawk) Sensors (Pixhawk) Embedded semi-automatic control with remote external control	The user commands altitude and planar position via remote control, which is automatically executed by the Pixhawk in PD mode	ArduPilot

Linkage and Uses with Mission Planner

This section is not intended to describe the extensive features of the Mission Planner interface. For more detailed information, we recommend reading more comprehensive texts, such as the one by Ty Audronis.

However, this section will describe the utilities of Mission Planner focused on the use of the ArduPilot libraries, which are as follows:

- Loading executable files to the autopilot: in this case, the utility is essential to program the autopilot with the software designed by the user. This utility will be described in this book as part of the installation and configuration process of the ArduPilot libraries.

CHAPTER 1   INTRODUCTION AND PREREQUISITES

- Using Mission Planner as a serial interface for message display: in this case, it is convenient to know that if you want to display a message, such as a "hello world" or sensor values or remote control values, it can be done through Mission Planner. However, the displayed data cannot be copied or saved, at least not in the most recent versions of Mission Planner. Therefore, we recommend the reader use another serial interface like Terminal or PuTTY.

- Using Mission Planner to recalibrate sensors: there are occasions when the autopilot becomes misconfigured, and it is necessary to perform a reset of its main sensors to use it again.

- Using Mission Planner to identify maximum values of the remote control: although codes can be written directly to display these values, Mission Planner has a graphical tool to display the extreme values of each button and lever of the remote control.

- Using Mission Planner to verify pre-programmed flight modes by the user: with this utility, we can determine if the flight modes defined by the user have been correctly programmed in the autopilot.

- Using Mission Planner to display SD card information: the purpose of these tools is to visualize the data stored on the SD card. This can be done in two ways: live with the SD card mounted on the autopilot or externally with the SD card outside the autopilot and viewed as a removable disk unit. In the latter case, direct visualization or transformation to a text file is possible for later use in a spreadsheet or directly in Matlab (R).

The following is a detailed description of the indicated tools.

Warning Previously, data would start synchronizing as soon as the autopilot was connected to Mission Planner. Currently, depending on the version of MP used, the autopilot must also be armed for communication with MP to begin.

Some of the indicated sequences require connecting in MAVLink mode, while in others this should not be done. We will repeat this comment where we consider it pertinent. Before proceeding, the users should verify the port to which their autopilots are connected from the device manager as indicated in Figure 1-8; this port should match the one that will be connected to Mission Planner.

CHAPTER 1 INTRODUCTION AND PREREQUISITES

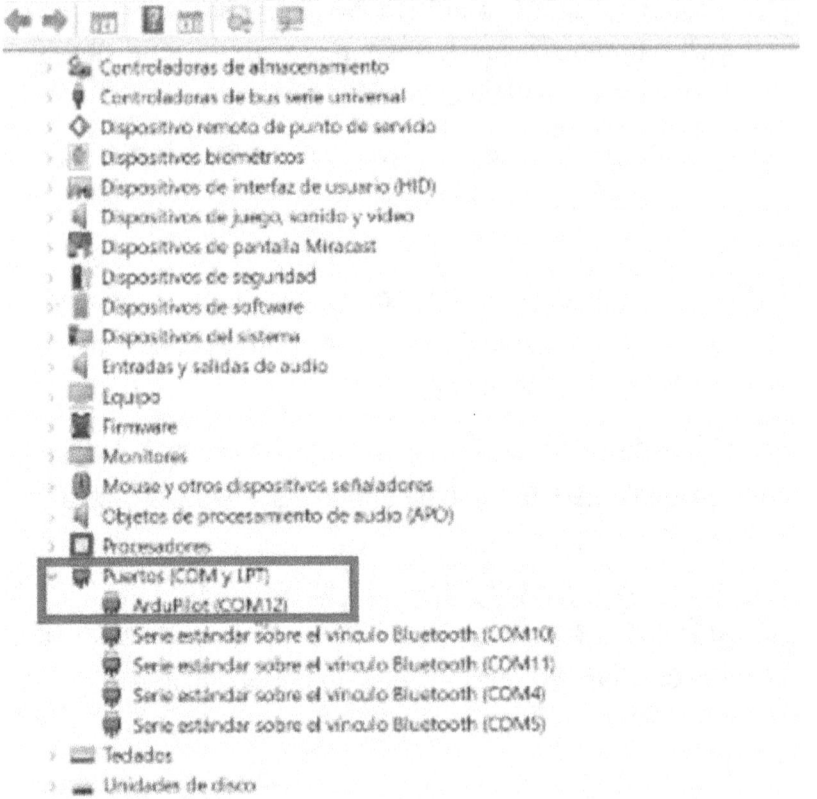

Figure 1-8. *How to verify the COM port number assigned to an autopilot from the Device Manager*

Using MP as a serial interface

To start, the reader should have a console message enabled anywhere in their code; for example, in the UserCode.cpp file, in the SLOWLOOP section, you can add the following line of code as a simplified "Hello World" like in Figure 1-9 (we'll see a more interesting version later).

CHAPTER 1 INTRODUCTION AND PREREQUISITES

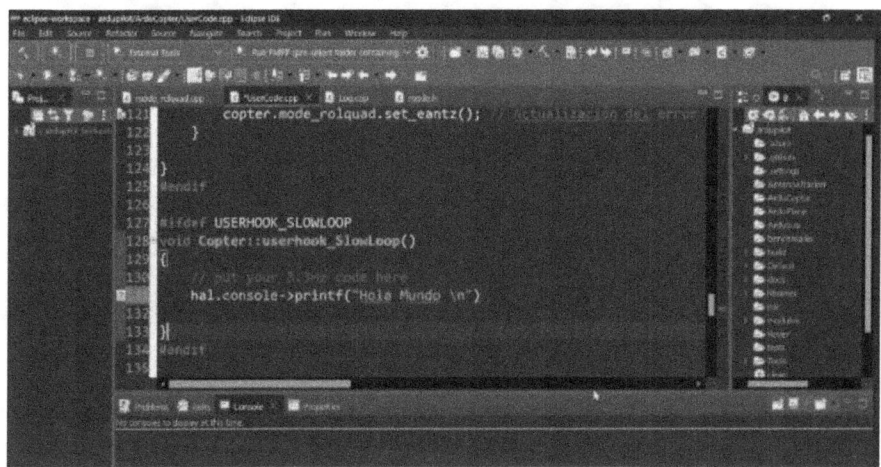

Figure 1-9. Using Mission Planner as a serial terminal 1

After compiling and uploading the code to the autopilot, open Mission Planner and without clicking the right icon that says "Connect", go to the "Setup" button.

Then to "Advanced", and finally to the "Terminal" button. Use Figure 1-10 as a guide.

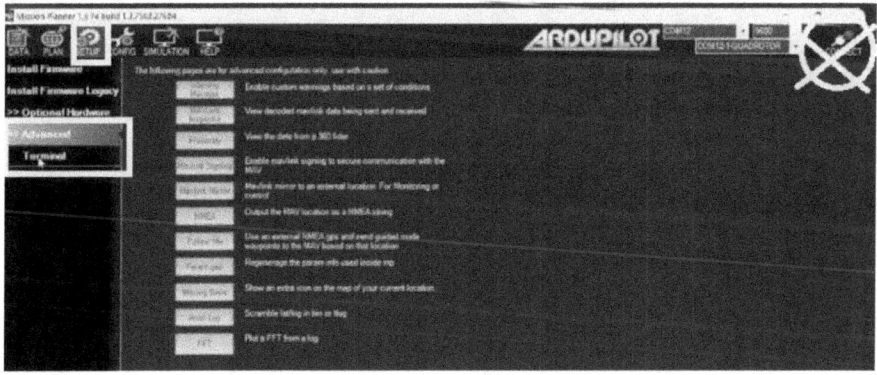

Figure 1-10. Using Mission Planner as a serial terminal 2

45

CHAPTER 1   INTRODUCTION AND PREREQUISITES

Once there, click the "Connect" option to visualize the sent data, as in Figure 1-11.

Figure 1-11. Using Mission Planner as a serial terminal 3

When you're sure you're receiving the desired information, don't forget to click "Connect" again to terminate.

Using Mission Planner to calibrate sensors

Occasionally, the autopilot won't arm (for example, in the case of the Pixhawk, the main LED may keep flashing orange).

To fix this, you'll need to have your autopilot with an external GPS and connect to Mission Planner using the top-right icon that says "Connect" as indicated in Figure 1-12.

Figure 1-12. Using Mission Planner to calibrate sensors 1

Once connected, go to the "Setup" menu.

Then to "Mandatory Hardware", and then to the "Compass" button. There, you'll need to verify at least two sensors: the external or GPS sensor, which has primary priority and another internal sensor with secondary priority. Refer to Figure 1-13 as a guide.

CHAPTER 1   INTRODUCTION AND PREREQUISITES

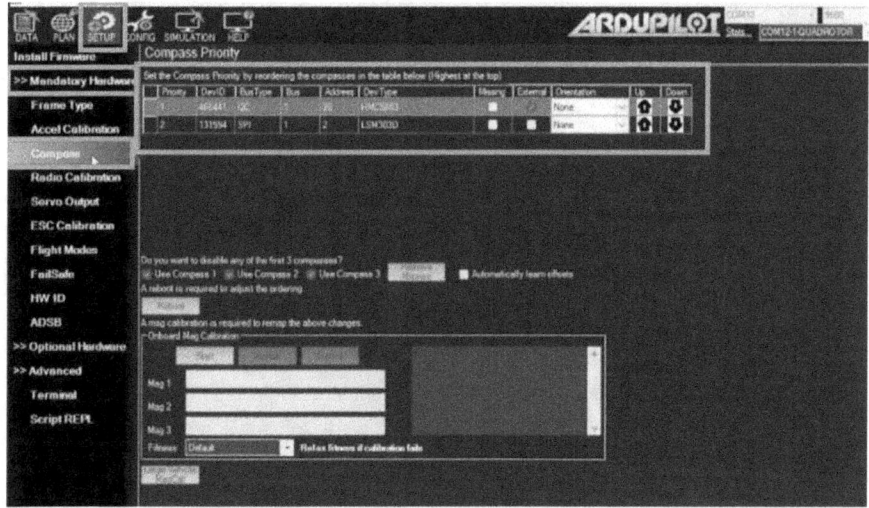

Figure 1-13. Using Mission Planner to calibrate sensors 2

Click on "Start" and follow the procedure indicated by the interface until the internal software recalibrates the main sensors of the autopilot through movement. Follow Figure 1-14 as a guide.

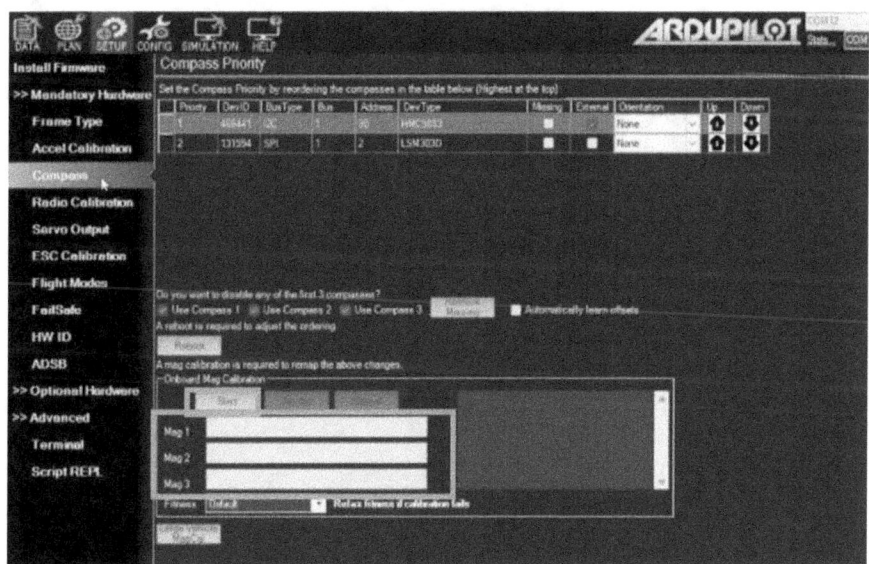

Figure 1-14. Using Mission Planner to calibrate sensors 3

47

CHAPTER 1   INTRODUCTION AND PREREQUISITES

After completing this procedure, go back to the "Data" menu and verify the "ARMED" legend on the main screen, see Figure 1-15. If there are any warnings, errors, or failsafe modes, repeat these calibrations.

Figure 1-15. *Using Mission Planner to calibrate sensors 4*

Note   Additional calibrations, such as the accelerometer, may be required, see Figure 1-16.

CHAPTER 1   INTRODUCTION AND PREREQUISITES

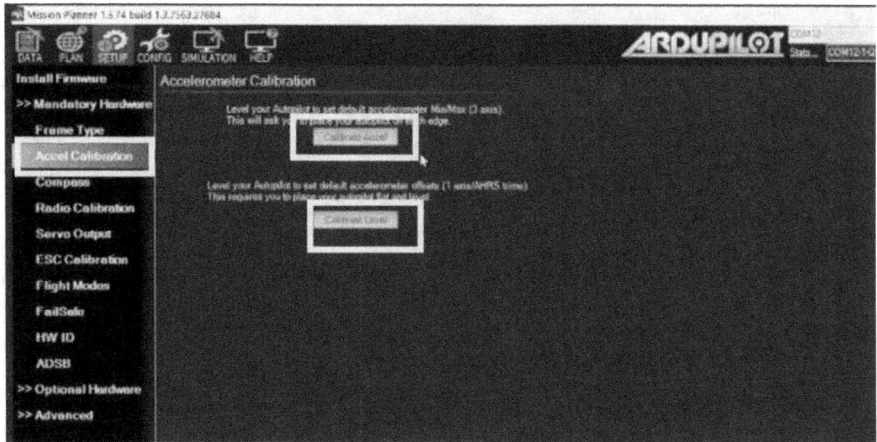

Figure 1-16. *Using Mission Planner to calibrate sensors 5*

Another possible error we've noticed is the following:

When trying to upload custom software, the system doesn't allow it.

We've solved this issue several times by setting a predefined frame type (even if it's not used). For some reason, when repeatedly flashing the autopilot, this option gets unchecked or auto-selected as undefined. Simply selecting a predefined multiple configuration, as indicated in Figure 1-17, solves the issue.

CHAPTER 1   INTRODUCTION AND PREREQUISITES

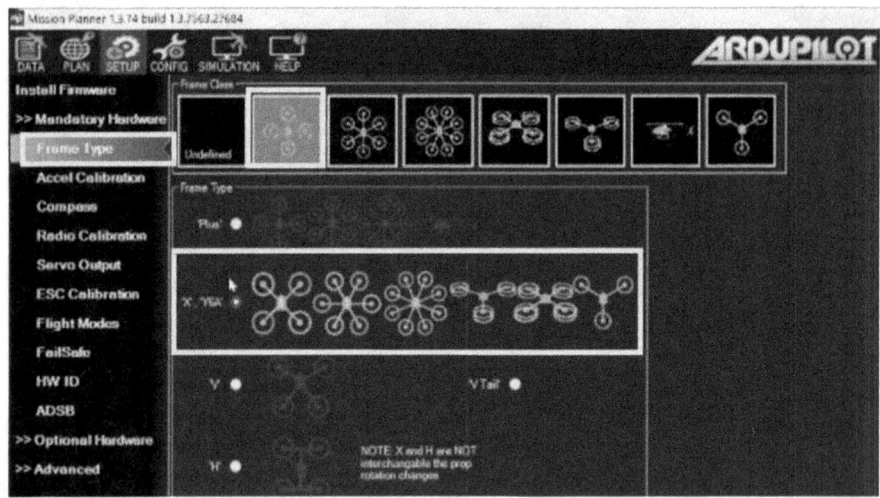

Figure 1-17. *Using Mission Planner to calibrate sensors 6*

Using Mission Planner to identify maximum remote control values

First, click the connection button in the top-right corner, see Figure 1-18.

Figure 1-18. *Using Mission Planner to identify maximum remote control values 1*

Turn on the remote control and go to the "Setup" menu, then "Mandatory Hardware", and finally "Radio Calibration," see Figure 1-19.

50

CHAPTER 1   INTRODUCTION AND PREREQUISITES

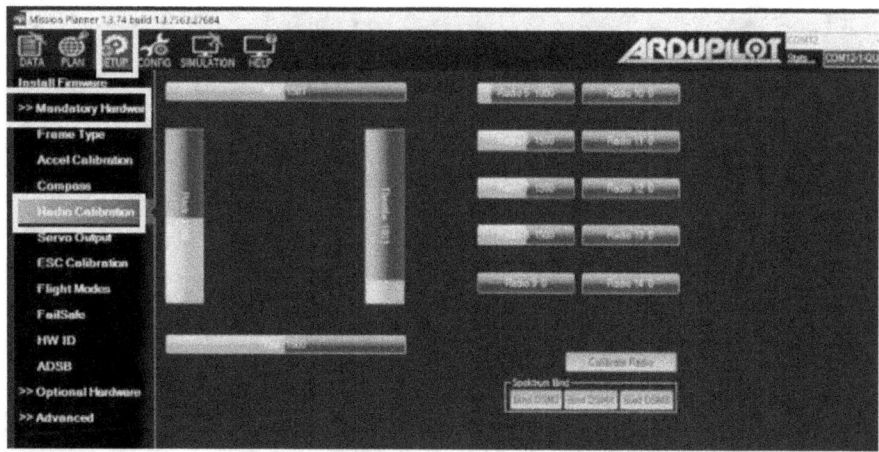

Figure 1-19. *Using Mission Planner to identify maximum remote control values 2*

Once there, start moving levers, knobs, or buttons and observe the minimum, maximum, and intermediate values available. Although this can be done directly in code, it's a quick way to observe the values available on the remote control.

Using Mission Planner to verify user-defined flight modes

In this case, we recall that the users will define their own flight modes to use their robotic vehicle designs.

To verify that these flight modes are working, it's convenient to do the following from Mission Planner (MP):

As will be seen later, the user will need to define their own flight modes in the Config.h file, see Figure 1-20.

51

CHAPTER 1   INTRODUCTION AND PREREQUISITES

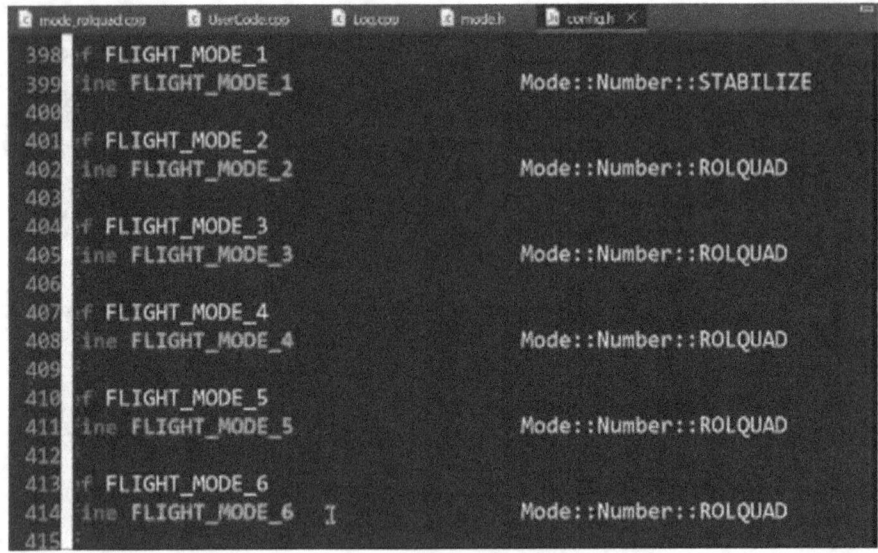

Figure 1-20. *Using Mission Planner to verify user-defined flight modes 1*

You will need to click the "Connect" button again, go to "Setup", "Mandatory Hardware", and the "Flight Modes" section.

There, you will see that the first flight mode is "STABILIZE", as defined in the code. Use Figure 1-21 as a guide.

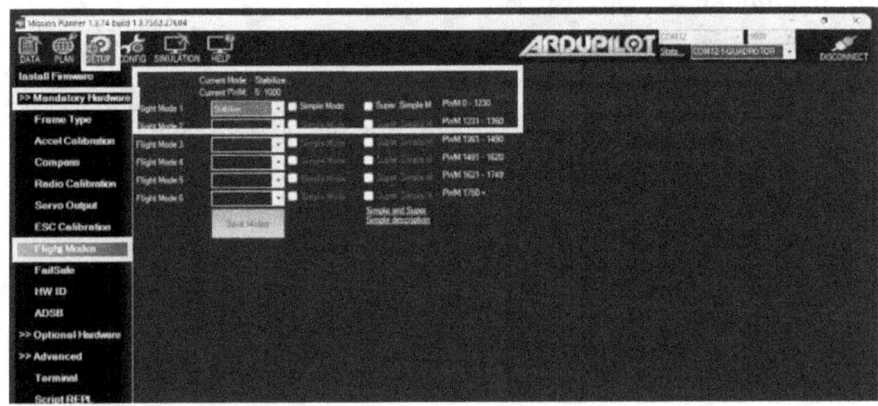

Figure 1-21. *Using Mission Planner to verify user-defined flight modes 2*

52

CHAPTER 1　INTRODUCTION AND PREREQUISITES

Then, with the designated lever to switch between flight modes, simply move it. You will notice that it switches to another unnamed flight mode, indicating that our flight modes have been loaded correctly, see Figure 1-22. It's not necessary to move the lever further; this verification is only done once to ensure our pre-programmed code operates correctly.

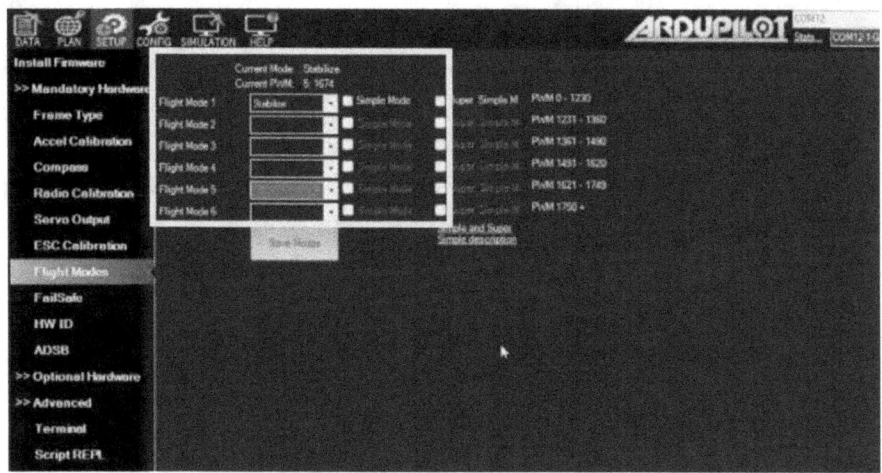

Figure 1-22. Using Mission Planner to verify user-defined flight modes 3

Using Mission Planner to display SD card information

Two methods are described:

On-board (directly from the autopilot without extracting the SD card): this method can be unstable, so it may require trying a few times.

Click the "Connect" button in the top-right corner, then the "Data" button, the "DataFlash Logs" option, and the "Download DataFlash Log Via Mavlink" box, see Figure 1-23.

CHAPTER 1   INTRODUCTION AND PREREQUISITES

Figure 1-23. *Using Mission Planner to display SD card information on-board 1*

In the auxiliary window, select the log of interest and click "Download Selected Logs", see Figure 1-24.

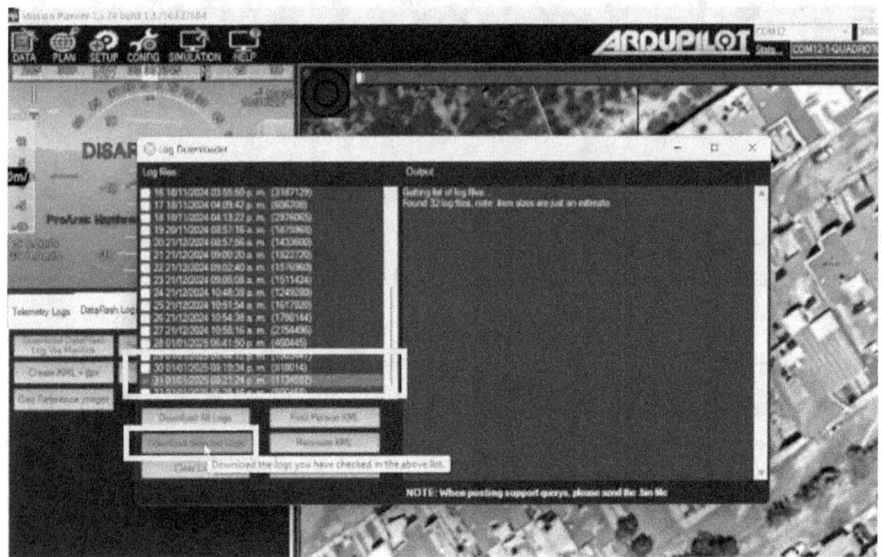

Figure 1-24. *Using Mission Planner to display SD card information on-board 2*

54

CHAPTER 1   INTRODUCTION AND PREREQUISITES

The necessary bin and log files will be saved to the specified folder on your computer, which can be used by spreadsheets or graphing software, see Figure 1-25.

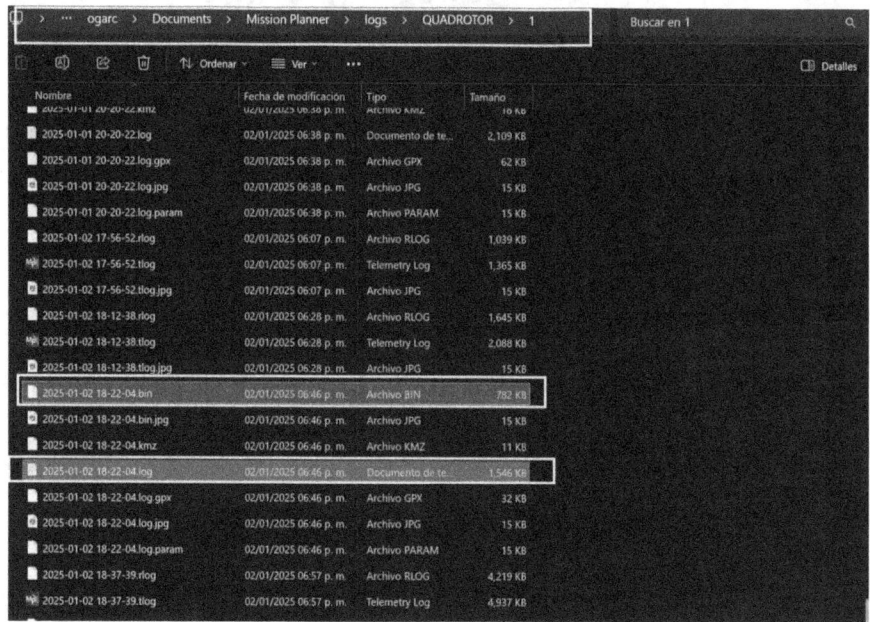

Figure 1-25. *Using Mission Planner to display SD card information on-board 3*

Note It's convenient to search the Mission Planner repository and forums to find where these logs are stored, see Figure 1-26.

55

CHAPTER 1   INTRODUCTION AND PREREQUISITES

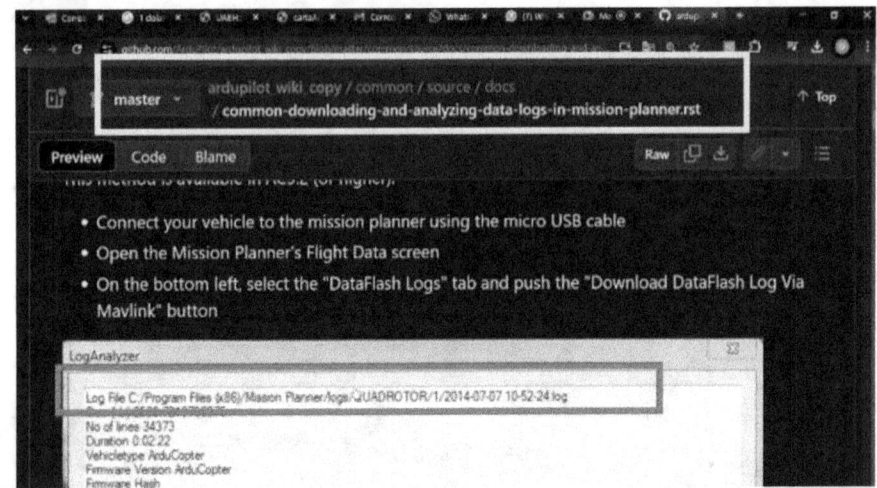

Figure 1-26. *Using Mission Planner to display SD card information on-board 4*

External (extracting the SD card from the autopilot and using a computer with a connector or adapter): in all external modes, the "Connect" button in the top-right corner of Mission Planner should not be clicked.

In the external mode, there are also several versions available, one of which is a simple viewer from Mission Planner.

To do this, click "Setup", "Terminal", "Log Browse", see Figure 1-27.

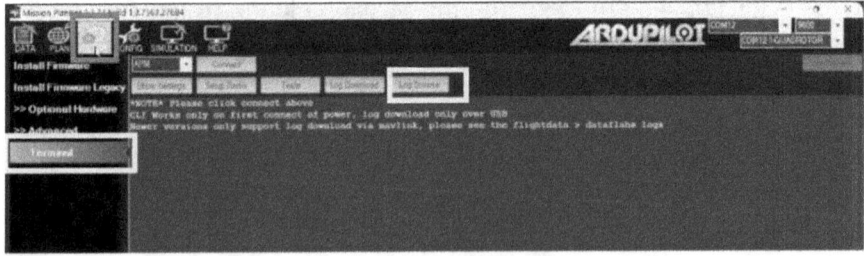

Figure 1-27. *Using Mission Planner to display SD card information, external mode 1*

CHAPTER 1   INTRODUCTION AND PREREQUISITES

Then select the SD adapter's address and the file of interest, see Figure 1-28.

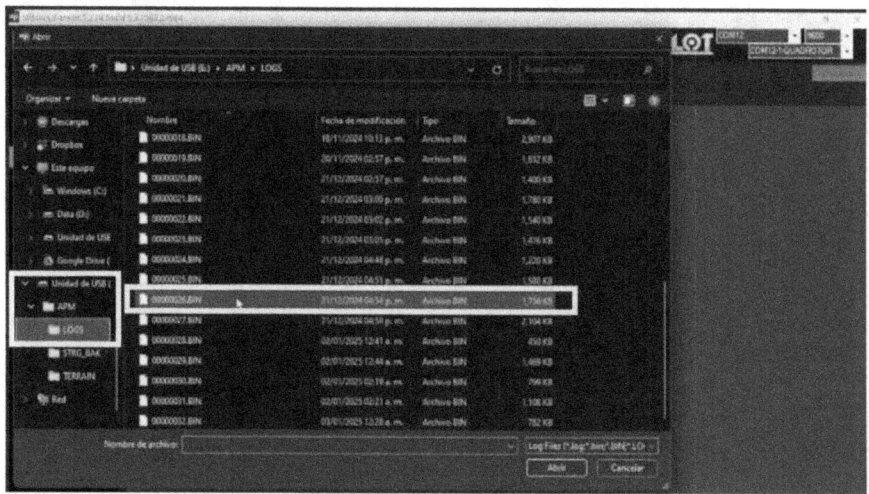

Figure 1-28. *Using Mission Planner to display SD card information, external mode 2*

Finally, choose the sub-data to plot directly in Mission Planner, see Figure 1-29. Remember that you need to know what data and packages you want to plot, so we recommend reading further in this book on how to save data to the SD card.

CHAPTER 1   INTRODUCTION AND PREREQUISITES

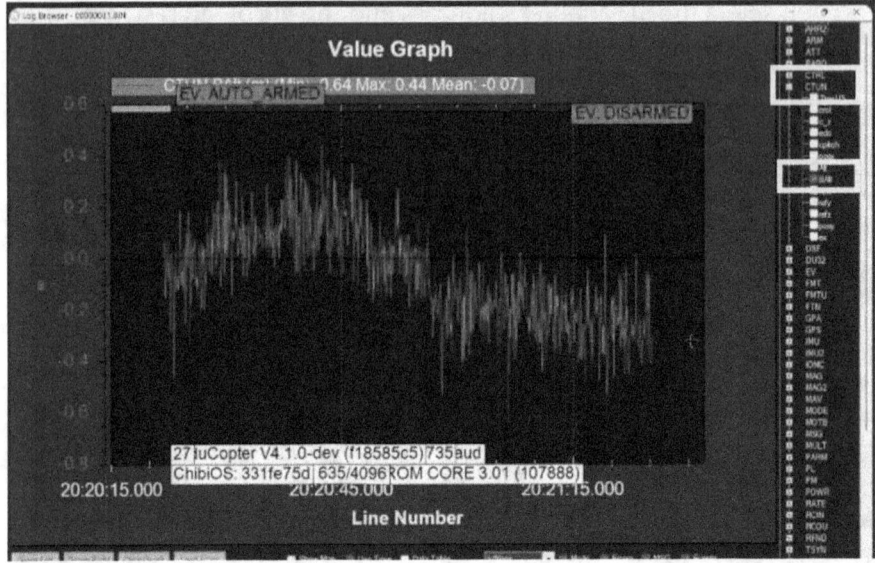

Figure 1-29. *Using Mission Planner to display SD card information, external mode 3*

Other external modes are used for converting SD card data to text files usable by spreadsheets or other generic graphing and editing software, or recently, to Matlab (R) files.

For these cases, without clicking the "Connect" button in the top-right corner, go to the "Data" button, the "DataFlash Logs" option, and any of the options you desire, such as "Convert Bin to Log" or "Create Matlab File", see Figure 1-30. When you click, you will be prompted to select the file of interest, and the conversion will be made to Log format, generic text format, or Matlab format. A detailed description of this operation can be found in our previous book, *Advanced Robotic Vehicles Programming*.

CHAPTER 1   INTRODUCTION AND PREREQUISITES

Figure 1-30. *External alternative to extract SD card data*

Chapter Summary

In this chapter, we provided an introductory approach to the new ArduPilot libraries (2023), covering a brief historical context to alternative ways of using them.

We also described a couple of examples based on Arduino code to facilitate understanding of the topic regarding Object-Oriented Programming (OOP) and modularity concepts.

Finally, we showed the interaction modes of Mission Planner with the ArduPilot libraries and the mechatronic methodology used in this text.

In the next chapter, we will describe the installation process of the ArduPilot libraries for Windows 10, a useful "Hello World" example to understand the invocation and usage of the different kinds of time, and a comparison between the latest ArduPilot libraries (2023) and the 2018 libraries discussed in our previous book, *Advanced Robotic Vehicles Programming*.

PART II

Installation and Description of Commands and Mechatronics of Generic Components Used in This Book

CHAPTER 2

Installation and Command Description

In this chapter, we will teach you three segments of knowledge. In the first one, you will learn how to install the libraries in a guided manner, exclusively for Windows. Although the ArduPilot libraries have many variants, we will use one of the most common ones to illustrate the installation process.

The second segment you will learn is the classic "Hello World", which in this book will have two variations: one for verifying the installation and another for introducing the concept of time management, which is one of the main features of the ArduPilot libraries.

Finally, we will show a tabular comparison of commands between the old ArduPilot libraries, previously described by us in the *Advanced Robotic Vehicles Programming book*, and the current ones that we used to write this text.

CHAPTER 2   INSTALLATION AND COMMAND DESCRIPTION

Basic Setup on Windows and Code Upload to Autopilot

The installation presented here is one of several possible configurations, which may vary in

- Operating system
- Version of the ArduPilot libraries
- Version of the C++ editor

among many other aspects.

Additionally, it should be noted that the installation of ArduPilot libraries can be the most cumbersome and unstable part, given that it is a constantly changing software.

Therefore, you should consider this section as a guide to install a relatively stable and recent version with which we developed this book.

We divide the installation process into the following parts:

1. List of requirements
2. Download process
3. Installation process
4. ArduPilot's code compilation
5. Loading the executable file with Mission Planner
6. Customization of the C++ editor (Eclipse in this case)

Part 1
Generic Requirements

- Windows 10 or later
- Any Pixhawk distribution or board compatible with ArduPilot
- A serial terminal

Specific Requirements

CHAPTER 2   INSTALLATION AND COMMAND DESCRIPTION

- copter 4.2 GitHub offline

  https://github.com/ArduPilot/ardupilot

- eclipse-inst-jre-win64.exe

  https://download.eclipse.org/justj/?file=oomph/products/latest

- gcc-arm-none-eabi-6-2017-q2-update-win32-sha2.exe

  https://developer.arm.com/downloads/-/gnu-rm/6-2017-q2-update

- install-prereqs-windows.ps1

  https://ardupilot.org/dev/docs/building-setup-windows-cygwin.html

- mission planner

  https://ardupilot.org/planner/docs/mission-planner-installation.html

Part 2

Download Process

Below is the download process for the specific requirements.

Note   DO NOT INSTALL ANYTHING, JUST DOWNLOAD.

For each specific requirement, follow these steps on the indicated web pages:

For Eclipse, see Figure 2-1.

CHAPTER 2   INSTALLATION AND COMMAND DESCRIPTION

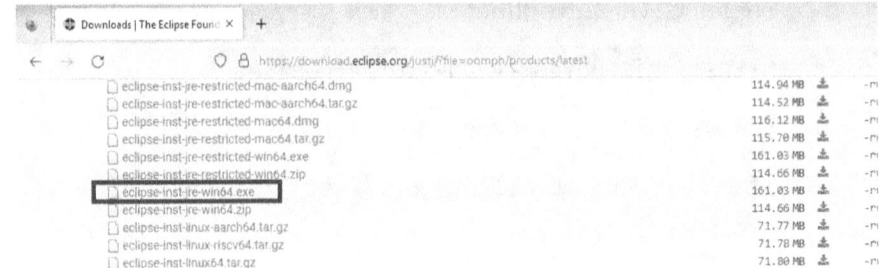

Figure 2-1. *Download process for the necessary files to install the ArduPilot libraries 1*

For the Copter folder, once inside the ArduPilot GitHub repository indicated, click the arrow next to "master", see Figure 2-2.

Once clicked, in the dialog box, type "Copter" starting with a capital letter.

The suggested libraries will appear; select Copter 4.2.

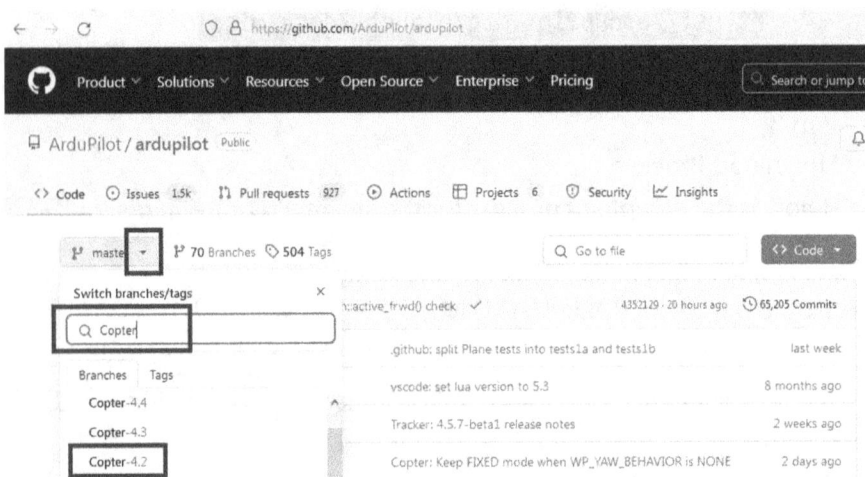

Figure 2-2. *Download process for the necessary files to install the ArduPilot libraries 2*

When clicking on the indicated option, the following web page of the repository will appear, see Figure 2-3.

CHAPTER 2   INSTALLATION AND COMMAND DESCRIPTION

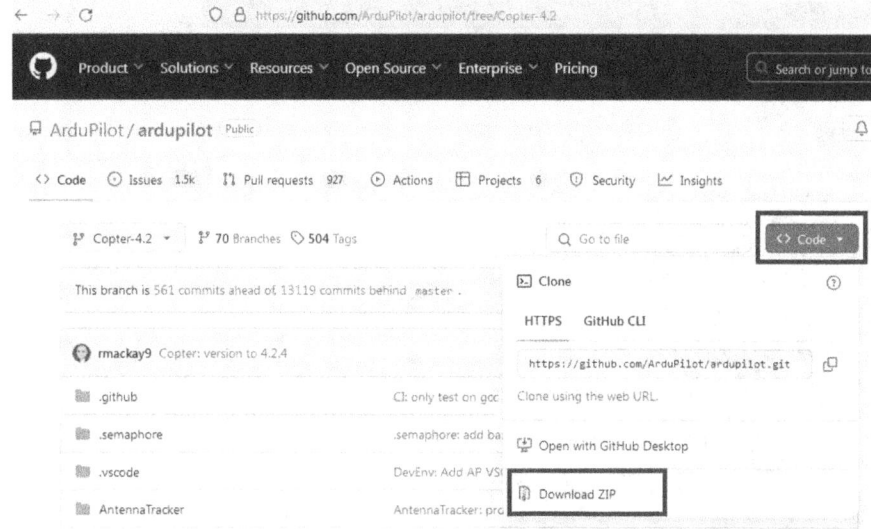

Figure 2-3. *Download process for the necessary files to install the ArduPilot libraries 3*

On it, click the green button called "Code" and then "Download ZIP". This will download the specified version of the libraries to a specific folder on your computer for offline installation.

For Mission Planner:

Simply download it from the official website in its latest version, see Figure 2-4.

CHAPTER 2 INSTALLATION AND COMMAND DESCRIPTION

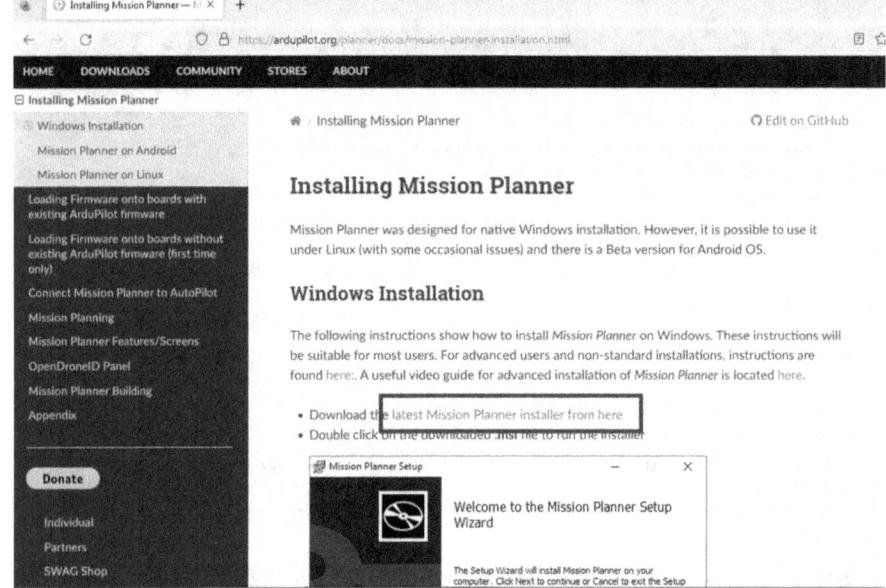

Figure 2-4. *Download process for the necessary files to install the ArduPilot libraries 4*

The same for install-prereqs-windows.ps1, see Figure 2-5.

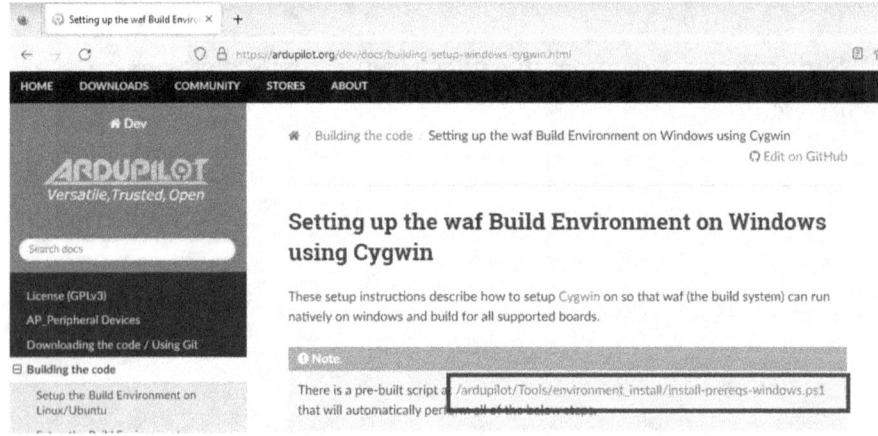

Figure 2-5. *Download process for the necessary files to install the ArduPilot libraries 5*

CHAPTER 2   INSTALLATION AND COMMAND DESCRIPTION

Finally for gcc-arm-none-eabi-6-2017-q2-update-win32-sha2.exe, see Figure 2-6.

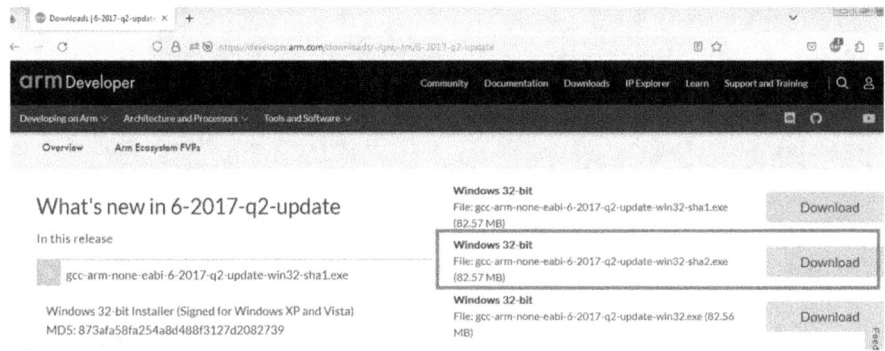

Figure 2-6. *Download process for the necessary files to install the ArduPilot libraries 6*

It's preferable to have the specific requirements available in a personal folder for the installation process to be described as in Figure 2-7.

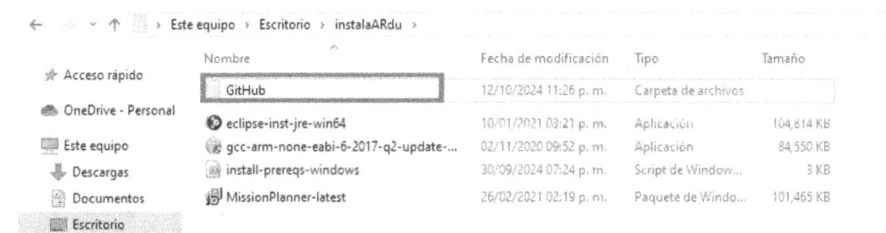

Figure 2-7. *Download process for the necessary files to install the ArduPilot libraries 7*

Part 3

Installation Process

Copy the GitHub folder to the "Documents" folder, see Figure 2-8.

69

CHAPTER 2 INSTALLATION AND COMMAND DESCRIPTION

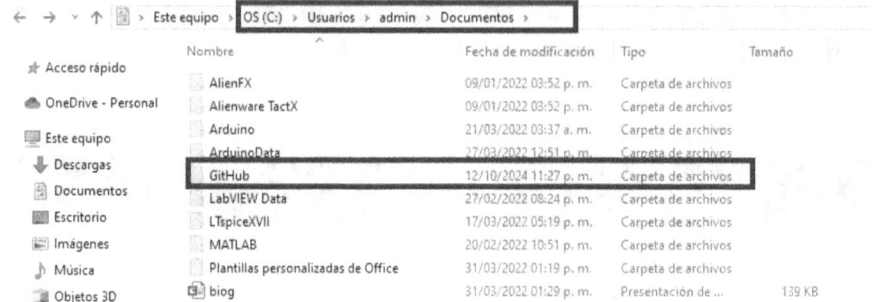

Figure 2-8. *Installing ArduPilot libraries and its dependencies 1*

Install Eclipse and create a shortcut. Choose the option for developers, see Figures 2-9, 2-10, and 2-11.

Note   This step requires Internet access.

CHAPTER 2 INSTALLATION AND COMMAND DESCRIPTION

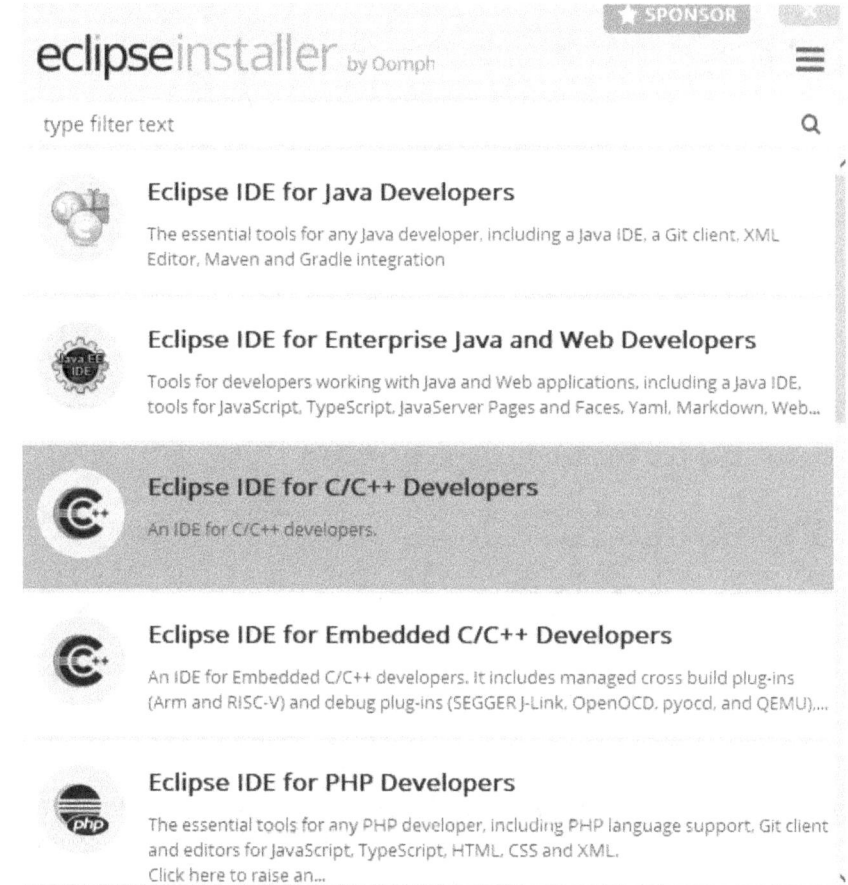

Figure 2-9. *Installing ArduPilot libraries and its dependencies 2*

CHAPTER 2   INSTALLATION AND COMMAND DESCRIPTION

Figure 2-10. *Installing ArduPilot libraries and its dependencies 3*

CHAPTER 2   INSTALLATION AND COMMAND DESCRIPTION

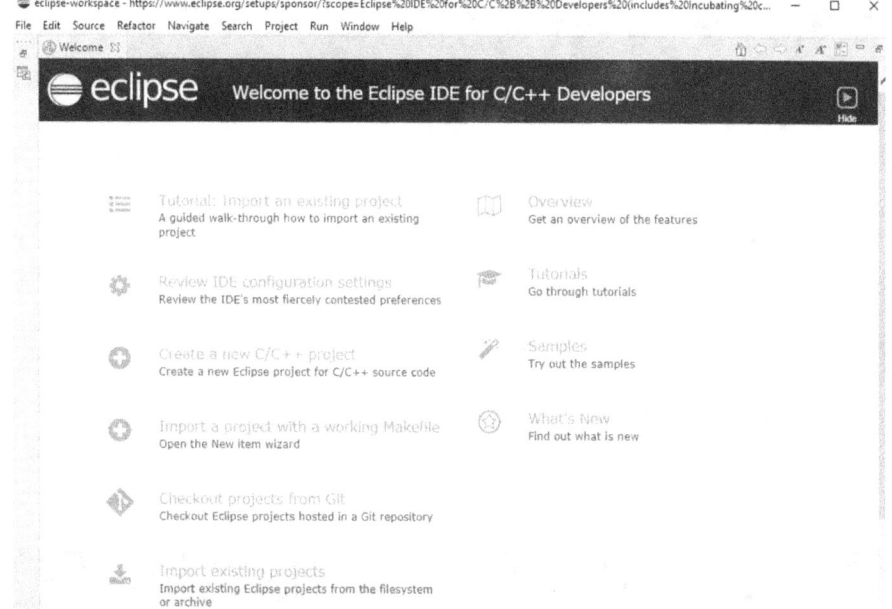

Figure 2-11. *Installing ArduPilot libraries and its dependencies 4*

Run the file: install_prereqs, and wait until it finishes. This may take more than 20 minutes. For this, right-click and then select "Run with PowerShell" as in Figures 2-12 and 2-13.

CHAPTER 2   INSTALLATION AND COMMAND DESCRIPTION

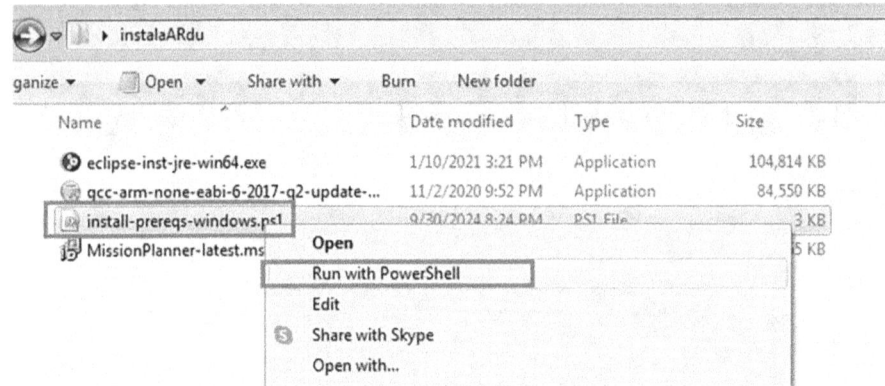

Figure 2-12.   Installing ArduPilot libraries and its dependencies 5

```
Windows PowerShell
Starting Downloads
Downloading MAVProxy (1/7)
Downloading Cygwin x64 (2/7)
Downloading ARM GCC Compiler 10-2020-Q4-Major (3/7)
Installing Cygwin x64 (4/7)
User has NO backup/restore rights
User has NO symlink creation right
note: Hand installation over to elevated child process.
Downloading extra Python packages (5/7)
Installing ARM GCC Compiler 10-2020-Q4-Major (6/7)
Installing MAVProxy (7/7)
Finished. Press any key to continue ...
```

Figure 2-13.   Installing ArduPilot libraries and its dependencies 6

CHAPTER 2 INSTALLATION AND COMMAND DESCRIPTION

If you're having trouble running the ps1 file in Windows 11, follow these steps:

- Open PowerShell: You can open PowerShell by pressing the Windows key + R, then typing "powershell" and pressing Enter.

- Change the execution policy: PowerShell has an execution policy that may prevent scripts from running. To change the execution policy, type the following command and press Enter: Set-ExecutionPolicy Unrestricted

- When you press Enter, it will ask you to confirm the new execution policy. Type "Y" and press Enter to confirm.

- Run your .ps1 file by right-clicking it and selecting the option: Run with PowerShell.

- Restore the execution policy: After running the script, it's recommended to restore the previous execution policy to avoid security issues. To do this, type the following command and press Enter: Set-ExecutionPolicy Restricted

- Confirm by typing "Y".

Now run the file gcc-arm-none-eabi-6-2017-q2-update-win32-sha2.exe. At the end of the installation, you should select this option: "Add path to environment variable". See Figures 2-14 and 2-15.

CHAPTER 2   INSTALLATION AND COMMAND DESCRIPTION

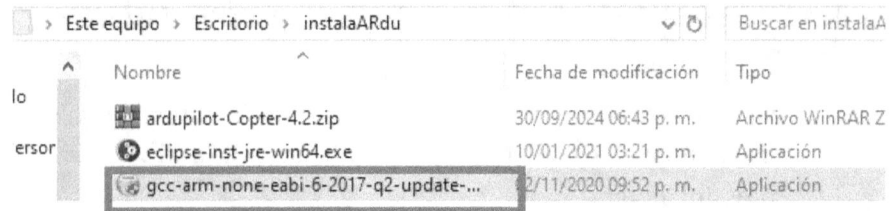

Figure 2-14.   *Installing ArduPilot libraries and its dependencies 7*

Figure 2-15.   *Installing ArduPilot libraries and its dependencies 8*

A terminal will open as indicated in Figure 2-16. Wait a few minutes and close it.

CHAPTER 2   INSTALLATION AND COMMAND DESCRIPTION

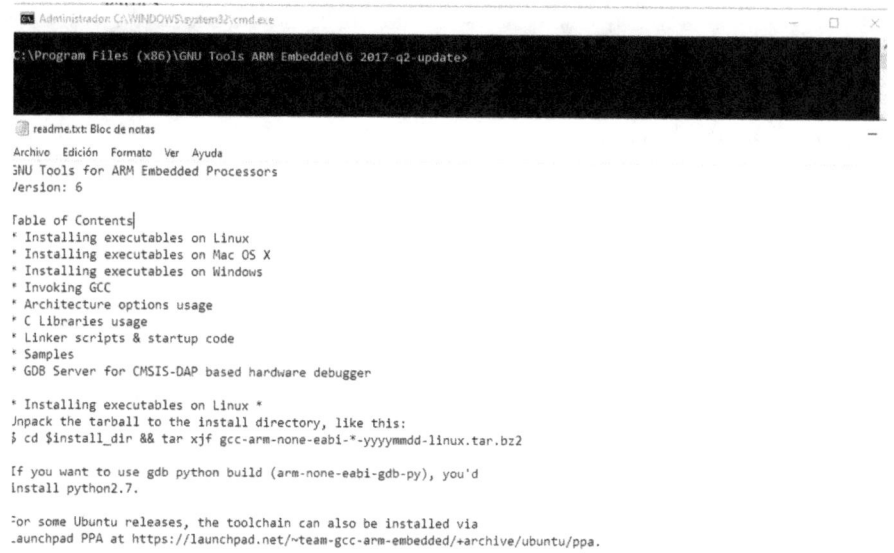

Figure 2-16. *Installing ArduPilot libraries and its dependencies 9*

Part 4

ArduPilot code compilation

Attention   We remind you of the high volatility of the procedures shown here. Each year, developers release at least 3–4 new versions. It's in this compilation part where we've noticed that recent autopilots require some additional steps beyond those described here. Therefore, it's advisable to also take a look at this website.

https://ardupilot.org/dev/docs/building-setup-windows-eclipse.html

---

Continuing with the procedure:

Open Eclipse and select the following option, see Figure 2-17.

CHAPTER 2 INSTALLATION AND COMMAND DESCRIPTION

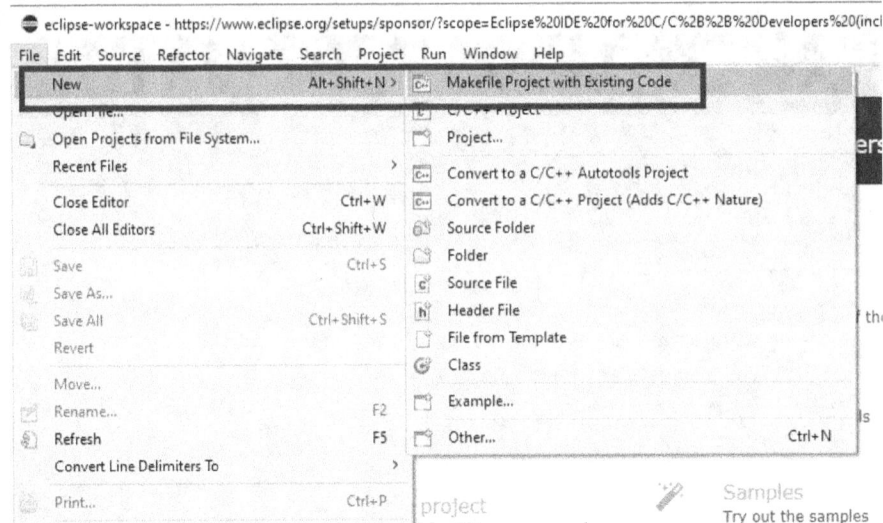

Figure 2-17. *ArduPilot code compilation 1*

Navigate through your files and find the ArduPilot folder within the GitHub folder.

Verify that it contains the information shown in Figure 2-18.

CHAPTER 2   INSTALLATION AND COMMAND DESCRIPTION

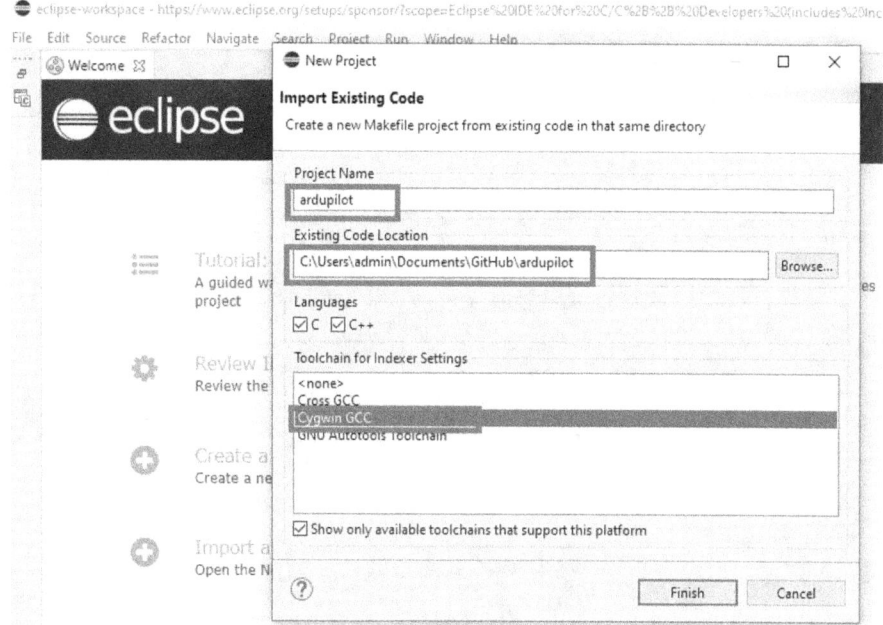

Figure 2-18. *ArduPilot code compilation 2*

Before continuing, close the Welcome tab.

Right-click the project name and select Properties (Figure 2-19), then make the modifications illustrated in Figure 2-20. After that, click Apply and Close.

Note   It's essential to verify which version of python3.xm you have in the following folder. When necessary, you'll need to indicate it along with its address and add the word waf, for example, in our case.

```
c:\cygwin64\bin\python3.7m waf
```

CHAPTER 2 INSTALLATION AND COMMAND DESCRIPTION

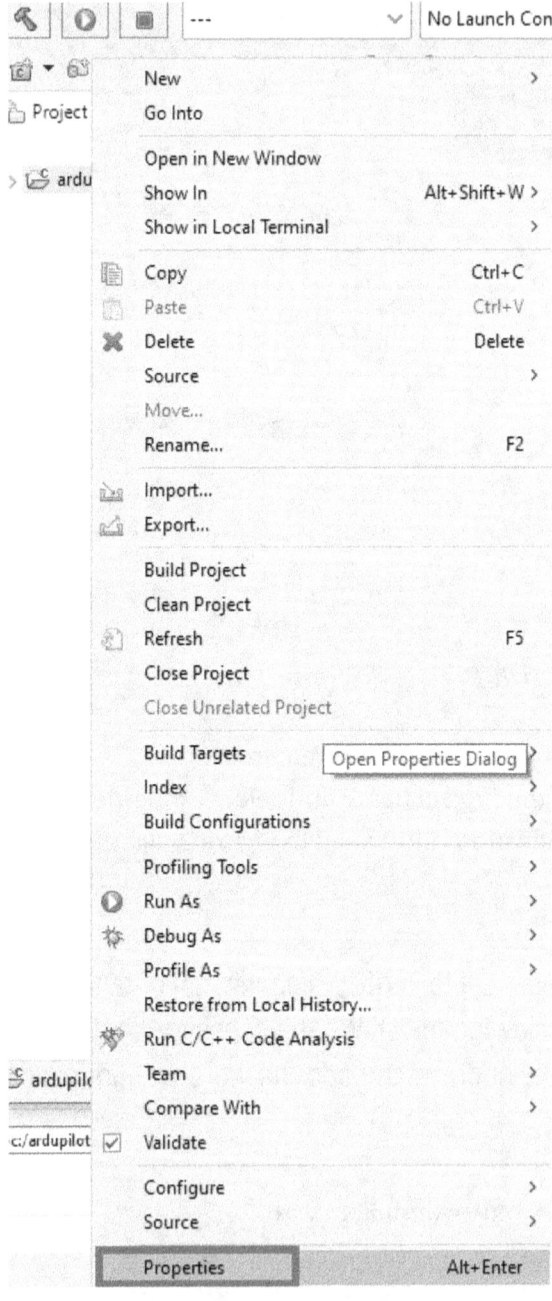

Figure 2-19. *ArduPilot code compilation 3*

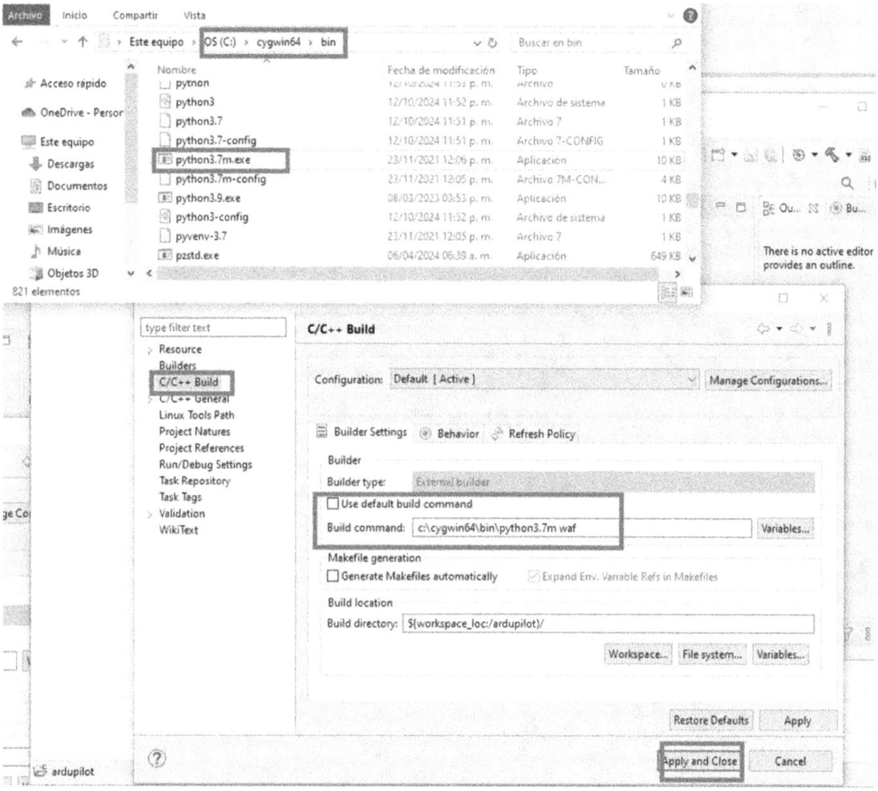

CHAPTER 2   INSTALLATION AND COMMAND DESCRIPTION

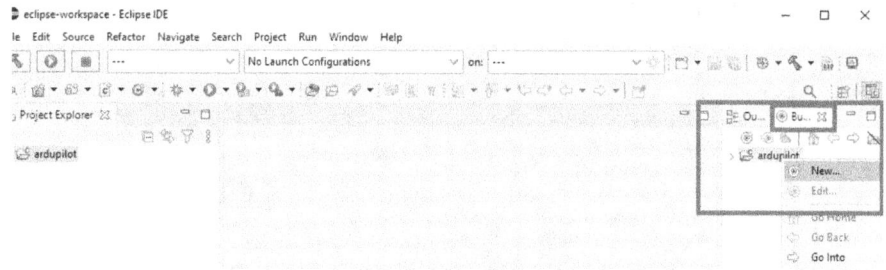

Figure 2-20. *ArduPilot code compilation 4*

Next, we'll create a new compilation Target. Right-click the project in the upper-right section as indicated in Figure 2-21.

Figure 2-21. *ArduPilot code compilation 5*

CHAPTER 2   INSTALLATION AND COMMAND DESCRIPTION

In the window that appears, write

configure --board fmuv2 --no-submodule-update as shown in Figure 2-22.

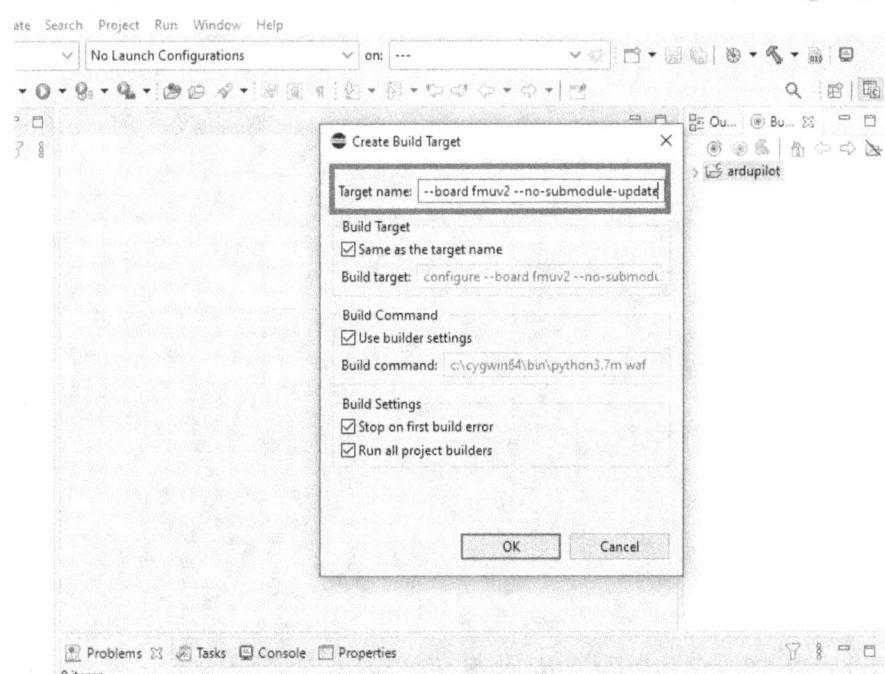

Figure 2-22. *ArduPilot code compilation 6*

The word fmuv2 will depend on the board you have. Other possible options are in Figure 2-23.

```
./waf configure --board bebop --static   # Bebop or Bebop2
./waf configure --board edge             # emlid edge
./waf configure --board fmuv3            # 3DR Pixhawk 2 boards
./waf configure --board navio2           # emlid navio2
./waf configure --board Pixhawk1         # Pixhawk1
./waf configure --board CubeBlack        # Hex/ProfiCNC Cube Black (formerly known as Pixhawk 2.1)
./waf configure --board Pixracer         # Pixracer
./waf configure --board skyviper-v2450   # SkyRocket's SkyViper GPS drone using ChibiOS
./waf configure --board sitl             # software-in-the-loop simulator
./waf configure --board sitl --debug     # software-in-the-loop simulator with debug symbols
```

Figure 2-23. *ArduPilot code compilation 7*

CHAPTER 2 INSTALLATION AND COMMAND DESCRIPTION

Create another compilation target with the following command: Copter, see Figure 2-24.

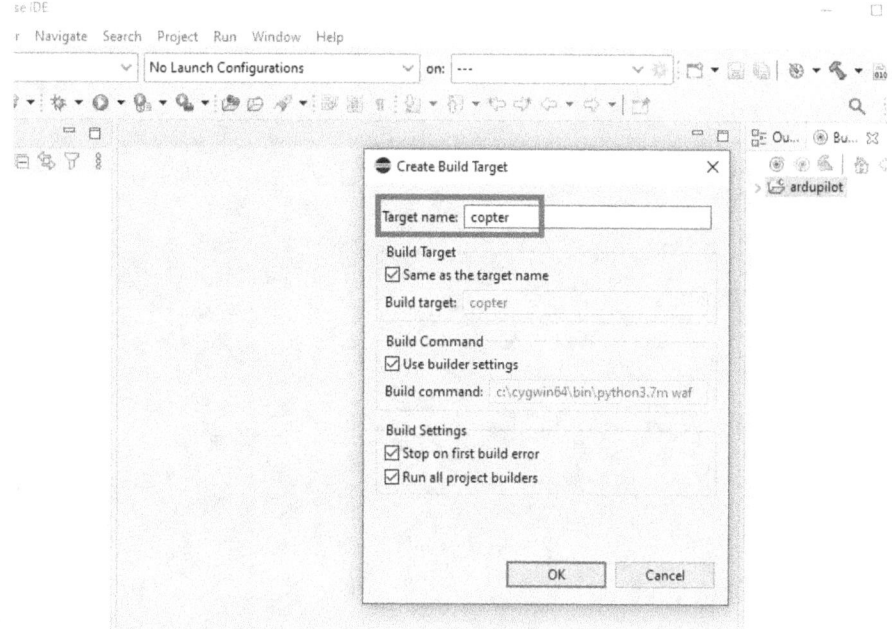

Figure 2-24. *ArduPilot code compilation 8*

Double-click the first target created and wait for it to finish executing, see Figure 2-25. You can see the process in the console at the bottom as shown in Figure 2-26.

> Note   For Windows 11 (if it sends an error in gcc-arm), restart.

83

CHAPTER 2 INSTALLATION AND COMMAND DESCRIPTION

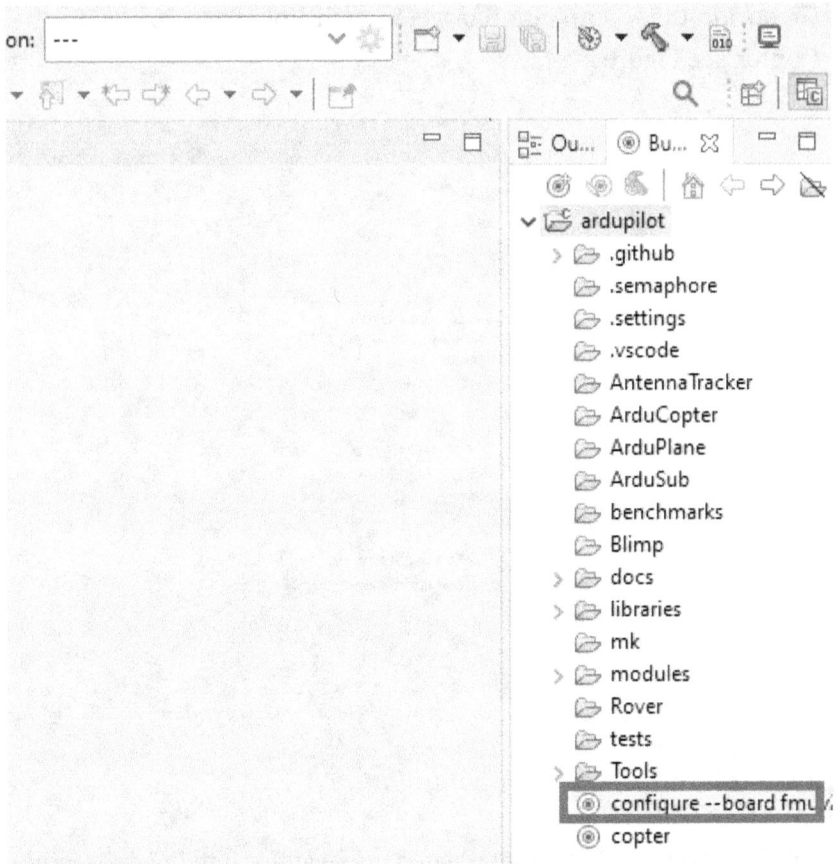

Figure 2-25. *ArduPilot code compilation 9*

CHAPTER 2 INSTALLATION AND COMMAND DESCRIPTION

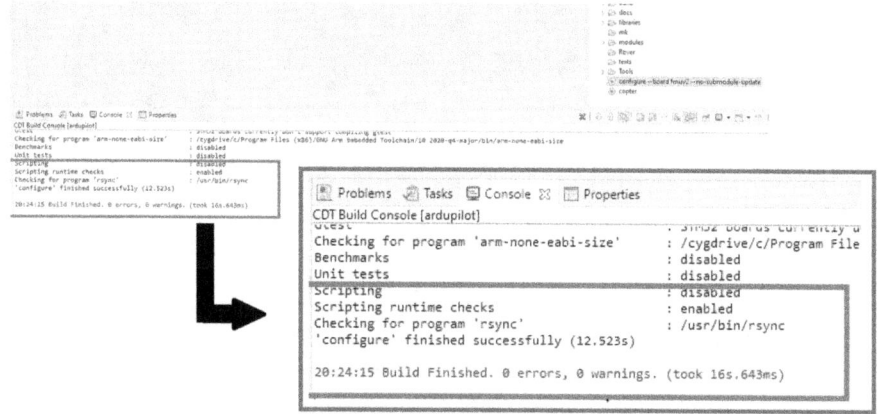

Figure 2-26. ArduPilot code compilation 10

Double-click the "copter" target and wait for it to finish, see Figure 2-27. The first time it might take more than three minutes, see Figure 2-28.

CHAPTER 2　INSTALLATION AND COMMAND DESCRIPTION

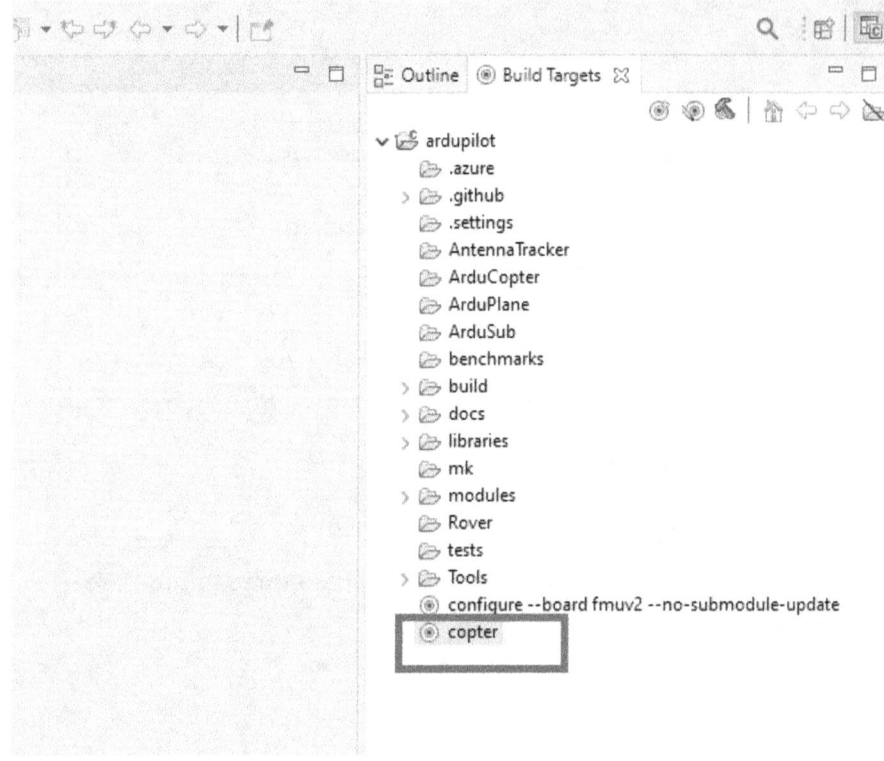

Figure 2-27. *ArduPilot code compilation 11*

CHAPTER 2   INSTALLATION AND COMMAND DESCRIPTION

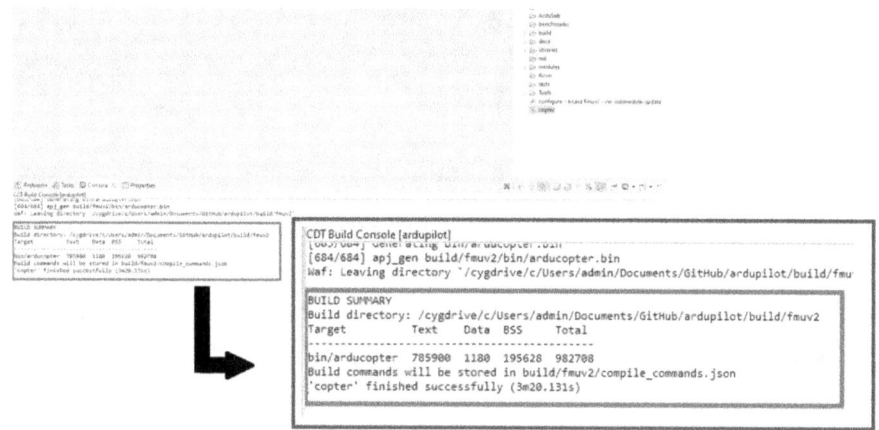

Figure 2-28. ArduPilot code compilation 12

Note   If it sends an error related to reconfiguring the project, delete the "build" folder inside the GitHub folder.

Issues have been found when executing -configure –board... with error messages like: Invalid lock file or simply not detecting the cygwin path.

Possible solution: Delete the .lock-waf... file from the ArduPilot folder within GitHub and also the Build folder; to do this, keep Eclipse closed. Then, re-run the compilation targets.

If the problem persists and a message appears "could not find the program ['arm-none-eabi-ar']", reinstall (without uninstalling anything) the gcc compiler (in administrator mode) and restart the PC. Then, delete the build folder.

If the compilation is successful, within the ArduPilot folder, a build folder should be generated containing a folder called fmuv2 (for the board used here) and within it, another folder called bin. Inside that folder will be our executable with the .apj extension and the name arducopter, see Figure 2-29.

87

CHAPTER 2   INSTALLATION AND COMMAND DESCRIPTION

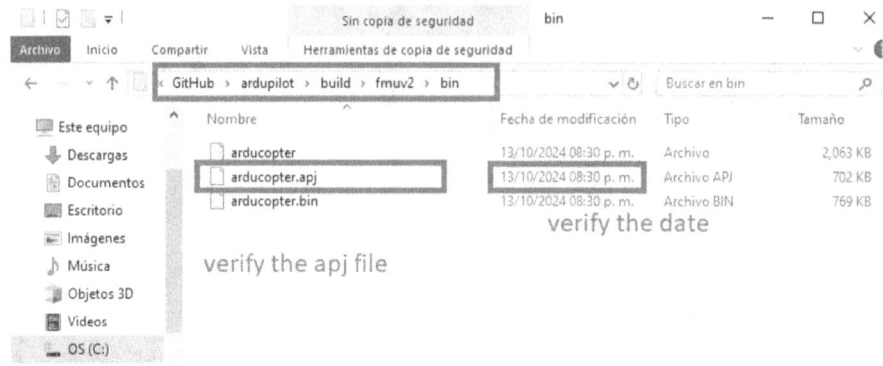

Figure 2-29. *ArduPilot code compilation 13*

Part 5

Loading executables to Autopilot from Mission Planner

First, install Mission Planner. This software is as straightforward as just clicking accept buttons and following the instructions.

Once installed, open it and select the SETUP option in the top left corner, see Figure 2-30.

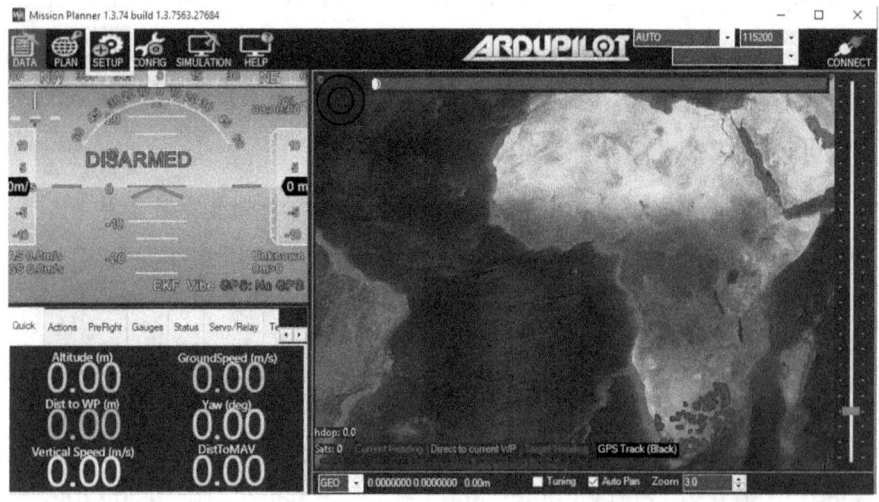

Figure 2-30. *Loading executables from Mission Planner 1*

CHAPTER 2   INSTALLATION AND COMMAND DESCRIPTION

Next, select the Install Firmware Legacy option, see Figure 2-31.

Figure 2-31. *Loading executables from Mission Planner 2*

Connect your autopilot to the computer, but don't click the CONNECT button in Mission Planner. Only select the COM port of your autopilot. The port should be enabled automatically if the drivers were installed correctly, see Figure 2-32.

Figure 2-32. *Loading executables from Mission Planner 3*

Select the option "Load custom firmware", see Figure 2-33.

CHAPTER 2   INSTALLATION AND COMMAND DESCRIPTION

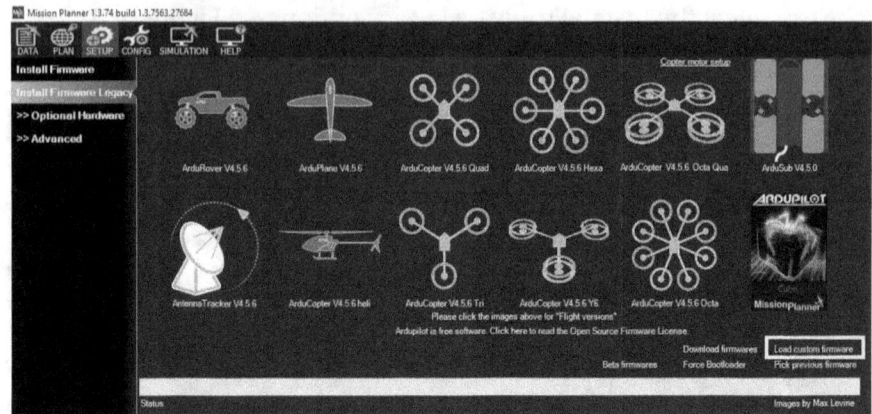

Figure 2-33. *Loading executables from Mission Planner 4*

Find the file with the .apj extension previously generated. Click open and follow the software's instructions, see Figure 2-34.

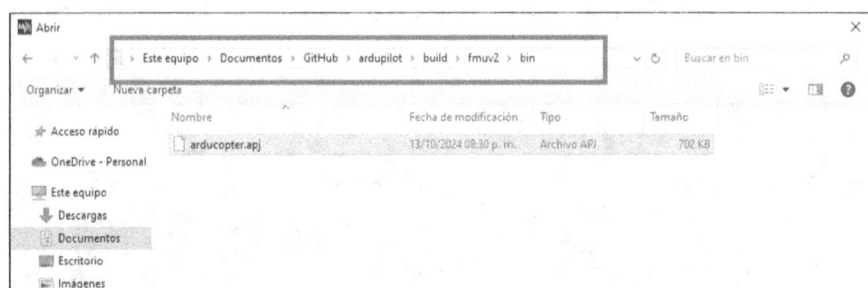

Figure 2-34. *Loading executables from Mission Planner 5*

DONE!! Your program has been uploaded to your autopilot.

Note   If issues occur with COM port changes, use the Install Firmware option to upload the .apj file and then use the Install Firmware Legacy option again.

CHAPTER 2   INSTALLATION AND COMMAND DESCRIPTION

Part 6

Customizing the Eclipse software interface

Open Eclipse and select the options indicated in Figure 2-35.

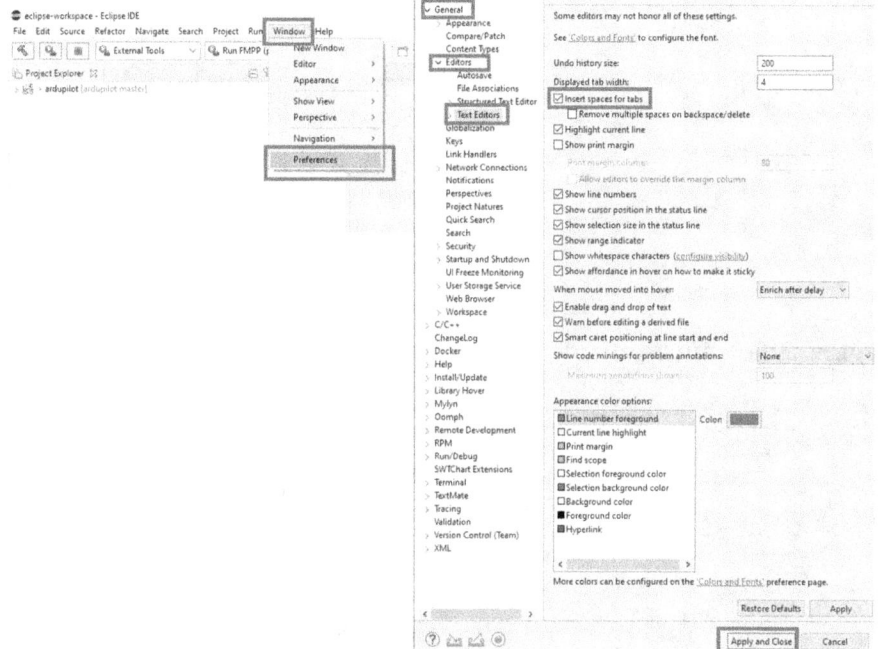

Figure 2-35. *Customizing the Eclipse software interface 1*

Add a new profile that uses only spaces called K&R Tab as in Figures 2-36 and 2-37.

91

CHAPTER 2   INSTALLATION AND COMMAND DESCRIPTION

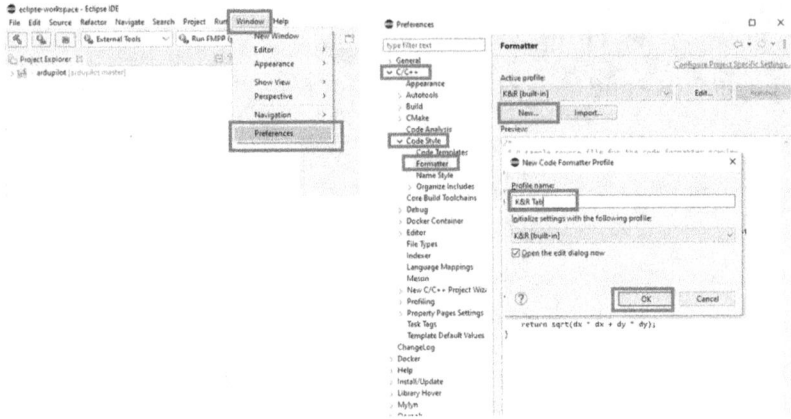

Figure 2-36. Customizing the Eclipse software interface 2

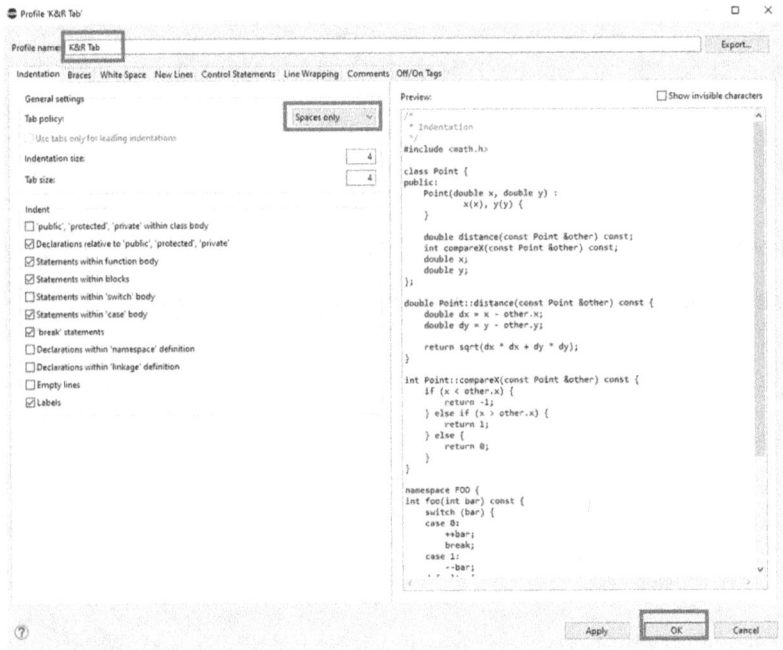

Figure 2-37. Customizing the Eclipse software interface 3

And that's it. End of installation.

CHAPTER 2   INSTALLATION AND COMMAND DESCRIPTION

Extended "Hello World"

The following "Hello World" is suggested after completing the installation process. Unlike other projects in this book, it doesn't require a custom file. You can simply modify the UserCode.cpp file by following these steps:

1. Go to the APM_config.h file and activate a predefined loop by uncommenting the line with the desired loop name; in this case, USERHOOK_MEDIUMLOOP. Remember that single-line comments in C++ are made with //. Specifically, remove these symbols from the predefined loops you want to use and add them to the ones you don't as in Figure 2-38.

```
//#define HIL_MODE                 HIL_MODE_SENSORS    // build for
hardware-in-the-loop simulation

// User Hooks : For User Developed code that you wish to run
// Put your variable definitions into the UserVariables.h file
(or another file name and then change the #define below).
#define USERHOOK_VARIABLES "UserVariables.h"
// Put your custom code into the UserCode.cpp with function
names matching those listed below and ensure the appropriate
#define below is uncommented below
//#define USERHOOK_INIT userhook_init();                       //
for code to be run once at startup
#define USERHOOK_FASTLOOP userhook_FastLoop();                 // for
code to be run at 100hz
#define USERHOOK_50HZLOOP userhook_50Hz();                     //
for code to be run at 50hz
#define USERHOOK_MEDIUMLOOP userhook_MediumLoop();             // for
code to be run at 10hz
//#define USERHOOK_SLOWLOOP userhook_SlowLoop();               //
for code to be run at 3.3hz
//#define USERHOOK_SUPERSLOWLOOP userhook_SuperSlowLoop();     //
for code to be run at 1hz
//#define USERHOOK_AUXSWITCH ENABLED                           //
for code to handle user aux switches
//#define USER_PARAMS_ENABLED ENABLED                          //
to enable user parameters
```

Figure 2-38. *Activation and deactivation of predefined loops in ArduPilot libraries*

CHAPTER 2   INSTALLATION AND COMMAND DESCRIPTION

2. Open UserCode.cpp and add the content of the previous predefined loop; this is described in Listing 2-1.

Listing 2-1. A more interesting Hello World inside the USERHOOK_MEDIUMLOOP in the UserCode.cpp file

```
#ifdef USERHOOK_MEDIUMLOOP
void Copter::userhook_MediumLoop()
{
    hal.console->printf("Hola...\n");
    hal.console->printf("%lu\n",(unsigned long)AP_
    HAL::micros64());
    hal.console->printf("%lu\n",(unsigned long)AP_
    HAL::millis());
    hal.scheduler->delay(1000);
}
#endif
```

In a very simplified way, the previous program will indefinitely display the message "Hola" followed by the time in microseconds and milliseconds, and repeat this sequence with a 1-second pause (1000 milliseconds).

Later, in the section on time management in this book, we'll discuss in detail the three types of time used in the previous code.

CHAPTER 2   INSTALLATION AND COMMAND DESCRIPTION

3. Once the files are compiled as previously indicated, use the Mission Planner serial monitor (a procedure also described in this book). You should see the output indicated in Figure 2-39:

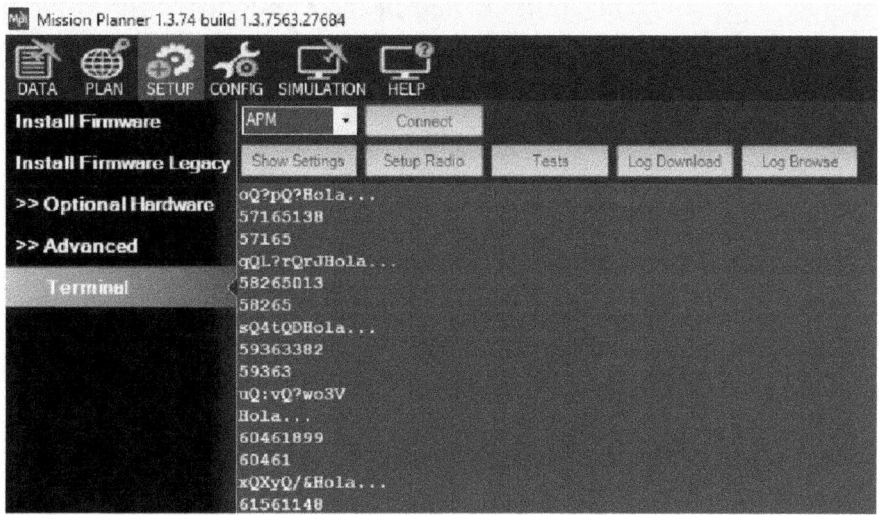

Figure 2-39. Visualization of the modified Hello World with timestamp printing

Before the "Hola" message, some random characters may appear due to communication issues and inadequate pauses (we'll explain this in the time management section, and it's a reason not to use delays). However, this should serve as a typical "Hello World" to verify that ArduPilot has been installed correctly on your system.

CHAPTER 2   INSTALLATION AND COMMAND DESCRIPTION

Comparison of Commands and Features of Current and Old ArduPilot Libraries

The differences between the ArduPilot libraries 2018 version and the 2023 version are presented below in a table. The most important observation we can make regarding the indicated versions is that we have found many false friends, either in the fact that the commands are the same but the procedure for their use varies significantly, or vice versa, where the procedure is practically the same but the commands change. In extreme cases, both things change (although this is less common).

Below in Table 2-1 is the list of commands used in this book. If another additional command is required, it is recommended to read the predecessor book, *Advanced Robotic Vehicles Programming*, to have a solid foundation on its use. Then, in the ArduPilot help, look for the new command or equivalent procedure.

Table 2-1. Comparison of commands and features of current and old ArduPilot libraries

Feature	ArduPilot 2018 (Advanced Robotic Vehicles Programming)	ArduPilot 2023 (This book)	Section or chapter of this book where it's used or explained
Programming paradigm	Semi-structured, very basic OOP with Arduino style: definition, setup, and main loop	Fully OOP, setup is unnecessary (predefined in copter's auxiliary files), declarations and loops are in user-defined codes and user-defined variables files	Chapter 1, section: Introduction to OOP work format
Files to modify	Main template and some auxiliary files	At least the seven files indicated throughout this text with modular intercommunication between them	Chapter 1, section: Description of the main files to modify simultaneously in the new ArduPilot libraries. Later on throughout the book.

(*continued*)

CHAPTER 2 INSTALLATION AND COMMAND DESCRIPTION

Table 2-1. (*continued*)

Feature	ArduPilot 2018 (Advanced Robotic Vehicles Programming)	ArduPilot 2023 (This book)	Section or chapter of this book where it's used or explained
Interaction with Mission Planner	Limited to flashing the autopilot and reading the SD card outside of the autopilot	The same case as the previous cell, and also for the definition and manipulation of data and sensors; additionally, Mission Planner can be used as a serial terminal to observe messages of interest	Chapter 1, Section: Linkage and uses with Mission Planner
Serial writing to screen (computer)	Use anywhere in the template hal.console-> printf("%kindOfData",Data)	Use hal.console-> printf("%kindOfData",Data) Preferably in a 10Hz loop like Userhook_MediumLoop() in the UserCode.cpp file	Throughout the examples in the entire book

CHAPTER 2 INSTALLATION AND COMMAND DESCRIPTION

Reading radiocontrol	`hal.rcin->read(NUMBER)` Where number goes from 0 to 3 for roll, pitch, yaw, and throttle and more than or equal 4 for the aux channels	`copter.channel_X->get_radio_in()` Where X=roll, pitch, yaw, throttle Or alternatively `rc().get_radio_in(NUMBER)` Where number goes from 0 to 3 for roll, pitch, yaw, and throttle and more than or equal 4 for the aux channels	In the chapters on the aeropendulum, the quadcopter mounted on a test stand, and the free flight quadcopter
Writing to BLDC or Brushed motors by using a PWM RC to PWM cycle converter like an Arduino or a specialized device	`hal.rcout->write(channel,value);` Where channel goes from 0 to the maximum number of motors available in the autopilot minus 1 and value goes from 1000 to 2000 (motors' minimum and maximum velocities, respectively) In this case a setup section was required `hal.rcout->enable_ch(channel);`	`hal.rcout->write(channel, value);` Where channel goes from 0 to the maximum number of motors available in the autopilot minus 1 and value goes from 1000 to 2000 (motors' minimum and maximum velocities, respectively) In this case, a setup section IS NOT required	In the chapters on the aeropendulum, the quadcopter mounted on a test stand, and the free flight quadcopter

(continued)

Table 2-1. (*continued*)

Feature	ArduPilot 2018 (Advanced Robotic Vehicles Programming)	ArduPilot 2023 (This book)	Section or chapter of this book where it's used or explained

Reading positions and angular velocities and translations	It is not as straightforward as with the new libraries; the same basic lines of the next cell need to be declared, then set up and finally used along with updating commands, all inside the same template file	In your customized code this must run at 400Hz
		
		Once there, use the following commands
		
		FOR ROTATIONAL MOTION USING THE EMBEDDED AUTOPILOT'S IMU
		
		`const AP_InertialSensor &ins = AP::ins();`
		
		`const Vector3f &gyro = ins.get_gyro();`
			In the chapters on the quadcopter mounted on a test stand, and the free flight quadcopter

	FOR TRASLATIONAL MOTION USING AN EXTERNAL GPS
	
	`Vector3f position = (inertial_nav.get_position() / 100);`
	
	`Vector3f velocity = (inertial_nav.get_velocity() / 100);`
	
	Then use
	
	ahrs.N where N = roll, pitch or yaw
	gyro.N where N= x,y,z
	position.N where N=x,y,z
	velocity.N where N=x,y,z	

Signal Filtering	filter.apply(signal) with previous declaration of a time delta and a filter window but not in a setup section	low_pass_filter.apply(signal,dt) with previous declaration in the pseudoSetup USERHOOK_INIT	Chapter 3, Section: Programming

(continued)

CHAPTER 2 INSTALLATION AND COMMAND DESCRIPTION

Table 2-1. (*continued*)

Feature	ArduPilot 2018 (Advanced Robotic Vehicles Programming)	ArduPilot 2023 (This book)	Section or chapter of this book where it's used or explained

Analog Inputs	ch=hal.analogin->channel(chan);
	
	ch->set_pin(chan number);
	
	ch->voltage_average( );
	
	With the procedure from the previous book, *Advanced Robotic Vehicles Programming*
		Although the commands are almost the same
		
		chan = hal.analogin->channel(NUMBER);
		
		chan->voltage_average();
		
		Where NUMBER is the analog channel to read
		
		The procedure is a false friend and it's better to read the one described in this book.
			Chapter 4, Section:
			
			About connectors and analog, serial, and real-time tests

Saving to SD	The procedure described in our previous book, *Advanced Robotic Vehicles Programming*	Practically the same procedure described in our previous book, *Advanced Robotic Vehicles Programming*	In the chapters on the aeropendulum, the quadcopter mounted on a test stand, and the free flight quadcopter

Serial Communication	`hal.uartX->begin(vel)` `hal.uartX->available()` `hal.uartX->read()` `hal.uartX->write(data);` Where X are the ports D or C, and vel is the serial velocity transmission With the procedure described in our previous book *Advanced Robotic Vehicles Programming*	Practically the same commands and procedure as the previous libraries but placed in various modular files including the PseudoSetup	Chapter 4, Section: About connectors and analog, serial, and real-time tests
Real time Scheduler	It's based on defining custom tasks and their assignment in a scheduler table, the extensive procedure is indicated in our previous book, *Advanced Robotic Vehicles Programming*	Although similar in content and operation to the old libraries, the use of the real-time scheduler is a false friend, and in this case, it's convenient to use the method described in this book.	Chapter 4, Section: About connectors and analog, serial, and real-time tests

(continued)

Table 2-1. (*continued*)

Feature	ArduPilot 2018 (Advanced Robotic Vehicles Programming)	ArduPilot 2023 (This book)	Section or chapter of this book where it's used or explained
Setup	Mandatory to set up ports; literally it's a section called setup	PseudoSetup USERHOOK_INIT	Chapter 3, Section: Programming
Time Stamps	hal.scheduler->millis() hal.scheduler->micros()	AP_HAL::micros64(); AP_HAL::millis();	Chapter 2, Section: Extended "Hello World" and Chapter 3, Section: Programming

Chapter Summary

In this chapter, a more extensive approach to the new ArduPilot libraries (2023 version) was shown, describing the installation process on Windows; also, a useful "hello world" with a first description on time management and a comparative table between the current 2023 ArduPilot libraries and the old 2018 ones were shown.

In the next chapter, the components and general knowledge that will be used in the three extensive projects of this book will be described with a mechatronic focus, including details such as the basics of PD control, the definition of a differential vehicle, the generic ArduPilot files to be modified, a description of autopilots, structural and electronic components, and the definition of a state machine, among other topics.

CHAPTER 3

Mechatronic Description of Generic Components Used in This Book

In the third chapter of this book, we describe the common components of each project developed in the following chapters. This description is divided into the four basic elements of mechatronics:

> Mechanics: In this section, we'll discuss the structural elements that comprise the projects, including fasteners, metal profiles, and couplings used throughout the text.

> Electronics: This section covers the electrical and electronic components used in the projects, including power sources, motors, remote controls, and sensors.

CHAPTER 3　MECHATRONIC DESCRIPTION OF GENERIC COMPONENTS USED IN THIS BOOK

Programming: We present two approaches: one focused on hardware, describing the autopilots used in this book, and the other on software, detailing common modifications for all guided projects.

Control: You'll learn about the difference between logical and arithmetic control, also a solid but easy understanding of the PD controller used in all projects, and you'll explore the concept of differential vehicles, which applies to our guided examples.

Finally, we include a section on verifying safe operation of flight modes.

In this book, prototypes are presented in an order that facilitates understanding of ArduPilot libraries, focusing on programming. All this from a design and operational manufacturing perspective, specifically in mechatronics, the prototypes followed a staggered design process from the simplest chassis to the most complex structure, see Figure 3-1.

CHAPTER 3   MECHATRONIC DESCRIPTION OF GENERIC COMPONENTS USED IN THIS BOOK

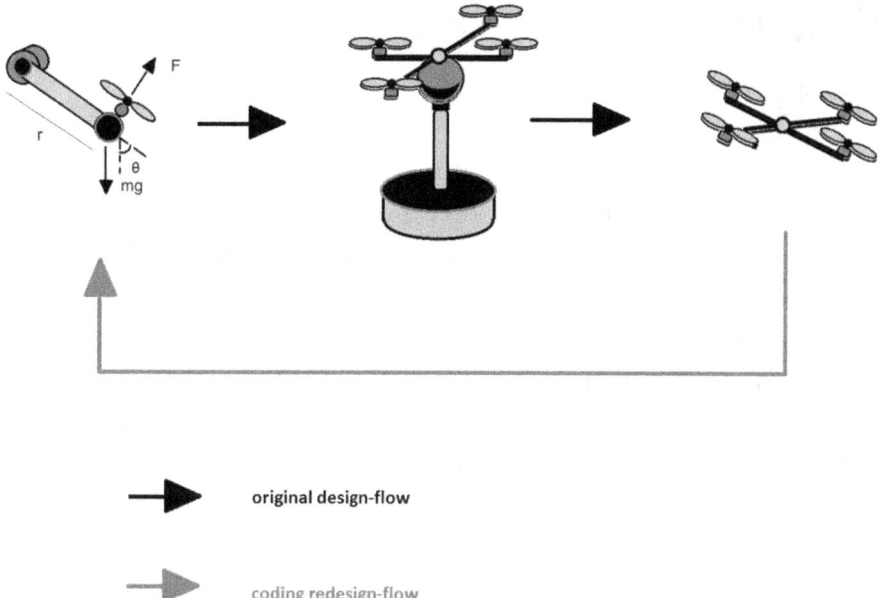

Figure 3-1. *Mechatronic design sequence and computational redesign of the extensive examples in this book*

Our process involved building and testing the aeropendulum first, followed by a quadcopter mounted on a test stand, and finally a free-flying drone.

The aeropendulum tests a single motor's balance and stability with its own propeller. The quadcopter mounted on a test stand ensures the entire drone's balance and response with four motors and vehicle-level communication, preventing crashes due to design flaws. Having gained knowledge from these phases, we then conduct free-flight tests.

The redesign process is then at the control and programming level, since if the final version of the design, in this case the free-flying drone, has any unforeseen flight issues or imbalance, we go back to the previous versions to correct these aspects.

CHAPTER 3   MECHATRONIC DESCRIPTION OF GENERIC COMPONENTS USED IN THIS BOOK

Mechanics

Shafts

Use: They are the elements that connect the motors or motor outputs, transmitting rotation, speed, and force directly between two distant points. They are often used for weight distribution or to avoid bending the main axis of the motors.

Types: They are the most varied element. In this case, we will limit ourselves to using straight shafts or threaded ones (studs or screws). The way to fix them or attach other objects is through set screws, keyways, or fasteners and nuts, see Figure 3-2.

Figure 3-2. *Drive shaft and some of its usual fixing elements*

CHAPTER 3   MECHATRONIC DESCRIPTION OF GENERIC COMPONENTS USED IN THIS BOOK

Description and operation: It is simply a rotational transmission element, designed to transmit torque and speed from a driving point to a driven one.

Care and recommendations: This should be the most resistant part of a mechanism, as it connects the motor to an output element. At a minimum, it should be considered that its material, diameter, and length can withstand a certain weight or torque, and if it's for high-speed applications, they should also support that rotation.

Couplings

Use: They are devices designed to connect two shafts in a machine; for example, a motor shaft with an angular sensor shaft such as a potentiometer or encoder. They are also often used to compensate for larger misalignments.

Types: Although there are many more varieties than those presented here, and they often occupy large catalogs and sections of books or even entire books on the subject, for the projects in this book we will only use three, these are

- Linear flexible couplings: In this case, there is a device designed to interconnect two shafts in a straight line (see Figure 3-3), compensating for some angular lag in the rotation of both shafts or small angular misalignments.

CHAPTER 3   MECHATRONIC DESCRIPTION OF GENERIC COMPONENTS USED IN THIS BOOK

Figure 3-3. *A linear flexible coupling frequently used in maker projects*

- Universal joints: It is a widely used and well-known coupling, especially in heavy machinery and automobiles. It is characterized by good power transmission and allowing wide roll and pitch misalignment movements between shafts, see Figure 3-4.

CHAPTER 3 MECHATRONIC DESCRIPTION OF GENERIC COMPONENTS USED IN THIS BOOK

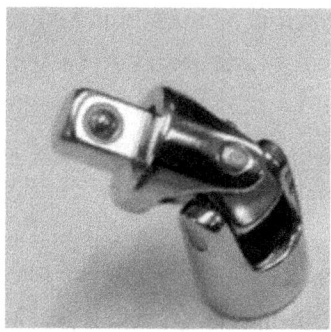

Figure 3-4. *Universal joints*

- Spherical or ball joints: These allow connecting two shafts with total spatial misalignment of 3 degrees of freedom in orientation (roll, pitch, and yaw), see Figure 3-5.

Figure 3-5. *Ball or spherical joint*

CHAPTER 3 MECHATRONIC DESCRIPTION OF GENERIC COMPONENTS USED IN THIS BOOK

Description and operation: As mentioned earlier, they are joints based on 2D or 3D hinges or flexible materials, which allow free angular movement with between 1 and 3 degrees of rotational freedom and interconnection between two shafts (e.g., a drone anchored to a base, as extensively developed in the chapter on the quadcopter mounted on a test stand in this book).

Care and recommendations: There are five key considerations; the first is respecting movement limits; the second is resistance to machining of parts, as modifications are sometimes necessary and some models may be hardened; the third consideration is related to their degree of stiffness in mobility; a fourth consideration is their weight, dimensions, and shape; and the last consideration is keeping them lubricated, as they can rust and become blocked.

Bearings

Use: They are specialized mechanisms widely used to facilitate the mechanical interaction of anchored or static parts with rotating ones.

Types: There are too many to include in the scope of this book; in fact, there are entire texts that specifically deal with bearings. However, for the purposes of this book, it is enough to use ball bearings with perpendicular load (the most common type).

Description and operation: A bearing has four basic components (see Figure 3-6):

> The outer ring: It has independent movement from the inner ring due to its sliding with the balls.
>
> The inner ring: It has independent movement from the outer ring due to its sliding with the balls.

The balls: These elements allow the independence of movement of the outer ring with respect to the inner ring.

The retainers: These are used to assemble the previous components, preventing the rings from separating and spacing the balls.

Figure 3-6. *Ball bearing*

Care and recommendations: They are specialized load and mobility elements, so if they are used beyond their limits, there is a risk of deforming or tightening them (resulting in lack of mobility due to high friction between their inner and outer surfaces). For the simplified prototypes in this book, and since the driving elements used generate very low torque and force, the selection criteria were omitted. However, for specialized designs, these criteria must be taken into account; for this, consult a book or course on machine element design.

CHAPTER 3   MECHATRONIC DESCRIPTION OF GENERIC COMPONENTS USED IN THIS BOOK

It is advisable to lubricate them periodically or when oxidation or high friction becomes evident or inadequate for the operation of the prototypes.

Although the next section will discuss pillow blocks, these systems are also treated as a separate topic because pillow blocks sometimes need to be custom-made according to the needs of each project (printed or machined). Thus, caution should be exercised, especially during their installation and adjustment.

Pillow Blocks

Use: They are used to support rotating shafts at one or more points. It is recommended to use at least two points to distribute the load (as in the axles of a tractor).

Types: They can be floor-mounted or wall-mounted; the choice depends on the reader's requirements.

Description and operation: In general, they consist of two parts; the first is a housing that can be attached to a fixed surface, and the second is a bearing or self-lubricating bushing where a shaft can rotate freely, see Figure 3-7.

CHAPTER 3   MECHATRONIC DESCRIPTION OF GENERIC COMPONENTS USED IN THIS BOOK

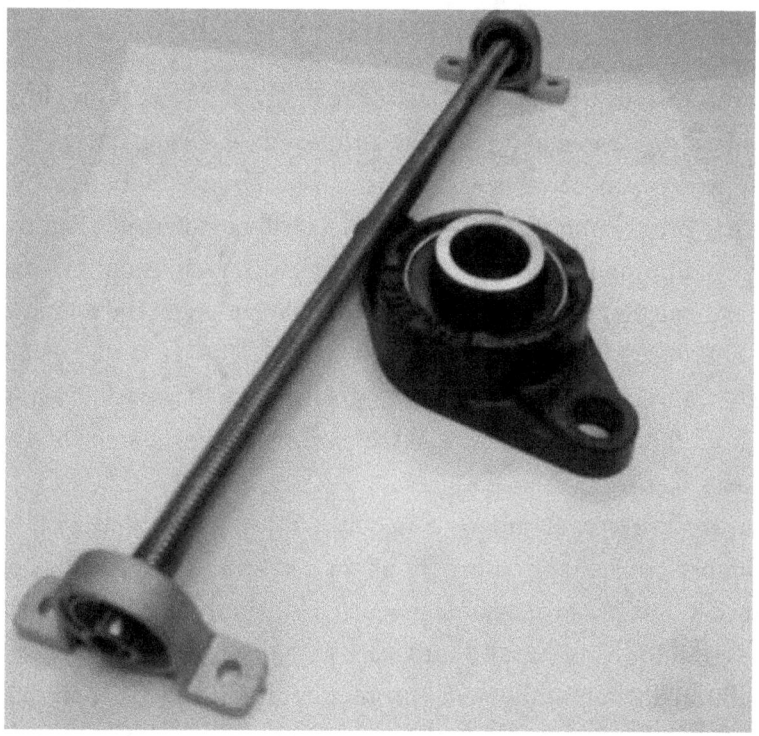

Figure 3-7. *Shaft supported by two pillow blocks and a big-size one*

Care and recommendations: If the pillow block has a self-lubricating material element, it can wear out or crack and affect the proper operation of the shaft's rotation over time. In the case of using bearings, they tend to rust and become blocked due to environmental action. It is enough to lubricate them periodically or after certain operating cycles.

Additionally, pillow blocks with bearings are recommended because many of them have self-aligning properties, meaning the bearing has partial spherical movement, making it easier to adjust moderate parallelism errors with another pillow block.

CHAPTER 3　MECHATRONIC DESCRIPTION OF GENERIC COMPONENTS USED IN THIS BOOK

Carbon Fiber or Engineering Plastics

Use: In this text, they will be used to make lightweight shafts and links with resistance comparable to metals like aluminum or certain types of steel. Therefore, in the following paragraphs, our preference for bars, tubes, and cylindrical profiles made of these materials will be noted, see Figure 3-8.

Types: Although there are many catalogs with various options, we will only use those that are commercially available and meet the diameter and length characteristics of our projects.

Description and operation: As already mentioned, we will use them throughout the text as shafts or links, as well as supports, spacers, and/or dowels.

Care and recommendations: Since they are special materials, it is convenient to select them properly, as their costs can vary greatly between similar scales. It is also advisable to learn a bit about machining curved surfaces (milling, drilling, and threading).

Additionally, remember that carbon fiber is an abrasive material at the powder level, so it is essential to read about its handling and reducing health risks.

CHAPTER 3   MECHATRONIC DESCRIPTION OF GENERIC COMPONENTS USED IN THIS BOOK

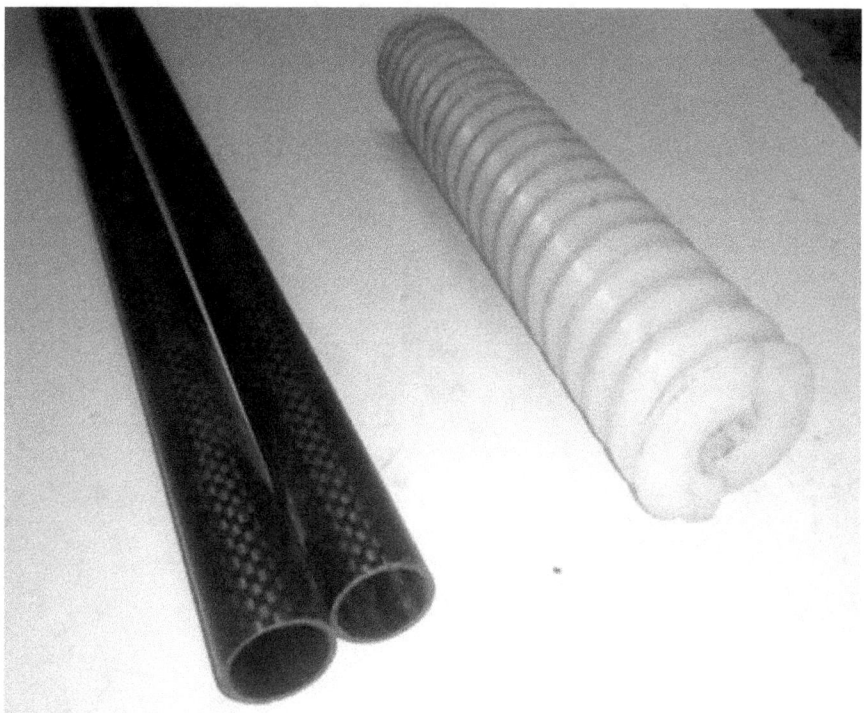

Figure 3-8. Carbon fiber tubes and nylon alloy skrew

Structural Profiles

Use: They serve as the foundation or structural base, allowing the rest of the elements to be fixed or anchored in a practical and visually appealing way.

Types: There are many, and in this book, the ones used will be indicated in each chapter. Some accessories will also be indicated to facilitate interconnection and assembly.

Description and operation: They are beams with channels and holes that are sufficiently hardened and rectified to provide a presentation and anchoring for a robotic prototype, see Figure 3-9.

CHAPTER 3   MECHATRONIC DESCRIPTION OF GENERIC COMPONENTS USED IN THIS BOOK

Care and recommendations: Use catalogs and preferably use locally available models, as importing them represents excessive costs. Preferably use aluminum profiles, as they do not rust, and whenever possible, buy connection accessories instead of making holes or adaptations.

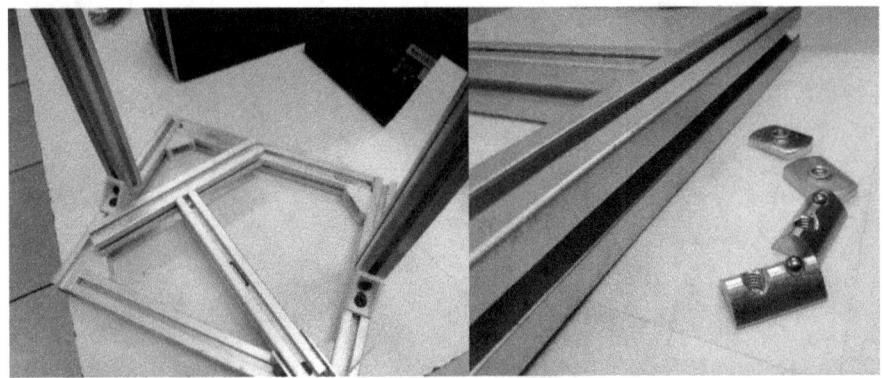

Figure 3-9. *IPS profiles and mounting accessories*

Supports

Use: They allow mounting the system's mobile components (pendulums, mobile links, etc.). This mounting is done toward the structural profiles.

Types: These are a wide variety, and in our case, we prefer right angles or wall types.

Description and operation: They are plates of various materials with holes and bends to facilitate their connection with sensor and driving elements, see Figure 3-10.

Care and recommendations: Choose those whose holes are compatible with the screws used with the structural profiles. Preferably buy at least two of each type used, as over time they may be modified, modernized, or discontinued, and it may be necessary to make adjustments or replace the entire piece.

CHAPTER 3   MECHATRONIC DESCRIPTION OF GENERIC COMPONENTS USED IN THIS BOOK

Figure 3-10. *Mounting or support with slots for placing motors, sensors, or other structural elements*

Specialized Fasteners

Use: The use is variable and depends on whether you want to operate with vibrations, pulls, or high speeds or forces and torques.

Types: In this text, we will use the following:

- Nilock, self-locking or safety: These nuts contain a plastic cover that can only be loosened with pliers, not manually, making it very difficult for them to separate with vibrations or free rotation, see Figure 3-11.

CHAPTER 3   MECHATRONIC DESCRIPTION OF GENERIC COMPONENTS USED IN THIS BOOK

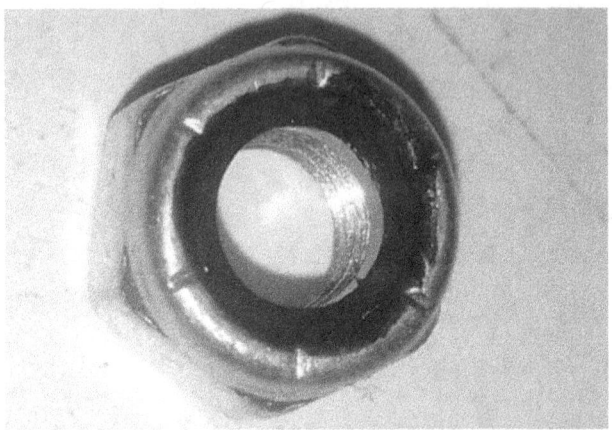

Figure 3-11. Self-locking or safety screw with plastic insert

- Washers: They are spacers for thin zones, allowing compensation of altitudes or distances or centering thinner elements in larger holes.

- Lugs: They are a type of washer used to connect electrical elements in a standardized way without using wire entanglements (which slowly break wires).

- Structural profile fasteners: They are special screws and nuts used directly with structural profiles.

- Allen screws: They are screws with special heads that allow tightening and loosening with screwdrivers instead of wrenches, particularly useful in tight spaces, see Figure 3-12.

CHAPTER 3   MECHATRONIC DESCRIPTION OF GENERIC COMPONENTS USED IN THIS BOOK

Figure 3-12. *Allen screw*

- Casings: They are nut-type connectors with internal and external threads to couple different diameters.

Description and operation: They are simple screws and nuts with specialized profiles and features for different fastening applications.

Care and recommendations: Ideally, use standardization and, whenever possible, use metric pieces with metric pieces and standard pieces with standard pieces (inch threads); avoid mixing parts. Also, check or estimate their load, torsion, and deformation limits.

Clamping Elements

Use: They allow anchoring a structure to a more solid element, such as a structural profile to a rigid table. This implies simply providing immobility or rigidity to a system without making it heavy or bulky.

Types: The ones we will use in this book are

- C-clamps: Also known as bar clamps, they allow fixing a structure to a worktable, see Figure 3-13.

CHAPTER 3   MECHATRONIC DESCRIPTION OF GENERIC COMPONENTS USED IN THIS BOOK

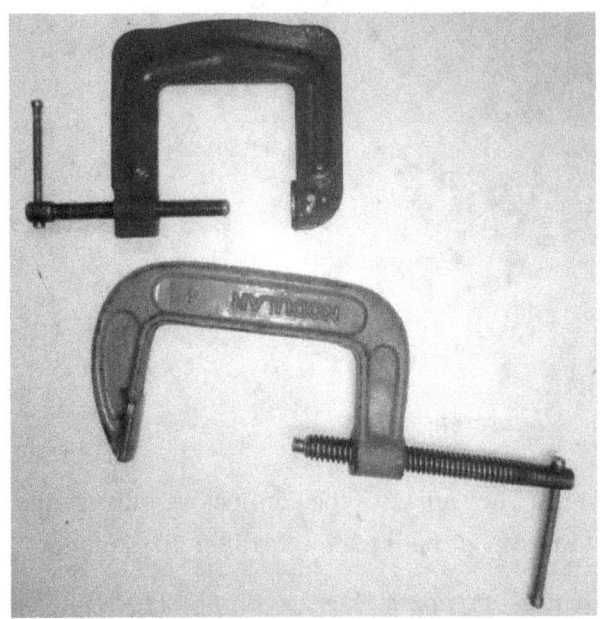

Figure 3-13. C-clamp

- Velcro straps, cable ties, etc.: In this case, they are useful for fixing small or light elements that require frequent or moderate replacement to a system, such as sensors, wireless transmission equipment, cables, etc., to keep them immobile or prevent them from hanging.

Propellers

They are the elements that transmit the power of the motor so that a body or vehicle can lift off. The types of propellers used or recommended in this text are the following:

For the aeropendulum, the quadcopter mounted on a test stand, and the free flight drone, we will normally use double-blade or double-edged propellers. Each blade on a propeller is equivalent to the wheels of a vehicle. A car with more wheels is intended to operate as a support for a

CHAPTER 3 MECHATRONIC DESCRIPTION OF GENERIC COMPONENTS USED IN THIS BOOK

heavy structure; however, this makes it slow due to the friction of so many wheels on the ground. Thus, speed applications require fewer wheels and less contact area.

Similarly, a propeller with several blades or wide blades is more focused on thrust (like a boat or the zeppelin mentioned in this book) or the load of a heavy aerial vehicle, but at the cost of draining the battery faster.

On the other hand, propellers with thin blades and few blades, having less contact area and friction with the fluid they push (air), are more focused on adapting to a system with faster changes or a lightweight vehicle. In this book, we recommend this type of propeller for the aeropendulum, the quadcopter mounted on a test stand, and the free flight drone.

The visual difference between both types of propellers is illustrated in Figure 3-14.

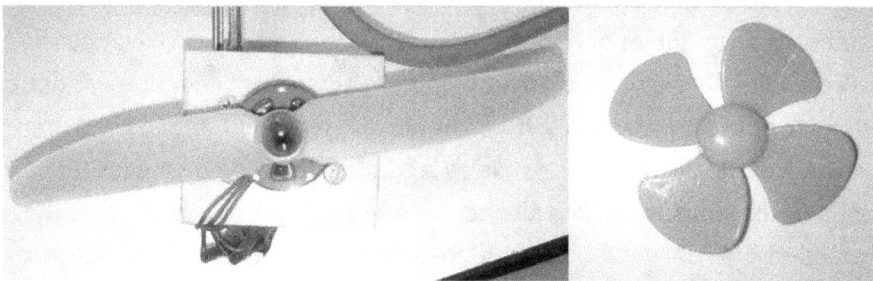

Figure 3-14. *Lift and thrust propellers*

Electronics

Brushless Motors

Use: They generate the force and torque needed for use with the systems described in this book, due to their standardization in the assembly of unmanned aerial vehicles with propellers. This standardization is partly due to their low friction and fast response to kinematic and dynamic changes by not having brushes.

Types: We will prefer high-speed ones; although there are low-speed ones, high-speed ones are used in aerial vehicle applications, regardless of whether they are outrunner or inrunner. Although reversible types will not be used in the prototypes in this text, they will be mentioned at some point.

Description and operation: They are a type of three-phase motor with an operating mode similar to stepper motors (see Figure 3-15), but designed generally for speed applications rather than positioning. Although they are three-phase, they are often used with an ESC that receives exclusively a PWM-RC pulse train and internally converts the pulse to the necessary phase logic to operate it.

Care and recommendations: If a racing aerial vehicle is desired, the response speed must be higher. In our case, since it is spatial positioning (the vehicle, not the motor), versions with slower electrical response will suffice. Another factor to consider is carefully analyzing the weight to be overcome to have at least a starting point in acquiring the motors and their corresponding power stages. In terms of care, it is advisable to keep them away from metal shavings or dust, as it can be absorbed by the motor's magnets and damage it. It is also recommended to properly balance the propellers and the vehicle to avoid forcing the use of the motors and reducing their lifespan.

CHAPTER 3   MECHATRONIC DESCRIPTION OF GENERIC COMPONENTS USED IN THIS BOOK

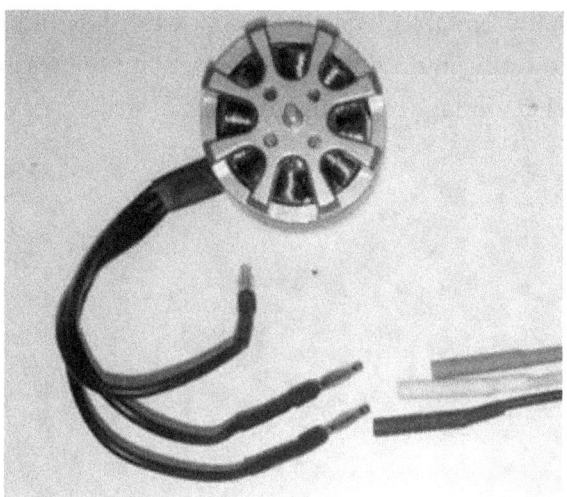

Figure 3-15. Brushless motor

Coaxial Contrarotating Brushless Motors

Use: The same as in the previous section, but they allow having a set of at least two motors on the same axis of action to perform load support or thrust-vectoring tasks, see Figure 3-16.

Types: Like in the previous case, the models are varied, but the same category is chosen, i.e., high-speed; in this case, necessarily outrunner (it is the known way to perform coaxial coupling), and non-reversible ones.

Description and operation: They are at least two brushless motors placed in tandem, one of them always rotating clockwise and the other counterclockwise. Their combination allows distributed load or a differential rotation effect on their main axis.

Care and recommendations: It is essential for the reader to know how to make them manually, given that although several models exist, they are difficult to obtain. Another issue is that the reader must take particular care with propeller balancing and also with the distance between them and other motors (otherwise, vortices capable of destroying the vehicle can be generated). Finally, as can be seen in the following illustration, spacers are required for mounting and a delicate placement for the wiring, which can be complicated to manage regarding the coaxial structure.

Figure 3-16. *Contra-rotating brushless motor*

ESCs (Electronic Speed Controllers)

Use: The ESCs or speed controllers are used to facilitate programming of brushless motors and reduce the number of channels to control; they are basically integrated circuits that transform a PWM signal (usually a PWM-RC protocol) into each of the signals that each phase of the brushless motor will use.

CHAPTER 3   MECHATRONIC DESCRIPTION OF GENERIC COMPONENTS USED IN THIS BOOK

Types: Although there are reversible and conventional ones, with electronic isolation and opto isolation, with or without BEC, and more variants even for brushed motors, we will use ESCs for conventional brushless motors with electronic isolation and incorporated BEC.

Description and operation: They are three-phase H-bridges (see Figure 3-17), where the speed in the triggering sequence of each transistor or electronic gate is a function of the pulse width received in the PWM input channel of the ESC.

Care and recommendations: Using ESCs with a slightly higher current rating than that consumed by the motor is a common practice, especially so that the motor can operate in its startup mode or certain conditions that demand a bit more from itself and not just in continuous or free load operations. Great care must be taken in the isolation and connection of the phases, using specialized wiring and connectors. It must be remembered that handling high currents leads to heating and fire.

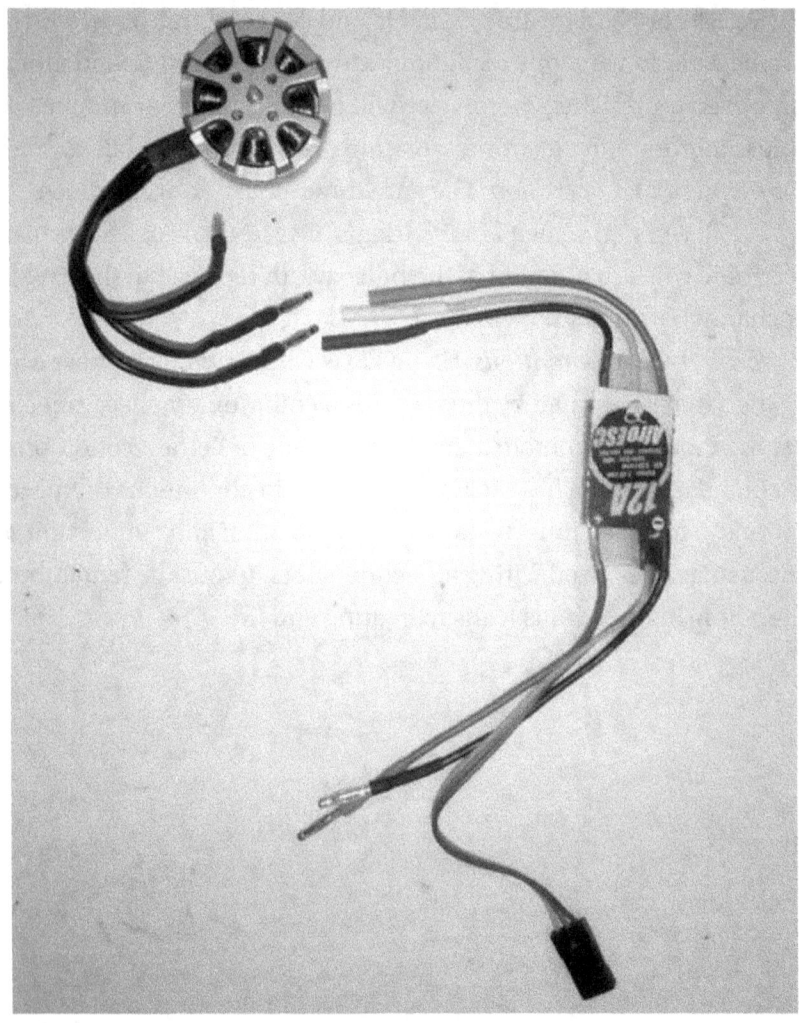

Figure 3-17. ESC or speed controller or brushless motor controller and a BLDC motor

CHAPTER 3 MECHATRONIC DESCRIPTION OF GENERIC COMPONENTS USED IN THIS BOOK

Insulation and Connectors

Use: Their utility lies in connecting the cables of the system in a relatively safe and standardized way (see Figure 3-18), such as motors to ESCs, ESCs to the distribution board, and the distribution board to the battery, etc.

Types: There are many, and they depend on the user's needs. The Figure 3-18 illustrates common 3mm connectors used to join ESCs with motors, known as bullet connectors.

Description and operation: They are semi-plug-and-play, designed to connect and use with some effort to prevent loosening or separation. Among other advantages, they prevent cable tangling, breakage, or overheating, and insulation melting.

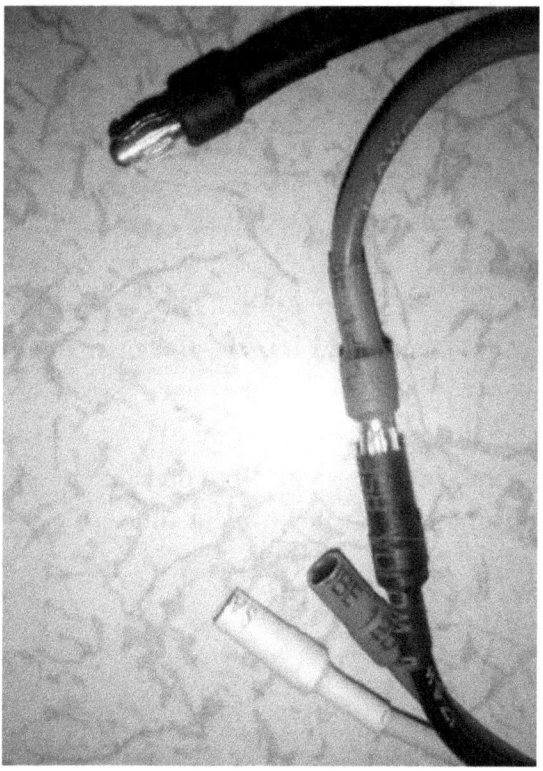

Figure 3-18. *Connectors with insulation for connecting BLDC motors with their ESCs*

CHAPTER 3　MECHATRONIC DESCRIPTION OF GENERIC COMPONENTS USED IN THIS BOOK

Care and recommendations: The most important parameters to consider are those related to maximum current and voltage supported, both in AC and DC. Also, compatible cable gauges and ease of use and replacement.

Batteries and/or Power Supplies

Use: They provide the necessary energy supply to power all system and motors.

Types: The most common in unmanned aerial systems is to use LIPO batteries. However, due to the characteristics of the projects described in this book, it is possible to use DC power sources, voltage reducers, or car batteries, see Figure 3-19.

Description and operation: Given the various ways to power our systems, we will focus on mentioning that the reader must ensure sufficient voltage and current to power the set of ESCs and other motors or devices (as sensors, servos, or autopilots).

Care and recommendations: If LIPO batteries are used, the reader must be careful when handling, charging, and storing them, as they are flammable and explosive. When using DC power sources, whether switched or linear, proper grounding and thermal dissipation are recommended and, of course, adequate thermal dissipation, either in the form of metal fins or fans. For car batteries, an easy connection system is necessary, as they can generate sparks, and precautions should be taken when handling them due to their weight and corrosive chemical components.

CHAPTER 3   MECHATRONIC DESCRIPTION OF GENERIC COMPONENTS USED IN THIS BOOK

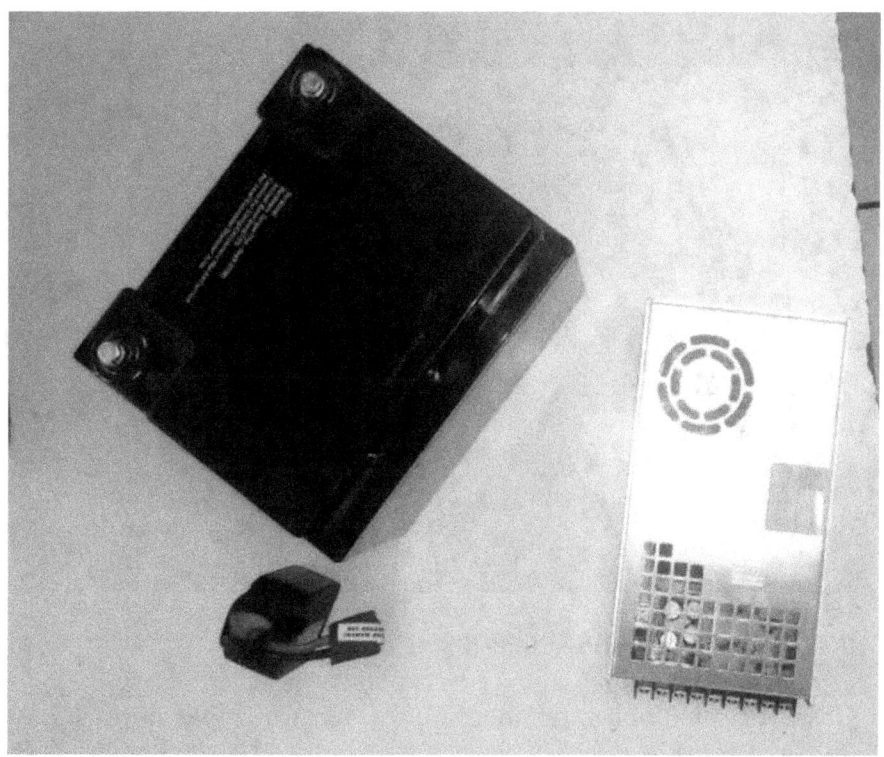

Figure 3-19. *Batteries and power supply*

Battery Chargers

If we talk about batteries, and unless they are disposable, a charger is necessary in everyday contexts. For car batteries and metal batteries, the charger is usually just a regulator with a certain voltage above the battery's nominal voltage for corresponding recharge. If we talk about Lithium and LIPO batteries, the situation changes, and the charger is more expensive and sophisticated, as it also has a balancing stage for the number of cells the battery has.

An example is shown in Figure 3-20.

CHAPTER 3   MECHATRONIC DESCRIPTION OF GENERIC COMPONENTS USED IN THIS BOOK

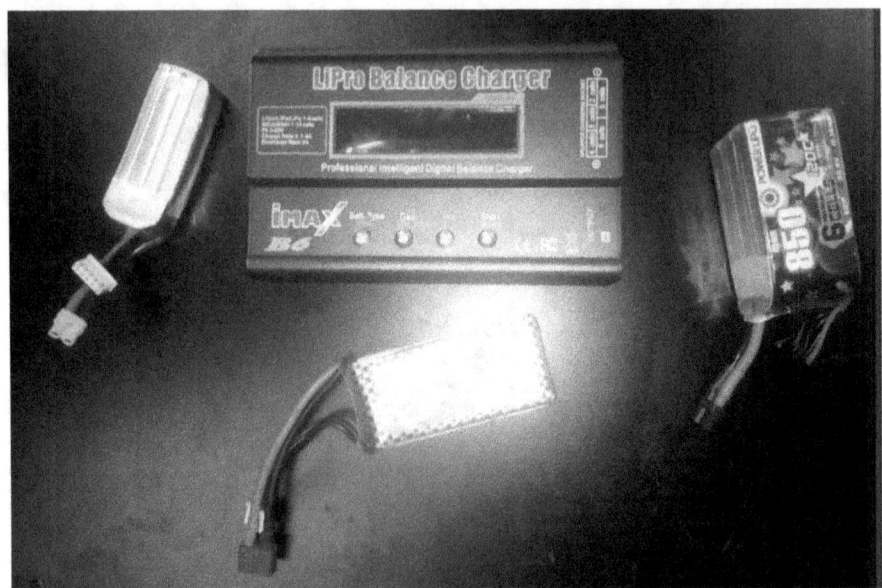

Figure 3-20. *LIPO battery charger*

It's worth mentioning that there are chargers with rapid, normal, single, or multiple battery charging modes, for one or several types of batteries, etc.

The main issues with a charger are its useful number of operating cycles, whether it has the right connector for the battery of interest, and whether it has any type of protection against overheating, etc.

Brushed DC Motors

The most commonly used DC motors, or brushed motors, function by contact and friction, not direct magnetic interaction. These motors usually have two terminals and are reversible by swapping the connection of these terminals. To be operated by an autopilot or computer, they require a power amplification stage called a driver.

There are some drivers that, in addition to amplifying the command signal, also have control over speed, torque, position, current, or voltage. For the purposes of this book, a regular driver is sufficient, and they are also more economical than control modules. Both the motors and their respective drivers are illustrated in Figure 3-21.

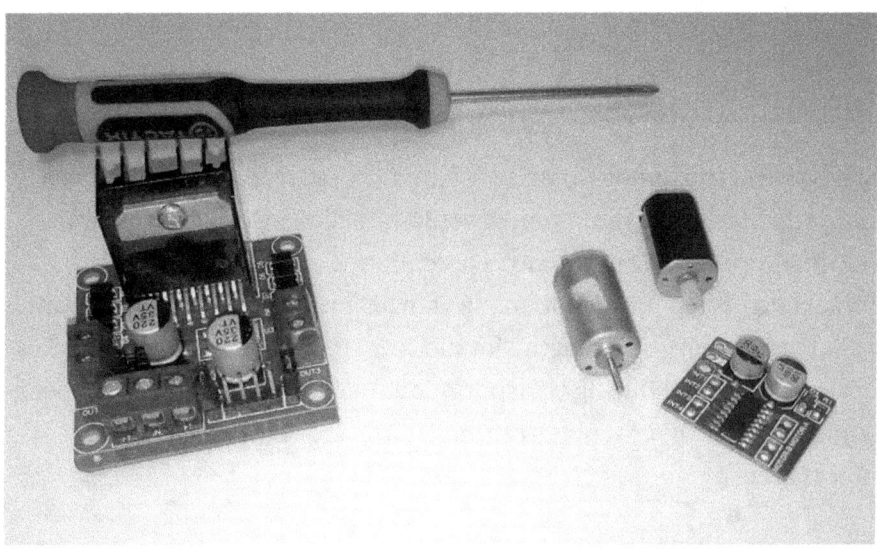

Figure 3-21. Brushed DC motors and a couple of power drivers for their operation

Motor Drivers for Brushed DC Motors

Figure 3-21 illustrates two frequently used drivers for small DC motors; one is the L298 module and the other is a compact model.

The difference is that the latter driver is a compact version without a heat sink. In addition to being compact, it is lightweight and suitable for projects like a zeppelin, where weight and dimensions are crucial factors for the vehicle's operation.

Its basic operating principle is a device called an H-bridge, which can control both output speed and motor direction. In essence, it's the automated version of manually reversing the motor cables using electronic switching. The BLDC has a similar device in its ESC, but it's a three-phase version (for the 3 control signal lines instead of the single signal of brushed technology).

Remote Control

This is one of the remote interface elements that every autopilot typically has, particularly every unmanned vehicle. It allows the user to operate it manually or revert autonomous operation to a safe mode. Figure 3-22 shows a suggested protection made with 3D printing (many designs are available online), given that the joysticks are its most fragile part and this serves as a defense during transportation (personally, we've experienced damage to these components during our travels, so this is how we protect them).

CHAPTER 3   MECHATRONIC DESCRIPTION OF GENERIC COMPONENTS USED IN THIS BOOK

Figure 3-22. Remote control with 3D-printed protection for its controls

Control

Logical and Analytical Control

First, we will make the distinction between two basic types of control.

> The analytical:
>
> This control is based on a mathematical analysis of equations. For the purpose of this book, we will limit to explain the standard PD controller.

The logical:

This control is based on an interaction of events and their corresponding decision-making. For the purpose of this book, we will revisit the basic logic of a differential vehicle already explained in the line follower example. Formally, it can be said that this kind of control is combinatorial logic or alternatively sequential logic.

Logical Control and State Machines

Let's revisit the example of the robot in differential configuration with two sensors given previously in the line follower example shown in Figure 3-23.

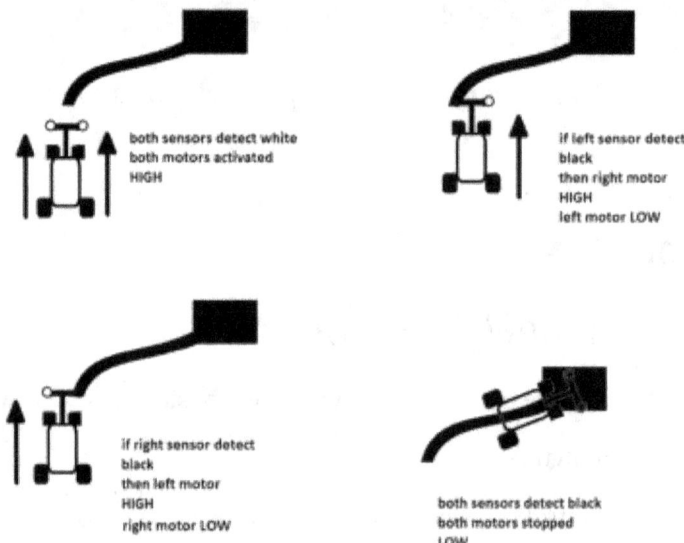

Figure 3-23. *Basic behavior of a line follower robot*

This behavior can be synthesized in Table 3-1.

Table 3-1. *Truth table with the synthesized logical behavior of the basic line follower robot*

INPUTS		OUTPUTS		State
Left Sensor	Right Sensor	Left Motor	Right Motor	
White	White	High	High	1
Black	Black	Low	Low	2
Black	White	Low	High	3
White	Black	High	Low	4

which, without the need for mathematical calculations and based more on operational logic, can be programmed with the help of conditionals (IF, SWITCH, etc.) or cycles in case of repetition (FOR, WHILE, etc.).

Unlike an analytical controller based on mathematical operations and calculations, the family of controllers based on logic has the following features:

1. Being based on logic, it has limited inputs and outputs, either binary (two-state, generally on and off, as in the given example) or fuzzy (although this case can have more than two states, these are usually countable and generally not continuous).

2. Since it is based on limited inputs and outputs, the working resolution will depend on the number of available inputs and outputs or the number of available states (in the previous example, there are only four states, resulting in more of a bang-bang behavior than a natural one in the car's displacement).

CHAPTER 3   MECHATRONIC DESCRIPTION OF GENERIC COMPONENTS USED IN THIS BOOK

3. If the previous bang-bang operation occurs at high frequencies, a destructive phenomenon called chattering occurs.

4. This type of controller is ideal for actuators that can switch between states, such as relays, logic gates, FPGAs, or power electronic devices.

5. An extensive operating logic requires a large-dimensional matrix and, therefore, more memory and processing for evaluating each state.

6. The logical operation is often free from the system's mathematical model and based on the power of the actuators.

7. Stability testing is at the same time much more flexible and complex than with analytical controllers since they require at least solving differential equations, whereas this family requires only logical equations.

To test the performance or at least imagine it, a state graph is designed (see Figure 3-24), and based on sensors, the change between one state and another is made. Note that for this example, there is a single final state or goal from which there is no exit, and between the other states, they can move from one to another until reaching that goal. Something interesting here is that the system can remain in a state while the change signals do not arrive, without having reached the goal. For example, the robot can abruptly leave the track (state 1) and continue moving outside the track without finding it.

CHAPTER 3   MECHATRONIC DESCRIPTION OF GENERIC COMPONENTS USED IN THIS BOOK

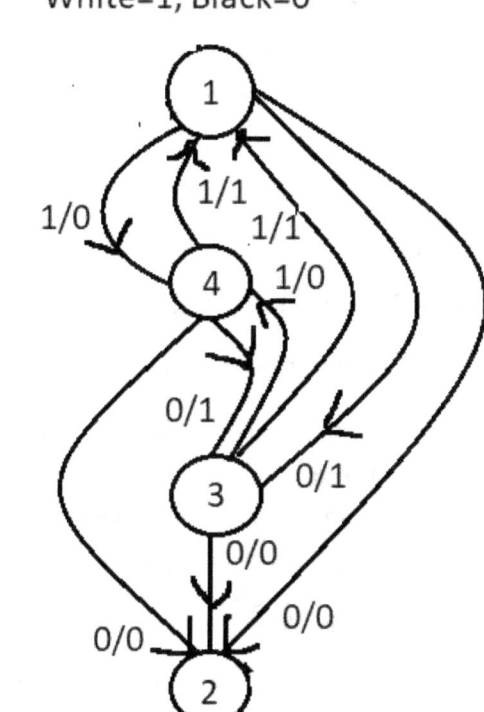

Figure 3-24. State machine of the line-follower robot illustrated in this example

The above would imply identifying certain problems with the algorithm and proposing some solutions; for example, if the robot has spent too much time without finding a line (states 3 and 4), then make random turns and movements until finding the lane again.

CHAPTER 3 MECHATRONIC DESCRIPTION OF GENERIC COMPONENTS USED IN THIS BOOK

PD-Type Analytical Control

Any of these definitions is compatible:

- It is a virtual spring-damper system.
- It is a type of damped harmonic oscillator.
- It is a useful zero.

Explanation: Note the following definition of PD:

$$PD=(Kp*E)+(Kd*Ed)$$

where Kp and Kd are the Proportional and Derivative gains, E is an error constituted by the subtraction of the operating value minus the desired value, and Ed is its derivative with respect to time.

Let's make the following changes of variable:

$$Kp=K;\ Kd=B;\ E=x;\ Ed=xdot$$

where K is a spring, B a damper, x a linear displacement, and xdot its derivative with respect to time.

As can be noted, the system is a spring-damper or a damped harmonic oscillator, see Figure 3-25.

$$(K*x)+(B*xdot)$$

Note that the proportional part acts as a spring, pulling the system to the desired value, but a dissipation part is required, provided by the derivative component. This dissipation allows the system to stop oscillating around the desired point and settle on it.

CHAPTER 3   MECHATRONIC DESCRIPTION OF GENERIC COMPONENTS USED IN THIS BOOK

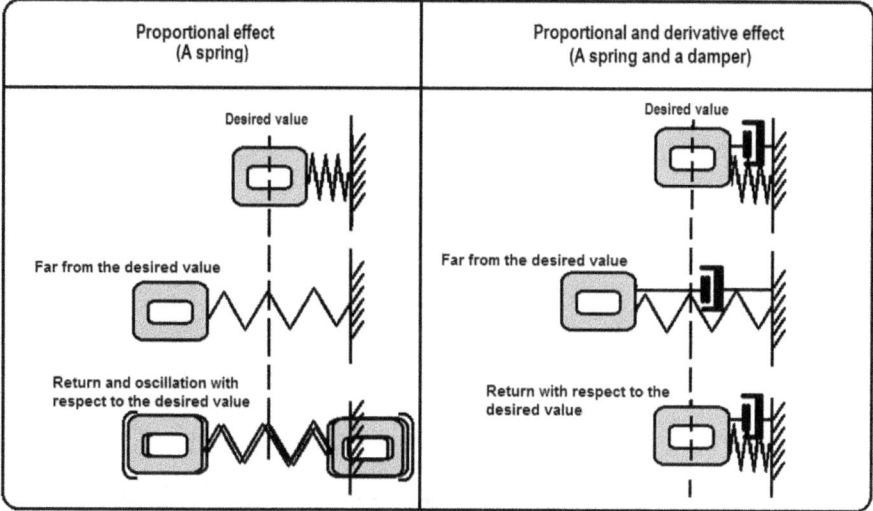

Figure 3-25. *Mechanical analogy of P and PD control*

The homogeneous solution of this system is (remember that a homogeneous solution for a system of differential equations is when it lacks an excitation force)

$$(K*x)+(B*xdot)=0$$

If we consider K and B to be positive constants:

The solution to this differential equation is an exponential that tends to zero, i.e., a USEFUL ZERO or a value that over time (steady state) tends to disappear, see Figure 3-26.

CHAPTER 3   MECHATRONIC DESCRIPTION OF GENERIC COMPONENTS USED IN THIS BOOK

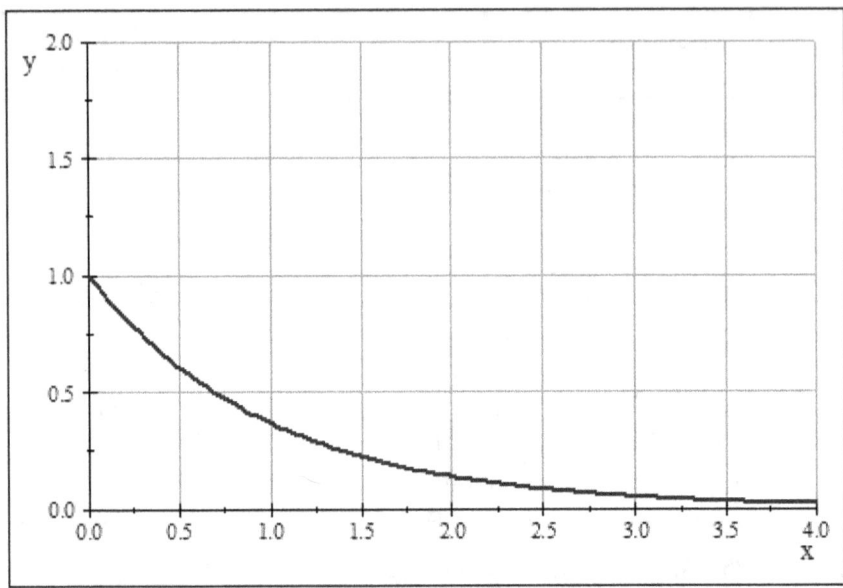

Figure 3-26. *Stable solution of the differential equation of the spring-damper system or first-order ODE*

If we return to our original system, it also implies that the variable E tends to zero, such that if the error tends to zero, it implies that the difference between the measured and desired values also tends to zero.

And this means that the system tends to reach a desired value.

Why do we use a PD control?

1. It is model-free (meaning you don't need to know the physical modeling of the system to apply it, unless an adaptive part is included).

2. It has decades of dominance along with PID because it's simple and robust.

3. More elements don't necessarily imply better performance. While the integral term represents better stabilization against constant or bounded

CHAPTER 3   MECHATRONIC DESCRIPTION OF GENERIC COMPONENTS USED IN THIS BOOK

external disturbances, it also implies calculating one or several integrators. Thus, if the computer is slow or doesn't have much processing capacity, adding it implies a delay and error accumulation.

4. Controller tuning is usually bounded by criteria of positivity and gain proportion, which is generally a heuristic or trial-and-error process (although there are extensive books on high-precision and even optimal control).

Robustness vs. Adaptability

Given a system to control, there are two types of controllers: dominant controllers and adaptive controllers. Both are based on the concept of the useful zero previously explained. In the first case, a dynamic is imposed on the system, and it is so large that the system's own dynamics are nullified or considered negligible (as long as the motors or actuators of the system can provide such an effect). In the second case, the goal is to directly compensate for the dynamics, disturbances, and most representative undesired values of the system, either through measurement or by mathematical estimation.

These concepts are explained in a simplified way with the following example:

Suppose a solid block capable of moving on an ice surface using a thruster as shown in Figure 3-27.

CHAPTER 3　MECHATRONIC DESCRIPTION OF GENERIC COMPONENTS USED IN THIS BOOK

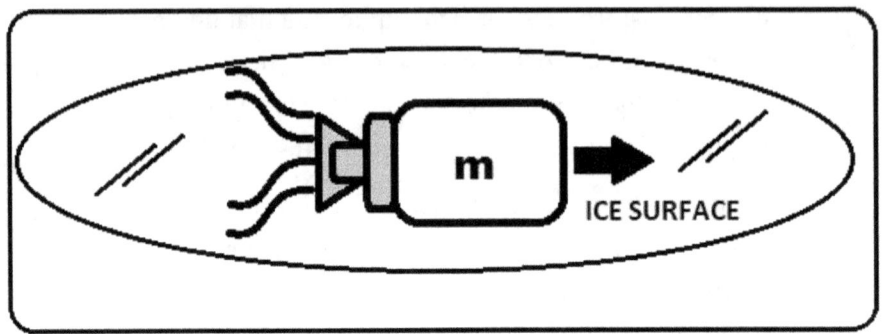

Figure 3-27. Simplified dynamic system to control: propelled mass on ice

Given this assumption, the equation that models the system is the following:

$$F=(m*a)$$

In this case, the input to the system is the force generated by the thruster (F) in the block.

Suppose our motor can provide the following force (a combination of the system's dynamics with a useful zero-type PD):

$$F=(m*a)+PD$$

By introducing this force into our original equation, we get

$$(m*a)+PD=(m*a)$$

It can be noted here that this control by compensation aims to cancel the original dynamics of the system (undesired) and leave the useful zero, resulting in

$$PD=0$$

In this way, the system will tend to behave like a spring-damper system, the error will tend to zero as time grows, and this will imply that the measured variable will tend to the desired value (reimagine our previously illustrated spring with the wall moved to a distinct non-zero xdes position).

$$E=0; E=x-xdes; x=xdes$$

However, adaptive control has the disadvantage that there may be unconsidered values. For example, let's consider an unmodeled dynamic to be a type of friction with the ice:

$$F=(m*a)+[b*sign(v)]$$

Given that we only compensate for the (m*a) term and the friction term survives in our dynamics, we cannot guarantee that the error will really tend to 0.

On the other hand, suppose now that the injected control is very large compared to the system's dynamics:

$$F=PD>>(m*a)$$

Then, injecting it into the original system:

$$PD=(m*a)$$

But given the fact that PD >> (m*a), ma tends to be negligible (considered null or zero).

Thus, PD = (m*a) = 0, and consequently, we still have the behavior where the error tends to zero, and the desired value or objective is achieved.

This is called dominant or robust control, and although it may have the same issue of interaction with unmodeled dynamics, as long as the motors allow it, the following can happen.

Suppose the unmodeled dynamics persists:

$$F=(m*a)+[b*sign(v)]$$

But since PD >> (m*a)

CHAPTER 3   MECHATRONIC DESCRIPTION OF GENERIC COMPONENTS USED IN THIS BOOK

It is also possible (as long as the motors allow it and a sufficiently large value is selected)

$$PD \gg (m*a)+[b*sign(v)]$$

By introducing this control into the system

$$PD = (m*a)+[b*sign(v)] = 0$$

And consequently, the effect of reaching the desired value persists.

As can be noted, dominant or robust control can even dominate unknown terms (it's based on brute force and is therefore model-free).

Differential Robot Concept

We must clarify that although there are fully functional aerial, terrestrial, or aquatic vehicles with odd-numbered wheels or propellers (three being a very common case), for the sake of simplicity in this text and especially for system control, which would otherwise require somewhat complicated geometric projections, we will focus on even-numbered or differential designs (with the exception of the aeropendulum due to its operational simplicity).

The word differential has a large number of definitions, from mathematics to automotive mechanics. In the particular case of this book, we will use the definition of differential according to the motor structure or allocation structure or propulsion structure that allows the movement of a vehicle as a difference in actions between pairs of actuators (propellers, wheels, fins, etc.).

In this way, a highly simplified differential wheel vehicle is illustrated in Figure 3-28.

CHAPTER 3 MECHATRONIC DESCRIPTION OF GENERIC COMPONENTS USED IN THIS BOOK

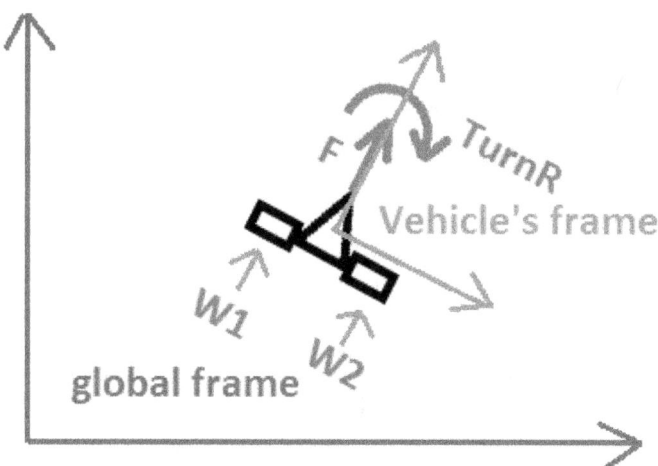

Figure 3-28. *A simplified differential wheeled mobile robot*

whose behavior is given as follows:

   Forward movement = speed wheel 1 + speed wheel 2

   Turn = speed wheel 1 - speed wheel 2

As can be noted, it is the second equation, where the subtraction determines the differential behavior of the vehicle.

Note from the drawing that in the case of the turn, it may seem ambiguous which speed is positive and which is negative. To determine this sign, it is necessary to consider several reference frames, which can be imposed as a standard, agreed upon by a work team, or simply decided by the designer or user according to their needs. These frames are the global frame, the body frame, and the motor or propulsion frame (for more details, see the books *Drones to Go* and *Advanced Robotic Vehicles Programming* by Julio Alberto Mendoza-Mendoza et al.).

Being so, the forward movement and turn of the vehicle seen from its own reference center (which for the sake of example was the geometric center, but is often also the center of mass, gravity, buoyancy, etc.) give rise to the following allocation matrix, see Figure 3-29.

CHAPTER 3   MECHATRONIC DESCRIPTION OF GENERIC COMPONENTS USED IN THIS BOOK

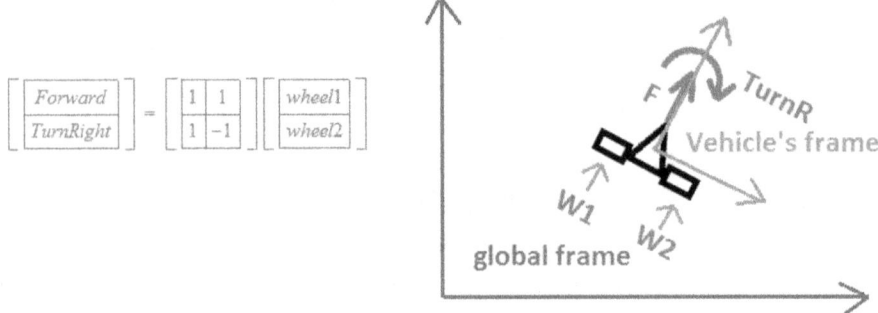

Figure 3-29. *Description of the movements through the differential combination of the wheels of the simplified differential robot using an allocation or propulsion matrix*

Extending the example to the quadcopter mounted on a test stand, which in turn is a doubly differential effect, see Figure 3-30.

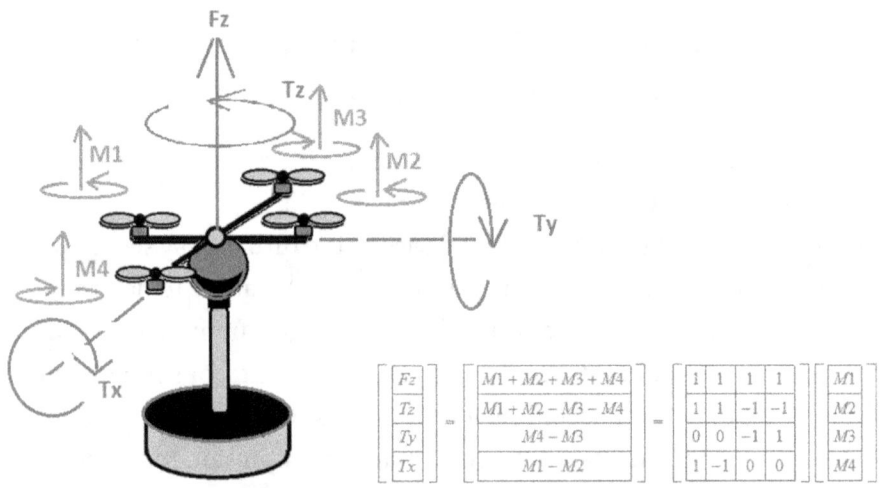

Figure 3-30. *Description of the movements through a simplified differential combination of the propellers of a quadcopter mounted on a test stand by using an allocation or propulsion matrix*

CHAPTER 3   MECHATRONIC DESCRIPTION OF GENERIC COMPONENTS USED IN THIS BOOK

Explanation of the Difference Between Logical and Arithmetic Control Based on the Differential Wheeled Robot

The fundamental differences between control based on logical operations and control based on mathematical operations are becoming increasingly less obvious due to the recent technological and scientific overlap between both techniques, as well as operational modes that fall right in between, such as basic sliding modes and on-off controllers.

It is clear that there are mixed or convergent controls that fuse both techniques, taking advantage of the benefits and eliminating the drawbacks of each. However, for the purposes of this book and to adequately distinguish the examples given throughout the text, we have decided to use and define both of them separately.

We will highlight these differences in Table 3-2 and Figure 3-31 using the differential configuration of a terrestrial robot, first in a case designed to follow a line drawn on the floor using only logic, and in a second instance, to follow a programmed trajectory (not drawn on the floor) using mathematical control (such as a PD controller, for example).

CHAPTER 3   MECHATRONIC DESCRIPTION OF GENERIC COMPONENTS USED IN THIS BOOK

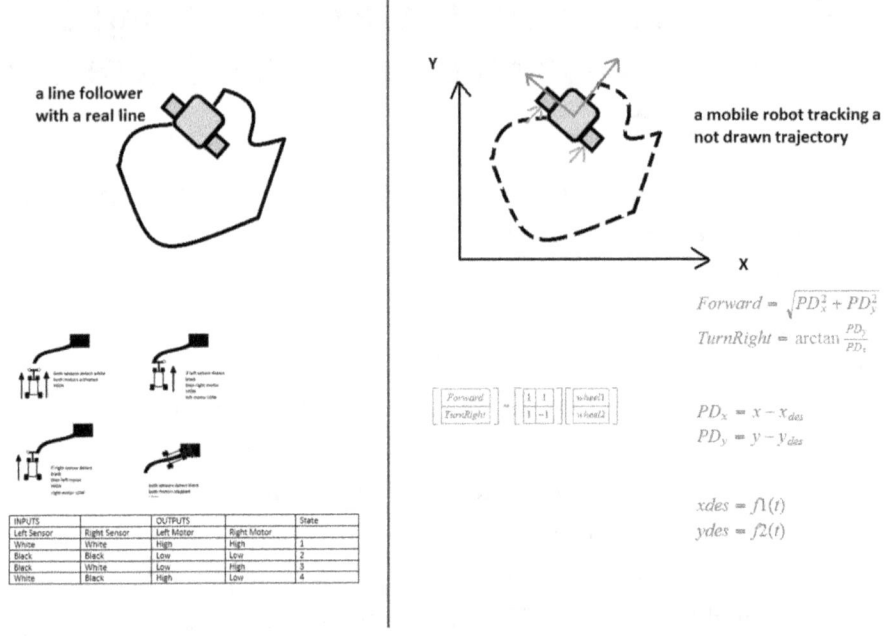

Figure 3-31. Graphic and summarized difference between an arithmetic controller and a logical one

Table 3-2. Extensive comparison between a logical controller and an arithmetic one

Logical or intelligent control	Mathematical or arithmetic control
The vehicle does not require location frames since the physical line provides it.	It may require up to three location frames (fixed, mobile, and motor frames).
The control action requires a logical table of actions for each motor based on line detection.	There is no physical line; the route to follow is arbitrary and is injected through kinematic equations and programming.
The sensors only have the function of detecting or not detecting the line.	The sensors must detect the vehicle's position.

(continued)

Table 3-2. (*continued*)

Logical or intelligent control	Mathematical or arithmetic control
The control objective is not to leave the line while the vehicle is moving.	The motor action depends on a propulsion or allocation matrix that relates a reference point of the entire vehicle to the location of its motors.
The control can fail if the line has knots or twists.	
Its speed and performance depend on the number of logical conditions, also known as a truth table.	The control objective is to minimize the difference between the measured and desired positions.
It requires a lower level of mathematical knowledge but a much higher level of logical thinking, making it useful for beginners and children to learn.	Since the trajectory to follow or desired value is generally a sequence of points in time, it doesn't matter if the path has twists, turns, knots, etc.
If you want to change the task to follow, you must physically modify the entire path.	The path to follow can be modified quickly by changing the path equation.
	It requires a higher level of mathematical knowledge.
Its reconfiguration, being physical, is slower, more laborious, and requires additional human action, making it a good example of automatization.	Its speed and performance depend on the processor and memory.
	Its rapid reconfiguration, sometimes without human intervention, allows for automations.
It converges with mathematical control in on-off techniques or basic sliding modes.	It converges with logical control in on-off techniques or basic sliding modes.

CHAPTER 3   MECHATRONIC DESCRIPTION OF GENERIC COMPONENTS USED IN THIS BOOK

Closed-Loop and Open-Loop Control

Regardless of whether it's logical or analytical, a controller can take two approaches: open-loop or closed-loop. In the first case, the controller relies entirely on proportionality and confidence in that proportionality. For example, if we have a speed range for a motor between 0 and 255, with 0 being zero speed and 255 being maximum speed, we would expect the value 127 to give us a speed around half of the maximum, based on proportionality and confidence. However, what if we place the motor shaft against mud or a very rough surface? Would it maintain the expected speed?

That's when open-loop control fails, and an adjustment is necessary based on feedback of what was expected versus what actually happened. This adjustment is known as closed-loop control, which is based on the error between the expected and measured values, specifically reducing that error to zero.

Most robotic systems are based on closed loops; but at some point, they reach a level of confidence or proportionality. For example, in the case of a drone, the closed loop in its automatic control is at the level of altitude and position, and then a combination of that closed loop (known as a propulsion or allocation matrix) is sent to the motors. However, these motors usually don't have a closed loop to maintain a desired operating speed, leaving the vehicle with a closed loop or feedback control for position and altitude but open-loop control for each motor's speed.

Gravity Compensation or Bias

Closed-loop control is a function dependent on error. Since the error can be above or below the operating point, the control can be negative or positive. However, BLDC motors only have a positive value for shutdown at 1000, which is not necessarily the startup value, and a maximum speed value at 2000.

Thus, the user must perform a rule of three or mapping to translate a minimum negative and maximum positive control value to the vehicle's operating values. In this case, it's recommended that the neutral or zero control value coincides with the minimum lifting value of the BLDC or bias. This startup value varies with the system's weight and inertia.

This is illustrated in Figure 3-32 for the case of the aeropendulum.

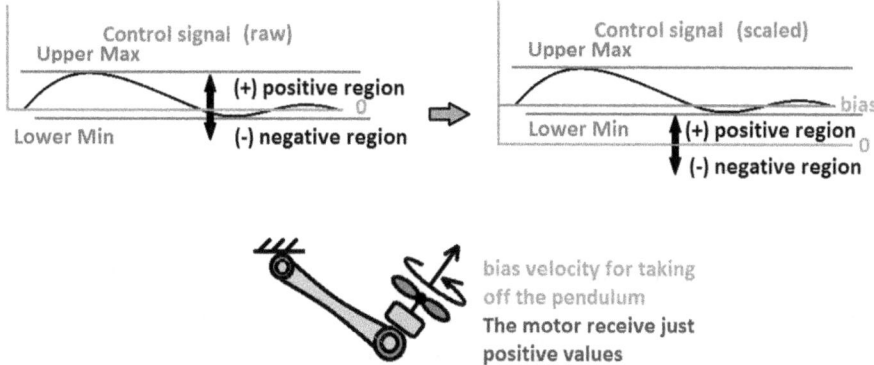

Figure 3-32. Illustration of gravitational compensation or bias

Direct and Indirect Control

If we have a pendulum with a motor at its center, the pendulum's position is directly controlled by manipulating the motor's angle.

If we have an aeropendulum where the mass is replaced by a motor with a propeller, the pendulum's angle is modified indirectly by using the propeller's speed. That is, the faster the propeller spins, the greater the angle reached, and the slower it spins, the angle reached tends to be minimal or in hanging configuration, see Figure 3-33.

CHAPTER 3 MECHATRONIC DESCRIPTION OF GENERIC COMPONENTS USED IN THIS BOOK

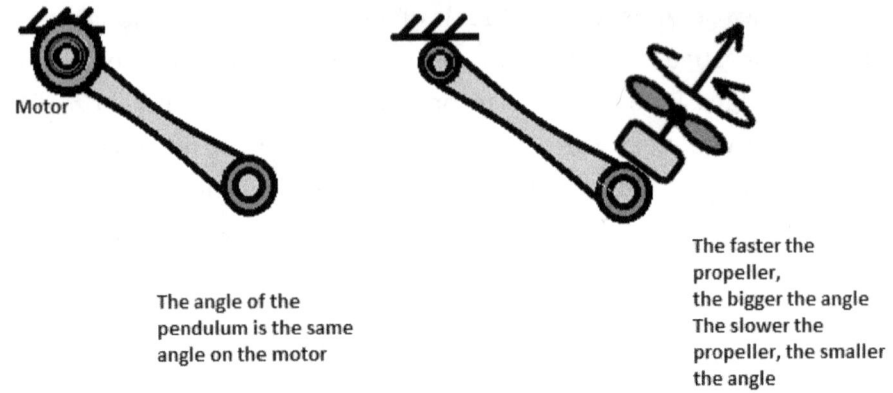

Figure 3-33. *Direct and indirect control of a pendulum's angular position*

Similarly, the position of a quadcopter is controlled indirectly through the combination of the speeds of the four motors. These speeds are not constant or directly controlled; on the contrary, according to the allocation matrix, if we perform the following calculations, we will notice that the speed of each motor is a combined function of the vehicle's position and orientation errors, see Figure 3-34.

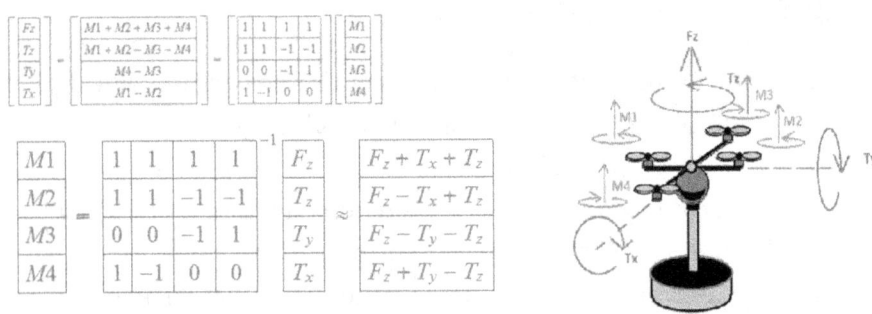

Figure 3-34. *Indirect control of a quadcopter's orientation and position through the differential combination of the speeds of each of its propellers*

CHAPTER 3   MECHATRONIC DESCRIPTION OF GENERIC COMPONENTS USED IN THIS BOOK

where the torques in X, Y, and Z, as well as the force in Z, are controllers (e.g., a PD controller) of the respective error in translation along the Z-axis and the angles around the X, Y, and Z axes.

Dirty Derivative

As previously mentioned, the PD controller consists of two terms: one with the proportional part multiplying the operating error of a particular system, defined as the measured value minus the desired value, and the second or derivative part multiplying the derivative of said error, also definable as the derivative of the measured value minus the derivative of the desired value.

The desired values typically don't represent a major problem, unless the user is unaware of the operational limits of their robotic vehicles (also known as workspace and speed and torque limits).

However, on the measured values side, we have more serious problems, starting with the fact that sometimes a particular sensor is not available or is too expensive, or the processor has few digital or analog inputs.

For example, to control the orientation of a quadcopter, autopilots usually have orientation sensors and angular velocity measurements, all in a single package known as an IMU (Inertial Measurement Unit).

On the other hand, in cases like the aeropendulum in the next chapter, the angular sensor is available as a potentiometer, but there is no angular velocity sensor (which could be a very expensive tachometer).

To address this, there are a couple of mathematical approximation techniques that can be used in the absence of physical sensors. One is known as a state observer, and the other, which is a variant of this and will be described in this chapter, is known as a "dirty derivative."

It is defined as follows:

Given a signal X, for example, an angle.

The dirty derivative of X, known as Xdi, is the following.

157

CHAPTER 3   MECHATRONIC DESCRIPTION OF GENERIC COMPONENTS USED IN THIS BOOK

$$Xdi = (xcurrent - xprev)/(timecurrent - timeprev)$$

where xcurrent and timecurrent are the current signal and time, and xprev and timeprev are the previous signal and time.

What is frequently done is to assume the initial value of xprev and timeprev as 0.

The process is iterative and is as follows:

1. Assign initial values to xprev and timeprev, usually 0.

2. Apply the dirty derivative formula with the current signal and time values xcurrent and timecurrent.

3. Update the values of xprev with xcurrent and timeprev with timecurrent.

4. Repeat the process indefinitely from step 2.

The dirty derivative can be used to provide an approximate value of the derivative of the measured value or directly the derivative of the error (in the aeropendulum example, we use both cases). The preference for which one to use will depend on the desired precision, required tuning, processing capacity, error propagation, and signal filtering capabilities.

The dirty derivative will be more imprecise if the difference between timeprev and timecurrent is large, and a better approximation to the real value if this difference or time delta is very small (due to the concept of differential known in calculus). On the other hand, a better dirty derivative implies that the processor has a high operating frequency, meaning low-frequency processors will produce imprecise dirty derivatives.

An Arduino, although capable of achieving time deltas of microseconds, usually saturates its processing with few of these values. Typically, a mid-to-low-end Arduino can control devices with 1-2 DOF relatively precisely. For more degrees of freedom, an embedded system like an autopilot is necessary.

CHAPTER 3 MECHATRONIC DESCRIPTION OF GENERIC COMPONENTS USED IN THIS BOOK

The dirty derivative will generate a lot of noise if the difference between xcurrent and xprev is very large (which is quite frequent). The dirty derivative is usually complemented with a low-pass filter.

The relationship between the dirty derivative and a filter is a trade-off. An unfiltered dirty derivative reaches the processing system very quickly but induces chattering. A filtered dirty derivative, on the other hand, produces delays in processing (a topic covered in the previous work *Advanced Robotic Vehicles Programming*).

Although it's common for the derivative part to have a lower gain than the proportional part, it's also common in very noisy systems for these proportions to be reversed, with larger derivative constants used as compensation.

To compensate for the effects of the dirty derivative, integrators are often used, which behave like filters. In electrical analogy, the derivative and integral parts compensate for each other, like the effects of a capacitor and an inductor. However, this implies more processing lines and delays.

Programming
Hardware: Autopilots

Tables 3-3 and 3-4 show the two autopilots we use most frequently.

CHAPTER 3   MECHATRONIC DESCRIPTION OF GENERIC COMPONENTS USED IN THIS BOOK

Table 3-3. *Hardware features of the RadioLink MiniPix autopilot*

Autopilot	Radiolink Minipix

Processor	STM32F405VGT6 ARM
Built-in sensors	Barometer, Accelerometer, and Compass
Additional features	Built-in software vibration damping technology
Dimensions	39x39x12mm
Weight	12 g without wires
ArduPilot compatibilities	Almost full with some important warnings
Main interfaces	6 PWM outputs, 1RC PPM input, 3 UARTS, 2ADCs, microSD slot, external I2C, external GPS
Website	https://ardupilot.org/copter/docs/common-radiolink-minipix.html

CHAPTER 3   MECHATRONIC DESCRIPTION OF GENERIC COMPONENTS USED IN THIS BOOK

Table 3-4. *Hardware features of the RadioLink Pixhawk autopilot*

Autopilot	RadioLink Pixhawk
	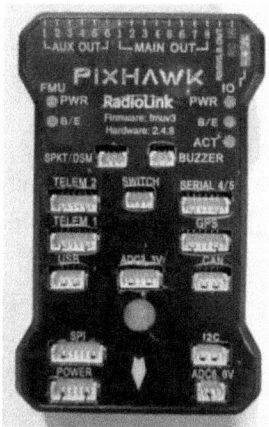
Processor	32bit STM32F427 Cortex M4
Built-in sensors	Barometer, Accelerometer, Magnetometer, and Gyroscope
Additional features	The classic Pixhawk design
Dimensions	16.5x51.8x82.2mm
Weight	38 g without wires or additionals
ArduPilot compatibilities	Almost full with some important warnings
Main interfaces	8 main PWM outputs, 6 aux PWM outputs, 1RC PPM input, 1RC spektrum, 2 UARTS, 1 GPS input, 2ADCs, microSD slot, external I2C, CAN, USB and SPI, external GPS
Website	https://www.radiolink.com.cn/doce/product-detail-116.html

161

CHAPTER 3   MECHATRONIC DESCRIPTION OF GENERIC COMPONENTS USED IN THIS BOOK

Software: Generic Modification Codes for All Book Projects

The following describes the common modifications to all projects that will be described in the following sections:

mode.h

In this file, you should look for the following code segment where the flight modes are defined and add your custom flight mode to the list, in our case ROLQUAD, see Figure 3-35. This code is at the beginning of the file.

```
class Mode {
public:
    // Auto Pilot Modes enumeration
    enum class Number : uint8_t {
        STABILIZE   =  0,  // manual airframe angle with manual throttle
        ACRO        =  1,  // manual body-frame angular rate with manual throttle
        ALT_HOLD    =  2,  // manual airframe angle with automatic throttle
        AUTO        =  3,  // fully automatic waypoint control using mission commands
        GUIDED      =  4,  // fully automatic fly to coordinate or fly at velocity/direction using GCS immediate commands
        LOITER      =  5,  // automatic horizontal acceleration with automatic throttle
        RTL         =  6,  // automatic return to launching point
        CIRCLE      =  7,  // automatic circular flight with automatic throttle
        LAND        =  9,  // automatic landing with horizontal position control
        DRIFT       = 11,  // semi-autonomous position, yaw and throttle control
        SPORT       = 13,  // manual earth-frame angular rate control with manual throttle
        FLIP        = 14,  // automatically flip the vehicle on the roll axis
        AUTOTUNE    = 15,  // automatically tune the vehicle's roll and pitch gains
        POSHOLD     = 16,  // automatic position hold with manual override, with automatic throttle
        BRAKE       = 17,  // full-brake using inertial/GPS system, no pilot input
        THROW       = 18,  // throw to launch mode using inertial/GPS system, no pilot input
        AVOID_ADSB  = 19,  // automatic avoidance of obstacles in the macro scale - e.g. full-sized aircraft
        GUIDED_NOGPS= 20,  // guided mode but only accepts attitude and altitude
        SMART_RTL   = 21,  // SMART_RTL returns to home by retracing its steps
        FLOWHOLD    = 22,  // FLOWHOLD holds position with optical flow without rangefinder
        FOLLOW      = 23,  // follow attempts to follow another vehicle or ground station
        ZIGZAG      = 24,  // ZIGZAG mode is able to fly in a zigzag manner with predefined point A and point B
        SYSTEMID    = 25,  // system ID mode produces automated system identification signals in the controllers
        AUTOROTATE  = 26,  // Autonomous autorotation
        ROLQUAD     = 27,  // Code Quad rol
```

Figure 3-35. *Illustration of the location and generic modification of the mode.h file*

Copter.h

Look for the line

`friend class Mode`

In that code section, various flight modes are also declared. Declare the custom one by adding Mode, in our case ModeRolQuad, see Figure 3-36.

162

CHAPTER 3   MECHATRONIC DESCRIPTION OF GENERIC COMPONENTS USED IN THIS BOOK

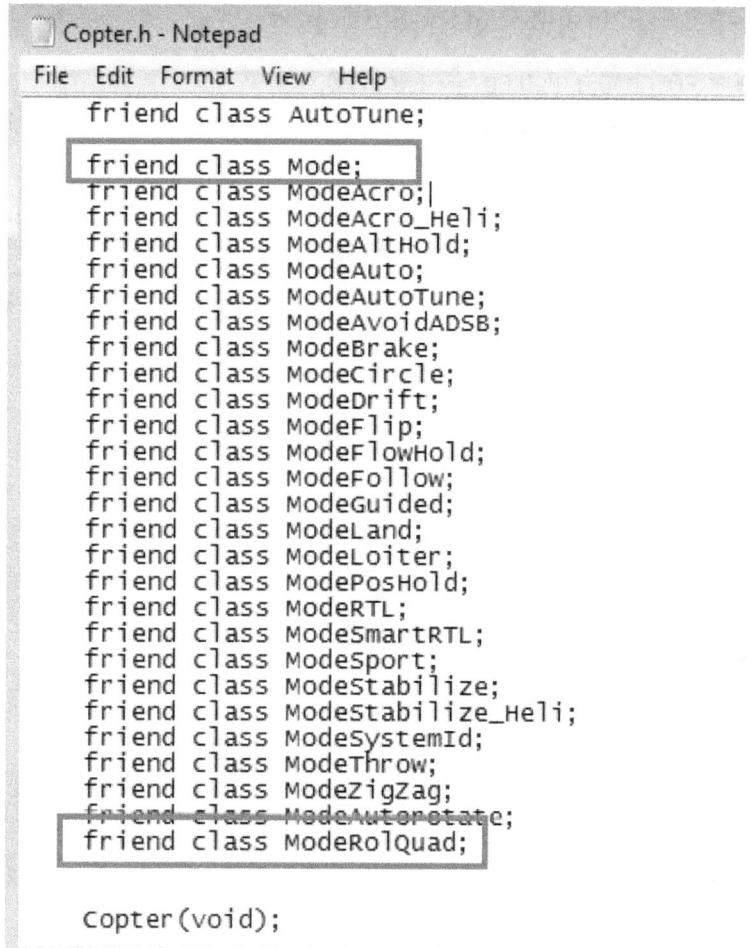

Figure 3-36. Illustration of the location and generic modification of the Copter.h file

Also, in the same file, look for the line

void failsafe_check();

Just before it, there are definitions of various flight modes, see Figure 3-37. You should also add the custom one.

In our case, we add what is described in Listing 3-1.

CHAPTER 3   MECHATRONIC DESCRIPTION OF GENERIC COMPONENTS USED IN THIS BOOK

Listing 3-1. Code added to the file Copter.h

```
#if MODE_ROLQUAD_ENABLED == ENABLED
ModeRolQuad mode_rolquad;
#endif
```

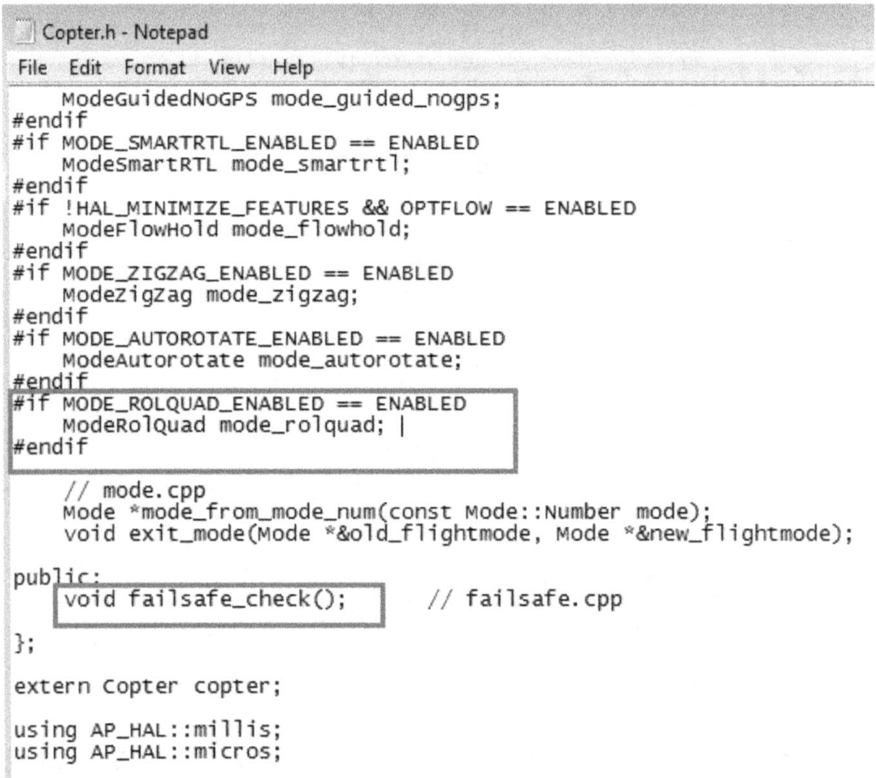

```
Copter.h - Notepad
File  Edit  Format  View  Help
    ModeGuidedNoGPS mode_guided_nogps;
#endif
#if MODE_SMARTRTL_ENABLED == ENABLED
    ModeSmartRTL mode_smartrtl;
#endif
#if !HAL_MINIMIZE_FEATURES && OPTFLOW == ENABLED
    ModeFlowHold mode_flowhold;
#endif
#if MODE_ZIGZAG_ENABLED == ENABLED
    ModeZigZag mode_zigzag;
#endif
#if MODE_AUTOROTATE_ENABLED == ENABLED
    ModeAutorotate mode_autorotate;
#endif
#if MODE_ROLQUAD_ENABLED == ENABLED
    ModeRolQuad mode_rolquad; |
#endif

    // mode.cpp
    Mode *mode_from_mode_num(const Mode::Number mode);
    void exit_mode(Mode *&old_flightmode, Mode *&new_flightmode);
public:
    void failsafe_check();         // failsafe.cpp
};

extern Copter copter;

using AP_HAL::millis;
using AP_HAL::micros;
```

Figure 3-37. *Illustration of the second location and generic modification of the mode.h file*

mode.cpp

Look for the first result for

`case Mode::Number::STABILIZE:`

CHAPTER 3 MECHATRONIC DESCRIPTION OF GENERIC COMPONENTS USED IN THIS BOOK

After that code segment (see Figure 3-38), add the custom one as indicated in Listing 3-2.

Listing 3-2. Code added to the file mode.cpp

```
#if MODE_ROLQUAD_ENABLED == ENABLED
    case Mode::Number::ROLQUAD:
        ret = &mode_rolquad;
            break
#endif
```

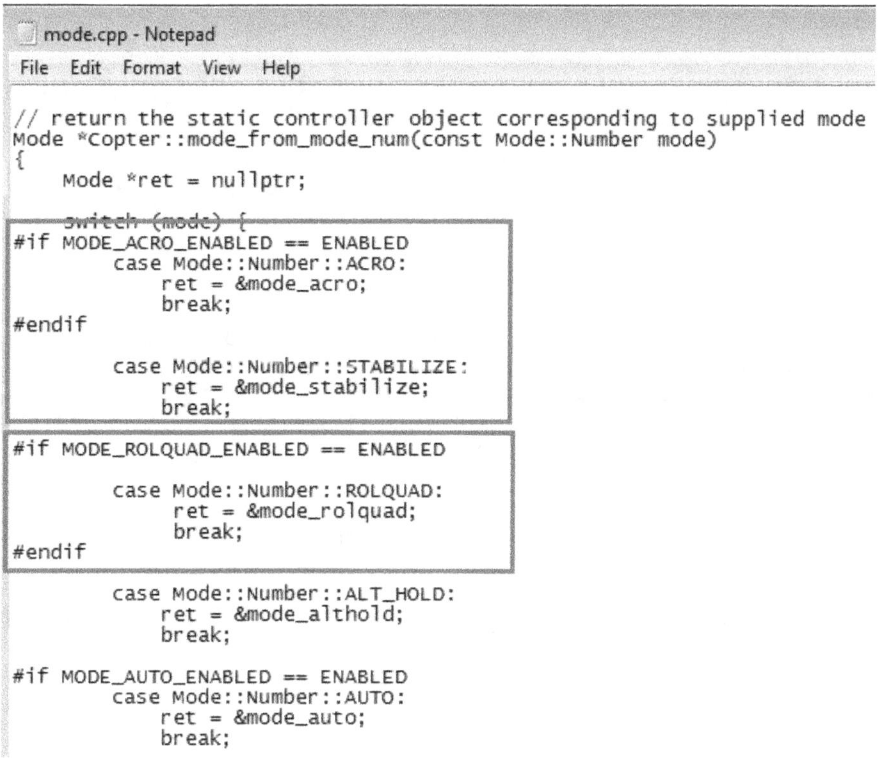

Figure 3-38. *Illustration of the location and generic modification of the mode.cpp file*

CHAPTER 3   MECHATRONIC DESCRIPTION OF GENERIC COMPONENTS USED IN THIS BOOK

config.h

Look for the first instance of

MODE_ZIGZAG_ENABLED

and add immediately after that block (see Figure 3-39) the code shown in Listing 3-3.

Listing 3-3. Code added to the file config.h

```
#ifndef MODE_ROLQUAD_ENABLED
    # define MODE_ROLQUAD_ENABLED ENABLED
#endif
```

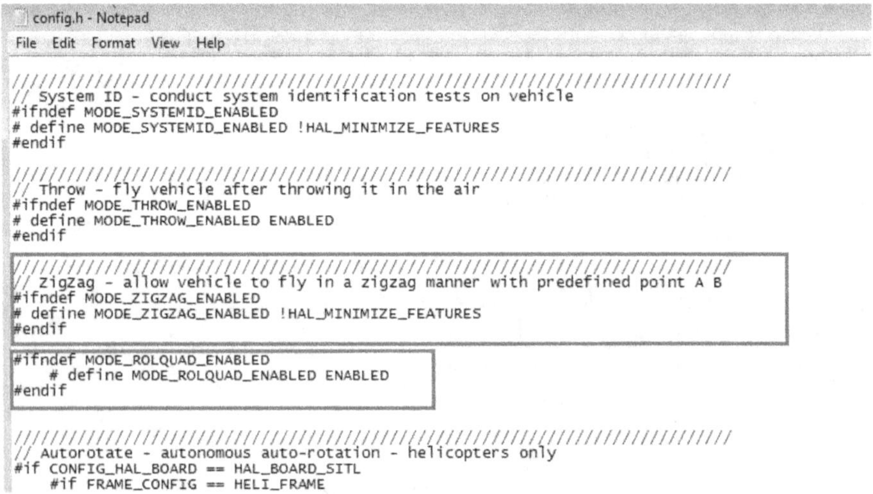

Figure 3-39. *Illustration of the location and generic modification of the config.h file*

In the same file, look for the first instance of

#ifndef FLIGHT_MODE_1

CHAPTER 3   MECHATRONIC DESCRIPTION OF GENERIC COMPONENTS USED IN THIS BOOK

and force all other flight modes to respond to the custom control; in this case ROLQUAD (see Figure 3-40).

This is because, in our code, the run method will not execute unless we activate our flight mode with the remote control via FLIGHT_MODE.

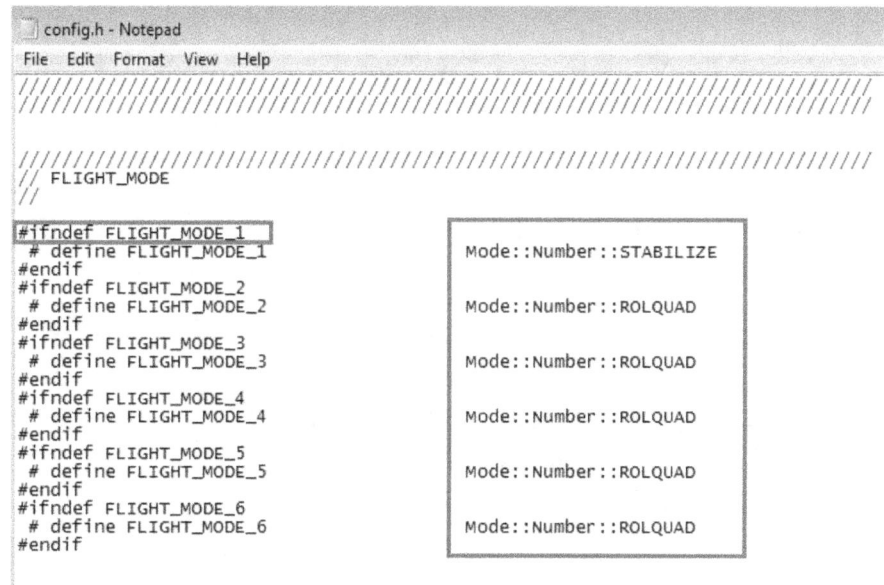

Figure 3-40. *Illustration of the second location and generic modification of the config.h file*

Copter.cpp

From this file, we only need to comment out the lines indicated in Figure 3-41.

We disable the orientation control, which is always being calculated

attitude_control->rate_controller_run();

We disable the motors output since it is our intention to manipulate it.

motors_output();

167

CHAPTER 3 MECHATRONIC DESCRIPTION OF GENERIC COMPONENTS USED IN THIS BOOK

```
#endif
#if OSD_ENABLED == ENABLED
    SCHED_TASK(publish_osd_info, 1, 10),
#endif
};

void Copter::get_scheduler_tasks(const AP_Scheduler::Task *&tasks,
                                 uint8_t &task_count,
                                 uint32_t &log_bit)
{
    tasks = &scheduler_tasks[0];
    task_count = ARRAY_SIZE(scheduler_tasks);
    log_bit = MASK_LOG_PM;
}

constexpr int8_t Copter::_failsafe_priorities[7];

// Main loop - 400hz
void Copter::fast_loop()
{
    // update INS immediately to get current gyro data populated
    ins.update();

    // run low level rate controllers that only require IMU data
    //attitude_control->rate_controller_run();

    // send outputs to the motors library immediately
    //motors_output();

    // run EKF state estimator (expensive)
    // --------------------
    read_AHRS();
```

Figure 3-41. *Illustration of the location and generic modification of the Copter.cpp file*

APM_Config.h

In this file, simply uncomment the lines shown in Figure 3-42, which will be used in the projects in the UserVariables.h and UserCode.cpp files that will be explained later.

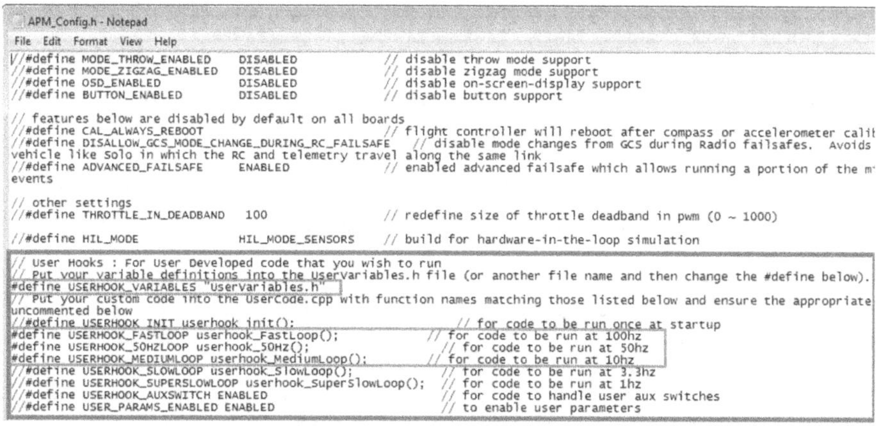

CHAPTER 3　MECHATRONIC DESCRIPTION OF GENERIC COMPONENTS USED IN THIS BOOK

Figure 3-42. Illustration of the location and generic modification of the APM_Config.h file (only uncomment the indicated lines)

Software: PseudoSetup

We say that the cycle called USERHOOK_INIT is a pseudo-setup because, in reality, all ports, components, and elements of the autopilot are executed all the time by the ArduPilot libraries. What is relevant here is that this cycle allows us to change or adjust parameters that would otherwise be performed in default mode.

This cycle, as its own comments indicate, is only executed once and, among other things, allows us to specify cutoff parameters for filters, indicate which analog or digital channels will be assigned, and initialize and set the speed of serial ports, etc.

This cycle replaces the old setup called SETUP in the ArduPilot libraries (see our previous book, *Advanced Robotic Vehicles Programming*) and will be used shortly in our aeropendulum project.

CHAPTER 3   MECHATRONIC DESCRIPTION OF GENERIC COMPONENTS USED IN THIS BOOK

Software: ArduPilot Time Management

A much more extensive description on time management can be found in our previous book, *Advanced Robotic Vehicles Programming*.

Here, we will only describe the three main modes of time management that we intentionally show in the "Hello World" example, see Figure 3-43.

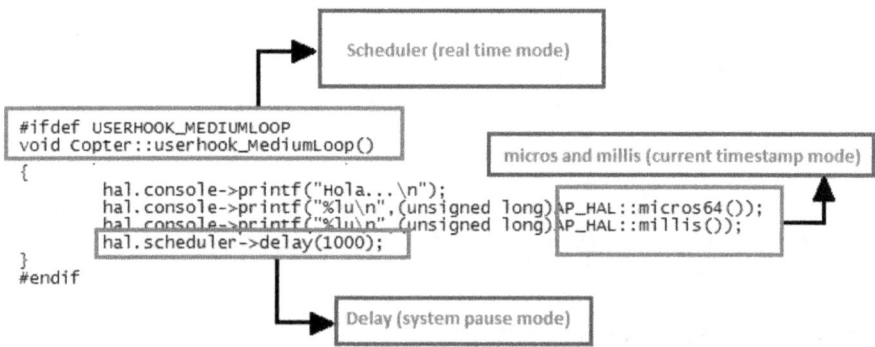

Figure 3-43. *The three most common types of time management in ArduPilot are delay, time stamps, and real-time*

Firstly, the pause, which is designed to stop the system from functioning for the specified time in milliseconds. Here, one-thousand milliseconds imply stopping the system for one second. The pause is the worst way to manage time, as it literally inactivates or suspends everything until it happens. We only mention it in case some user might need it, but it is not recommended. In its operation, it can be likened to an alarm clock.

The other way to manage time is with time stamps; this is done by using two commands: one returns the milliseconds elapsed since the system started and the other returns the microseconds. Each of these two commands has a precision prefix that can be 64, 32, 16, etc., which only affects the amount of time that can be saved or overflowed and, of course, the type of integer variable where the time should be stored. In its operation, it can be likened to a clock.

The last mode is the most relevant, as it gives the autopilot real-time functions and task execution assignment. In its operation, it can be likened to a precision stopwatch. This mode is explained in detail in the guided prototype on the aeropendulum later in this book.

Software: Signal Filtering

This is another generic utility command, either to reduce noise in a sensor or to deal with the effects of noise inherent in a controller like the PD, where it is known that the derivative part introduces or amplifies noise in a system.

The procedure is as follows:

1. First, you need to declare the low-pass filter object (or any other available filter) within UserVariables.h; this is done with the line described in Listing 3-4.

   Listing 3-4. Line of code for declaring a low-pass filter object in the USerVariables.h file

   ```
   LowPassFilterFloat low_pass_filter;
   ```

2. Then, in UserCode.cpp, in the initialization cycle USERHOOK_INIT, as displayed in Listing 3-5, declare the cutoff frequency using the previously declared object.

   Listing 3-5. Filter initialization in the UserCode.cpp file

   ```
   #ifdef USERHOOK_INIT
   void Copter::userhook_init()
   {
       // put your initialisation code here this will be called once at start-up
   ```

```
        low_pass_filter.set_cutoff_frequency(1.0f);
        //The "f" is a floating-point precision indicator
    }
    #endif
```

3. To use the filter, simply call the line of code in Listing 3-6 where necessary.

Listing 3-6. Filter implementation wherever you need it

```
low_pass_filter.apply(measuredAngle, 0.1f));
// The format is:
// low_pass_filter.apply(signal,dt));
// Where signal is the signal that needs to be filtered
and dt is the signal sampling time
```

Safety Requirements for the Aeropendulum and Quadcopters

Before moving on to the extensive prototypes in this book, we will discuss some general safety details for their operation.

Always wear goggles during propeller operation; the projects may seem like toy prototypes, but the propellers can reach higher speeds and torque than a blender's blades.

Wear comfortable long-sleeved clothing; due to the previous point, we have known cases and personal experiences where propellers have torn users' arms, leaving permanent scars in some cases. It is recommended to wear a lab coat or at least a long-sleeved shirt if the user doesn't have one.

Tighten the propellers adequately, as we have noticed that our students often fix them with minimal force, and when they spin, they literally fly off the prototype.

Verify in the connections and code that there is no false or immediate motor startup, and preferably condition it to the autopilot's arming. This ensures that the operator is not accidentally cut by the propellers.

Verify that there are no short circuits in the connections, as the batteries or power sources used, even with the smallest BLDC motor, have a risk of electrocution or burns due to the current demanded (the motors used in this book, although small, have a consumption of 10 A and possibly higher due to their startup currents).

Avoid using propellers until you are sure of achieving a proper prototype operation. This can be done by using it without propellers and verifying that the motors spin at their maximum speed, reach their differential speeds, or stop as expected; the following are examples.

Verification of the Desired Operation of the Aeropendulum Without Propellers

This case is relatively simple to verify without propellers, see Figure 3-44. The following can be done:

1. Define a desired operating angle and its control, as in the extensive code example in the following chapter of this book.

2. Connect the entire system and arm it.

3. If the pendulum exceeds the desired value, the motor speed should decrease to ensure that it returns to that operating point due to the effect of gravity and fall.

4. If the pendulum has an angle lower than the desired value, the motor speed should increase. This verifies that the system will return to the desired operating point due to motor action.

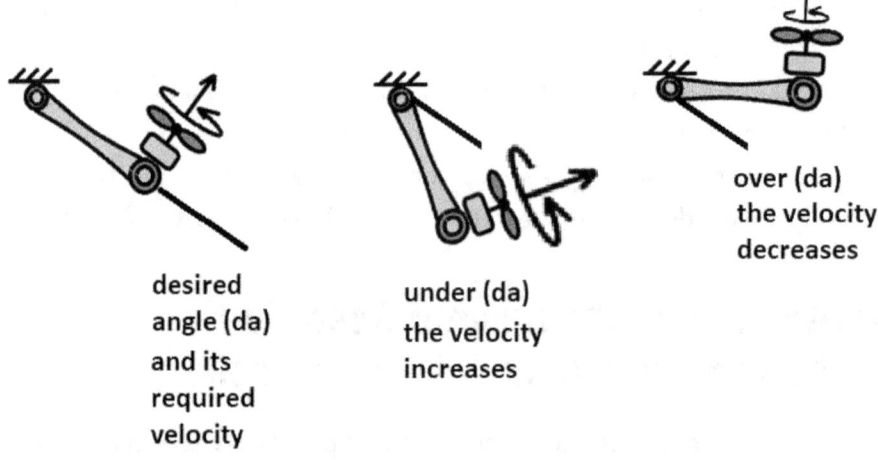

Figure 3-44. *Verification of the desired operation of an aeropendulum with or without propellers based on motor speed*

CHAPTER 3 MECHATRONIC DESCRIPTION OF GENERIC COMPONENTS USED IN THIS BOOK

Verification of the Desired Operation of the Quadcopter Mounted on a Test Stand and the Free Flight Quadcopter Without Propellers

In the case of the quadcopter mounted on a test stand, a balance orientation control is pursued, meaning the angles tend toward 0. If the vehicle's configuration is as shown in Figure 3-45, a differential effect of the motors will be noticeable, as shown in Table 3-5. Observe that the positive direction is indicated by the red arrowheads, both for yaw, roll, and pitch rotations, and for X, Y, and Z translations.

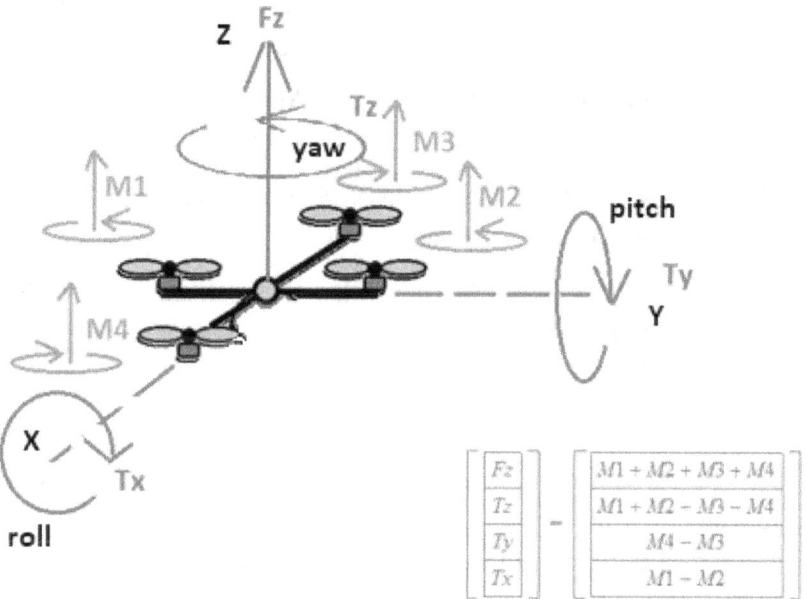

Figure 3-45. *The movements of a quadcopter with respect to its center of analysis (in this case the center of symmetry) related to the speeds of its motors*

CHAPTER 3   MECHATRONIC DESCRIPTION OF GENERIC COMPONENTS USED IN THIS BOOK

Table 3-5. *Verification of the desired operation of a quadcopter mounted on a test stand with or without propellers based on its motors' behavior*

Behavior with or without propellers	Motor 1	Motor 2	Motor 3	Motor 4
Above yaw target	Brakes	Brakes	Accelerates	Accelerates
Below yaw target	Accelerates	Accelerates	Brakes	Brakes
Above roll target	Brakes	Accelerates	Null or minimal action	Null or minimal action
Below roll target	Accelerates	Brakes	Null or minimal action	Null or minimal action
Above pitch target	Null or minimal action	Null or minimal action	Accelerates	Brakes
Below pitch target	Null or minimal action	Null or minimal action	Brakes	Accelerates

In the case of a free flight drone, as indicated in Table 3-6, the following modes are incorporated, considering that the XYZ positions are not anchored and that the X and Y positions depend on the roll and pitch angles; X is tied to the negative of pitch and Y to roll directly.

CHAPTER 3   MECHATRONIC DESCRIPTION OF GENERIC COMPONENTS USED IN THIS BOOK

Table 3-6. *Verification of the desired operation of a free flight quadcopter with or without propellers based on its motors' behavior*

Behavior with or without propellers	Motor 1	Motor 2	Motor 3	Motor 4
Above Z target	Brakes	Brakes	Brakes	Brakes
Below Z target	Accelerates	Accelerates	Accelerates	Accelerates
Above X target	Null or minimal action	Null or minimal action	Brakes	Accelerates
Below X target	Null or minimal action	Null or minimal action	Accelerates	Brakes
Above Y target	Brakes	Accelerates	Null or minimal action	Null or minimal action
Below Y target	Accelerates	Brakes	Null or minimal action	Null or minimal action

We also want to remind the reader that using these motors without propellers for too long could cause damage due to operation without load. A safer way to perform this type of test extensively is by placing small pieces of paper or foam on the axes, ensuring that these pieces are not sharp but represent a useful inertia for the motors.

In addition, it is essential for the user to verify that the connection and reference numbering of the motors match the autopilot numbering. This determines the correct functioning of the propulsion matrix, which in turn determines the vehicle's behavior. Similarly, the user must verify the positive and negative sense of the reference axes for both position and orientation.

In the case of the quadcopter mounted on a test stand and aeropendulums, it is advisable to keep them away from any type of liquid and food. We have had negative experiences with students spilling water or coffee on the power supplies or connections.

In the case of the quadcopter mounted on a test stand and aeropendulums, the user must verify that the joints, bearings, or bushings are properly lubricated to move. Additionally, the movement should be controlled by some stop or barrier so that the prototypes do not damage themselves.

In the case of the quadcopter mounted on a test stand and aeropendulums, it must be verified that they are properly anchored to a table or sufficiently heavy surface using clamps. We have had at least one experience where students forgot to secure them, resulting in damage to the motor and propeller due to the prototype's fall.

Before using drones in free-flight modes, it is advisable to have a flight mode in which it does not move away from the operating point. This way, it is avoided that the drone gets lost, infringes or damages private property, or crashes into a person or living being. This can be achieved in the following ways:

- Conducting tests in a closed space
- Conducting tests anywhere under a net
- Conducting tests anywhere with the vehicle anchored by a rope to the ground or to a user, like a kite
- Conducting tests anywhere but having a remote control with a safe operation mode
- In the case of a free flight drone, always use it away from or without the presence of electrical system networks or pipelines

- Finally, it is recalled that all of the above likely require usage or flight permits, so the reader is advised to always check current legislations for the operation of these devices.

Chapter Summary

In this chapter, the generic components used in the projects of the next chapters were illustrated and classified from a mechatronic point of view.

Among other things, the main structural and electronic elements were shown—the basics of logical and analytical control with the PD algorithm as the chassis—and finally the computational approach divided into hardware and software, where the details of the autopilots used in this book and standard modifications of the ArduPilot libraries were presented.

Finally, a section on the safe verification of the drone flight modes was included.

In the next chapter, we will extensively cover the aeropendulum project, which is the basis for the rest of the prototypes of this book.

PART III

Extensive Examples

CHAPTER 4

Aeropendulum

This chapter extensively covers the first guided project: the aeropendulum. It begins with its definition, uses, and variants, which are complemented in the theoretical context with references to the device at the end of the book. Following this, we proceed to the development of the prototype, covering a suggested list of components and knowledge, assembly instructions, and mechatronic design. Finally, the chapter concludes with the complete code using ArduPilot 2023 libraries in modular OOP mode and its corresponding experimental results.

Additionally, and for comparison purposes, an operational code using Arduino sequential programming is also presented.

Description and Applications of the Aeropendulum

This is a variation of the motorized simple pendulum, except that instead of having the motorized element at the pivot, it is located at the end in the form of a propeller (see Figure 4-1), which means it has an actuator based on speed variation; see the following figure. Due to the effect of gravity, only one motorized propeller is necessary (lift is achieved with the propeller, and descent is achieved with gravity).

CHAPTER 4 AEROPENDULUM

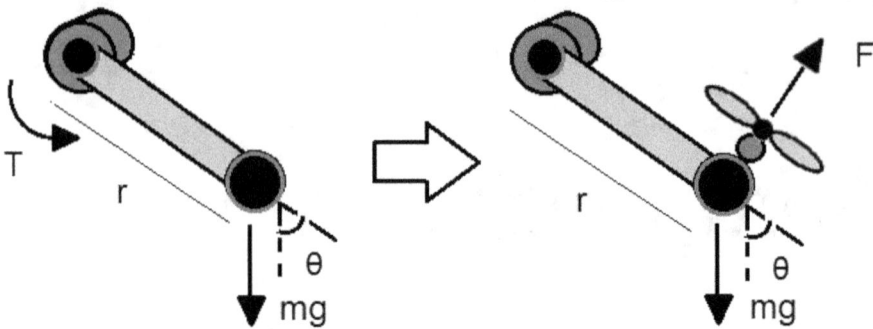

Figure 4-1. *Standard motorized pendulum and aeropendulum*

Perhaps one of the most pedagogical and immediate approaches to aerial robotics and applied control is the aeropendulum; this is because the aeropendulum and the simple pendulum are very simple robots to assemble and put into operation.

Of course, it carries a risk, which is the use of propellers at high speeds; but with proper care, it is a fairly intuitive and complete platform.

More complex versions of it are commercialized by the company Quanser or can be developed with certain dedication and research by the interested user, see Figure 4-2.

CHAPTER 4　AEROPENDULUM

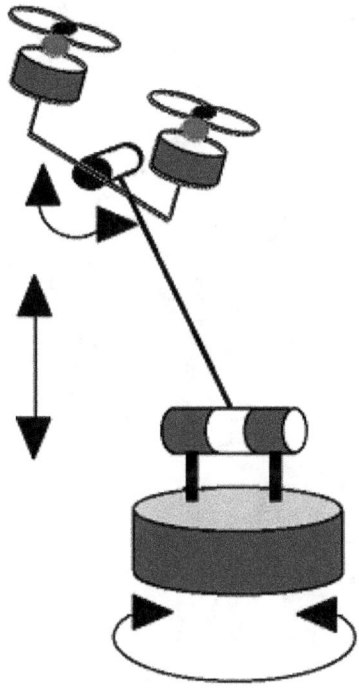

Figure 4-2. *Two-degree-of-freedom aeropendulum with two propellers in differential configuration*

Other variants may be those illustrated below:

In Figure 4-3, an aeropendulum with disturbances provided by a motor placed over its pivot is shown; this is in order to create controllers that resist turbulences or vortices.

CHAPTER 4 AEROPENDULUM

Figure 4-3. *Aeropendulum with turbulent perturbations induced by another motor at its pivot*

In Figure 4-4, an aeropendulum with anti-rotational propulsion effect is shown; also an aerobot, which is simply a succession of aeropendulums; and a snake aerial manipulator, which is a succession of aeropendulums not anchored to the ground (see "Snake Aerial Manipulators: A Review," Mendoza-Mendoza et al.).

CHAPTER 4   AEROPENDULUM

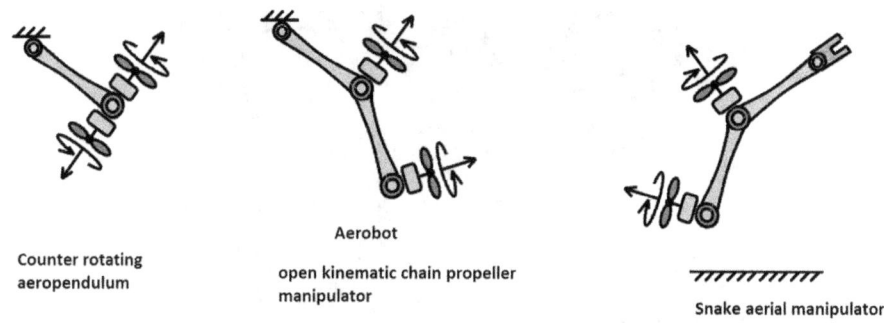

Figure 4-4. *Other three variants of the aeropendulum including a 2DOF aerobot and a snake aerial manipulator*

The objective of the aeropendulum is simple: to keep a structure at a desired angle through the combined effect of propulsion from one or more propellers and/or gravity or another counter-movement action. It's so simple to make that with a well-characterized potentiometer, some glue, and a stick, it can be done. In the following photographs, we present two versions, one very simplified (Figure 4-5) and the other with a higher degree of complexity (Figure 4-6), developed by our students.

187

CHAPTER 4　AEROPENDULUM

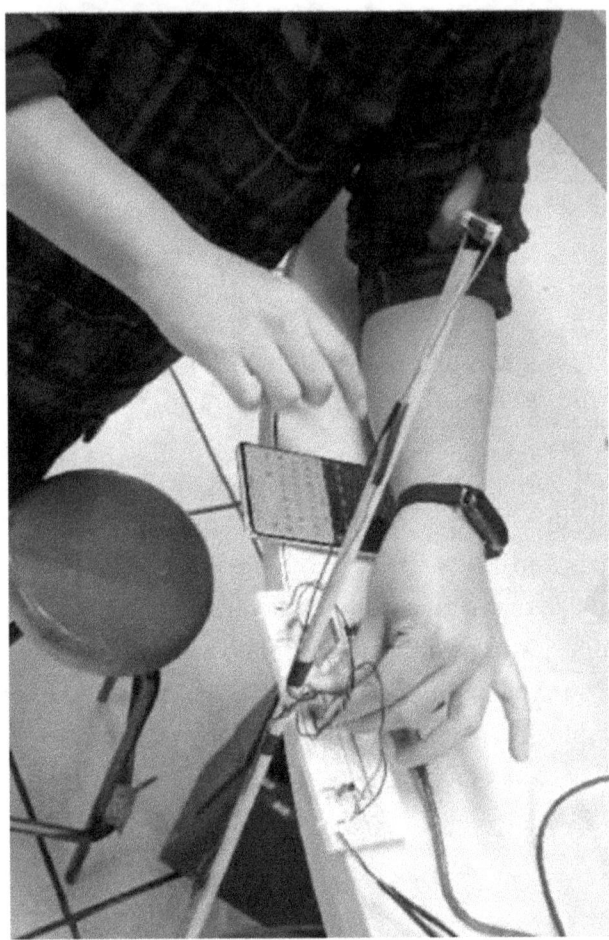

Figure 4-5. *A very simplified version of the aeropendulum made by our ESCOM students (courtesy of Professor Rene Baltazar Jimenez Ruiz)*

CHAPTER 4   AEROPENDULUM

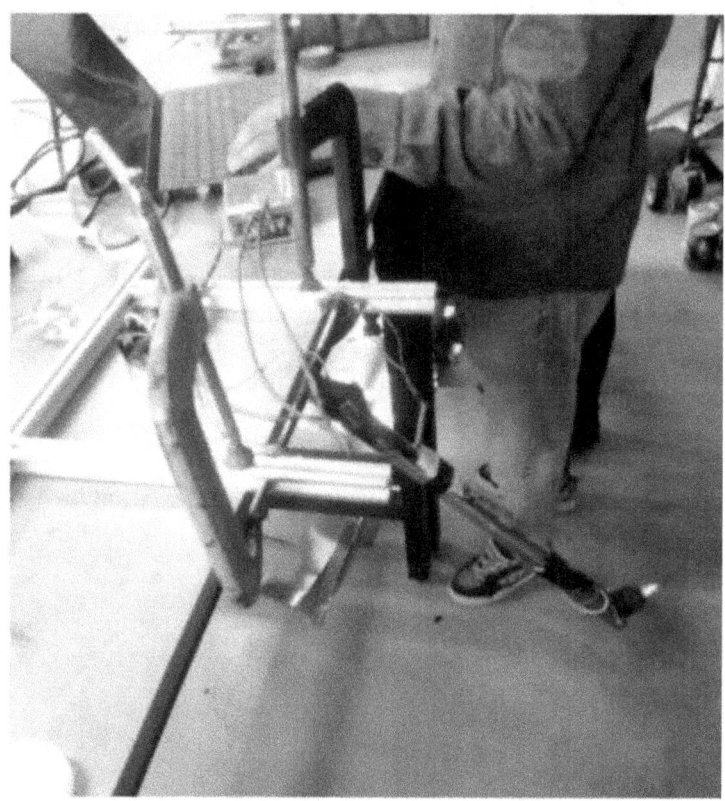

Figure 4-6. *A not-so-simple version of the aeropendulum made by our students from UPIITA*

For more details on this project, including extensive mathematical models and additional applications and control modes, we recommend reading the selected references section of this book.

CHAPTER 4 AEROPENDULUM

List of Materials and Minimum Knowledge Required to Build an Aeropendulum

Mechanics

Materials and Tools

- One lever arm between 30 and 35 cm long, lightweight and resistant
- Two pillow blocks with inner bearing
- One flexible metal connector (accordion-type)
- At least two meters of IPS profile or other material for the structure
- Propellers compatible with the BLDC motor
- Screws and nylock or security nuts
- IPS screws (if using that profile)
- Cutting tools for aluminum or steel profiles
- Various drill bits if necessary
- Oil for lubricating bearings if necessary
- Bench drill
- Screwdrivers or wrenches compatible with the screws
- Electronic scale for small elements (one gram to half kilogram)
- Sandpaper or emery if required
- One pair of clamps to secure the aeropendulum to a heavy surface (such as a table)

CHAPTER 4 AEROPENDULUM

Knowledge

- Basic machining operations using drills (parallel, perpendicular, and in-line holes)
- Basic finishing operations using sandpaper or emery

Electronics

Materials and Tools

- One BLDC motor (preferably)
- One ESC (Electronic Speed Controller) compatible with the motor
- One power supply compatible with the ESC
- One remote control with PPM receiver compatible with the autopilot
- One precision potentiometer with low friction (preferably)
- Power cables and connectors (AWG, bullet connectors, etc.)
- Data transmission and sensor cables and connectors (jumpers)
- One soldering iron with solder and flux
- One multimeter

Knowledge

- Know how to solder
- Know how to interpret connection diagrams
- Know how to interpret datasheets
- Know how to perform basic electrical measurements

CHAPTER 4   AEROPENDULUM

Programming

Materials and Tools

- One computer with ArduPilot libraries and Mission Planner

- One microSD adapter (in case you want to download autopilot's data)

- One serial data interface (it can be Mission Planner, PuTTY, etc.)

- One USB data cable compatible with the computer and the autopilot

Knowledge

- Object-oriented C++

- ArduPilot commands to read radio control

- ArduPilot commands to read analog port (potentiometer)

- ArduPilot commands to write to a BLDC motor

Control

Materials and Tools

- One Pixhawk autopilot with analog ports and its analog connectors kit

Knowledge

- Understand and program a simple PD algorithm (for BLDC control)

- Understand and program a logical algorithm (for remote control logical states)

CHAPTER 4   AEROPENDULUM

Assembly and Component Details

Assembly of mechanical parts:

    IPS structural elements
    Supports for the main shaft and angular sensor
    Main shaft
    Coupling for the shaft and sensor
    Pillow blocks with bearing, see Figure 4-7.

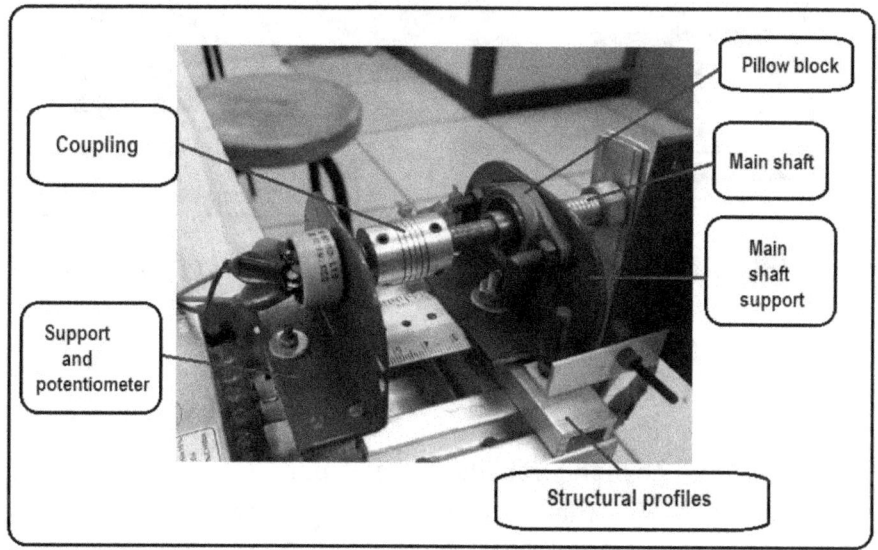

Figure 4-7. *Detail of the mechanical assembly of the aeropendulum 1*

    Motion limit stop
    BLDC motor with propeller
    Motor support
    Various screws and locknuts or safety nuts, see Figure 4-8.

CHAPTER 4   AEROPENDULUM

Figure 4-8. Detail of the mechanical assembly of the aeropendulum 2

Assembly of electrical parts:

Power supply

Connection terminals

ESC to power the motor from the power supply

Connectors and electrical insulation, see Figure 4-9.

CHAPTER 4   AEROPENDULUM

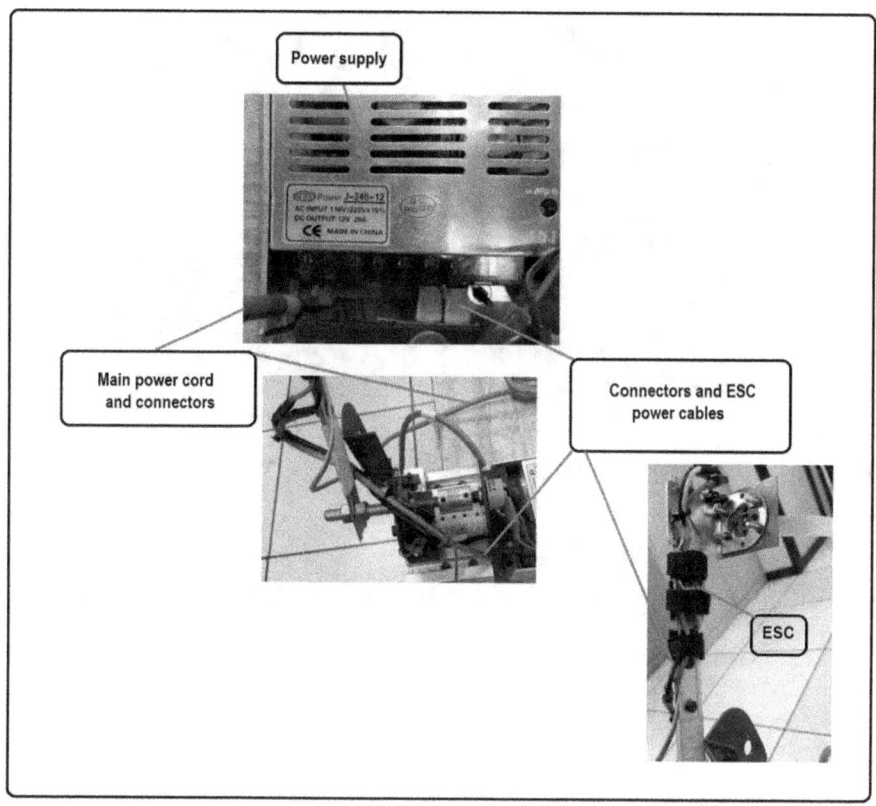

Figure 4-9. *Detail of the electrical assembly of the aeropendulum*

Assembly of control parts:

Unlimited rotation potentiometer for angle measurement, see Figure 4-10.

CHAPTER 4   AEROPENDULUM

Figure 4-10. *Detail of the potentiometer*

Assembly of programming parts:

Arduino as a computer for sensor reading, control processing, and task monitoring, see Figure 4-11.

Figure 4-11. *Detail of the first version of the aeropendulum based on Arduino, the three crocodile cables come from the potentiometer, and the two remaining cables go to the ESC of the BLDC motor (only PWM signal and ground)*

Assembly recommendations

The assembly also has the following special design considerations shown in Figures 4-12 and 4-13.

- The sensor cables and ESC control cables that connect to the Arduino have spacers every two centimeters, in order not to obstruct the pendulum's rotation.

- All ESC cables were placed forming a curvature such that the maximum radius of that curvature is present when the pendulum is at rest and reduces when the pendulum is in its extreme position from the rest angle (this is to avoid breaking or twisting the wiring).

CHAPTER 4   AEROPENDULUM

Additionally, they are kept away from the propellers by means of Velcro fastening and plastic zip ties, see Figures 4-12 and 4-13.

Figure 4-12. *Additional assembly recommendations for the aeropendulum 1*

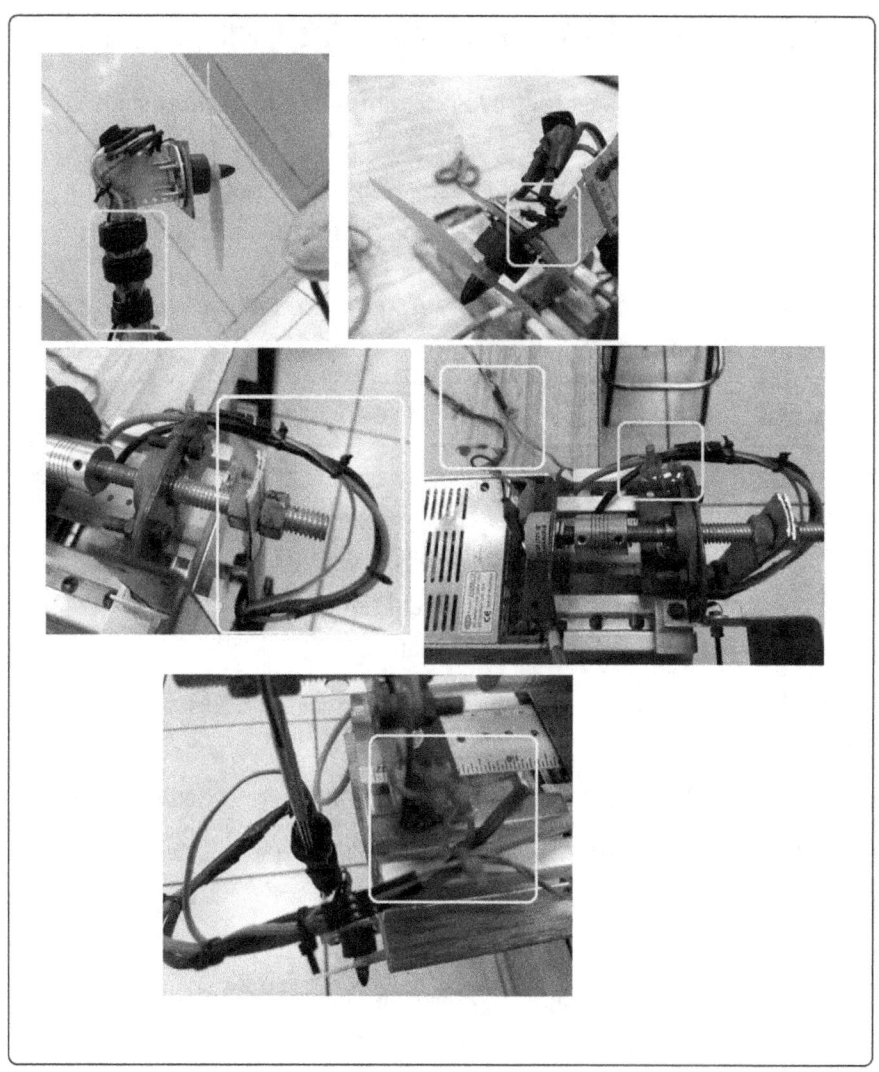

Figure 4-13. *Additional assembly recommendations for the aeropendulum 2*

CHAPTER 4　AEROPENDULUM

Electrical and Electronic Analysis

What type of sensor is best to use? For example, potentiometer, encoder, or IMU (gyroscope).

We opted for the potentiometer due to its quick implementation, but if you want, you can use another rotary sensor; for this, use Table 4-1.

Table 4-1. *Comparison between rotary sensors to measure the angle of the aeropendulum*

Sensor type	Potentiometer	Relative encoder	IMU (gyroscope)
Startup value	Yes, different from 0	It's always 0; it's recommended to use gravity or weight for system startup, or its Z channel.	Yes, different from 0
Rotational friction	Low to very high	Low to very high	Null
Signal type	One analog signal	Digital and dual	Serial generally
Linearity degree	Low to high	Depends on the DAC converter	Low to high
Noise level	Low	Low to medium	High
Resolution	Depends on the resolution of the input analog port	Depends on the number of pulses per revolution	Depends on the cost of the IMU
Measurement type	Pivot's rotation	Pivot's rotation	Rotation of a reference plane over the pivot (if the pivot is tilted, it changes)

(continued)

Table 4-1. (*continued*)

Sensor type	Potentiometer	Relative encoder	IMU (gyroscope)
Price	From very economical to expensive	Generally expensive	Intermediate
Requires filtering or other adjustment	Linearization algorithms	Algorithms to prevent loss of steps or excess of them, algorithms to determine limit values	Filtering due to its high noise level
Size	Small to large	Small to large	Very small
Ease of placement	Requires alignment and coupling, preferably with pillow blocks	Requires alignment and coupling, preferably with pillow blocks	Related to the plane to be measured
Measurement range	Generally with limits, even those without stop have a range that repeats	There is no limit, just the processor's memory	Limited with respect to the reference axis, normally the Earth's magnetic reference
Other variants	Multi-turn, without stop, high precision	Absolute, with analog channels (resolver)	Mechanical, magnetic, from 2 to 12 or more channels

It's also worth clarifying that most potentiometers exhibit high non-linearities and sudden changes in resistance, as well as high friction. The sensor we specifically used is of very low friction; and its linearity is quite acceptable, in this case, the BI 6187R5KL1.0.

What type of power source to use?

CHAPTER 4 AEROPENDULUM

In this case, consulting the same motor datasheet operating at 11V and consuming 6A, it was recommended to use an ESC or driver for said motor that is 12V and a maximum of 20A (a bit higher in its current due to the motor's stall effect). The driver should then be operated by a source in that operating range. For this, there were car batteries, LiPo batteries, or power supplies available. Below, Table 4-2, shows the selection criteria.

Table 4-2. *Comparison between power sources for the aeropendulum and in general all projects in this book*

Type of power source	Wired to powerline	LiPo battery	Car battery
Size	Small to Medium	Small	Medium
Weight	Relatively medium	Relatively light	Heavy
Operation time	Continuous as long as not disconnected	Generally tens of minutes to an hour	Hours to half a day
Special features	There can be regulated (heavier and bulkier but less noisy) or switched-mode (noisier and lighter)	Its voltage value should not be reduced to less than 70% of its nominal value, as it can be damaged	They withstand frequent engine start transients
Additional equipment required	Input regulator or surge suppressor	Specialized charger with balancer	Their operating value has low ripple
Risks	Electric shock	Explosion, combustion	Usually a standard charger

(continued)

Table 4-2. (*continued*)

Type of power source	Wired to powerline	LiPo battery	Car battery
Costs	For these applications, on average, all these technologies cost about the same per watt delivered	For these applications, on average, all these technologies cost about the same per watt delivered	Spill of hazardous substances
Most suitable use	Fixed or anchored devices	Light mobile devices, such as aerial drones	For these applications, on average, all these technologies cost about the same per watt delivered

Therefore, since the aeropendulum is a fixed test platform, a continuous operation wired power source that doesn't discharge like batteries was convenient, see Figure 4-14.

CHAPTER 4   AEROPENDULUM

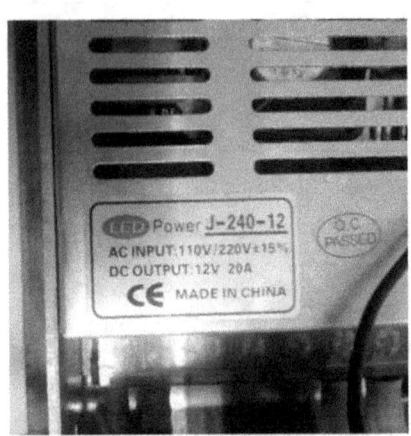

Figure 4-14. *Relationship between voltage and current supplied by the wired power source and our required ESC values*

About Connectors and Analog, Serial, and Real-Time Tests

To control the aeropendulum, we need to measure its angle, and as mentioned, this will be done using a potentiometer. Even if we weren't using a potentiometer and instead used an IMU, in both cases, the signal needs to be input to the autopilot.

In the case of the autopilot we used, specifically the Radiolink Pixhawk, it has 1.25mm Molex connectors like the ones shown in Figure 4-15 (you should verify the type of connector your autopilot has).

CHAPTER 4   AEROPENDULUM

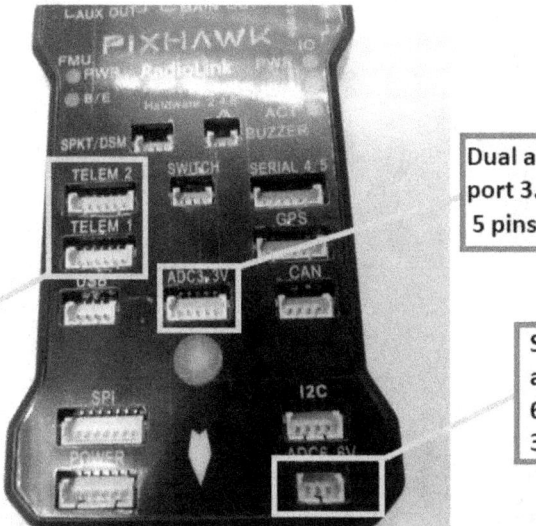

Figure 4-15. *Description of the Pixhawk ports used in our serial and analog testing*

In our case, we will input analog and serial UART-type information through the ports indicated in the previous figure.

Note In the appendices of this book, specifically the appendix on the robotic manipulator mounted on a mobile robot, several possibilities are indicated for input and output of information to the autopilot, depending on the type of motors available and whether serial, analog, or direct connection is preferred.

This implies knowing the pinout of the Pixhawk, which is more or less standardized as shown in Figure 4-16 (it's the reader's responsibility to verify).

205

CHAPTER 4 AEROPENDULUM

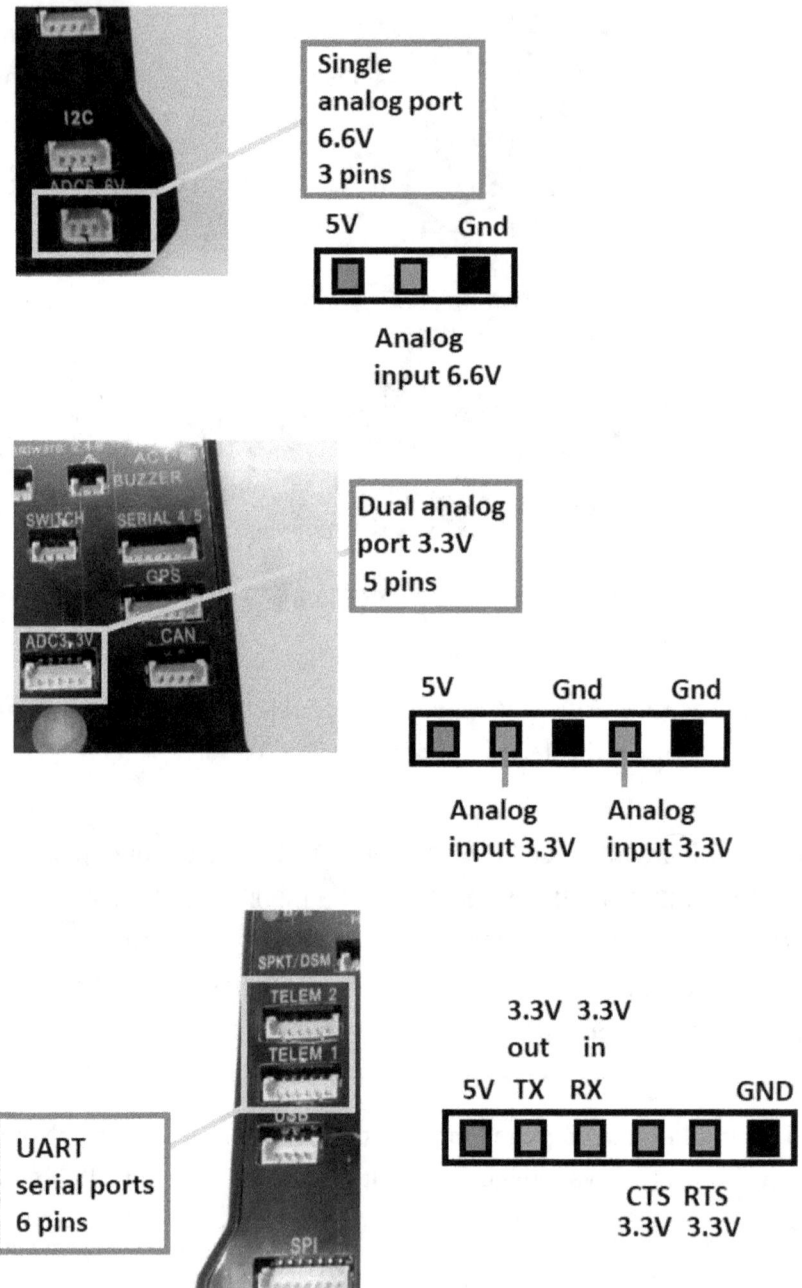

Figure 4-16. *Detailed description of the Pixhawk pins used*

CHAPTER 4 AEROPENDULUM

To input data to the Pixhawk from external hardware, we will outline the assembly process:

First, the components and tools, which can be seen in Figure 4-17:

- One soldering iron
- Solder and flux (preferably for better soldering, but not necessary)
- One multimeter to test continuity between cable terminals
- Molex connectors or the required ones (6, 3, or 5 terminals depending on the port to use) preferably pre-wired
- Jumpers to adapt the Molex connectors to the analog device of interest (in this case, the potentiometer)
- Wire strippers or pliers
- Electrical tape or heat shrink tubing

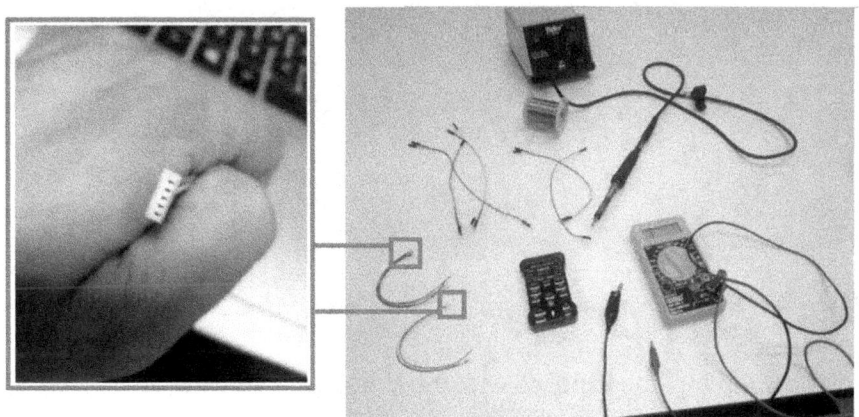

Figure 4-17. Wire assembly for the Pixhawk ports 1

207

CHAPTER 4   AEROPENDULUM

The next step is to solder the jumpers to the wires of the Molex connector (or the connector used by your autopilot), see Figure 4-18.

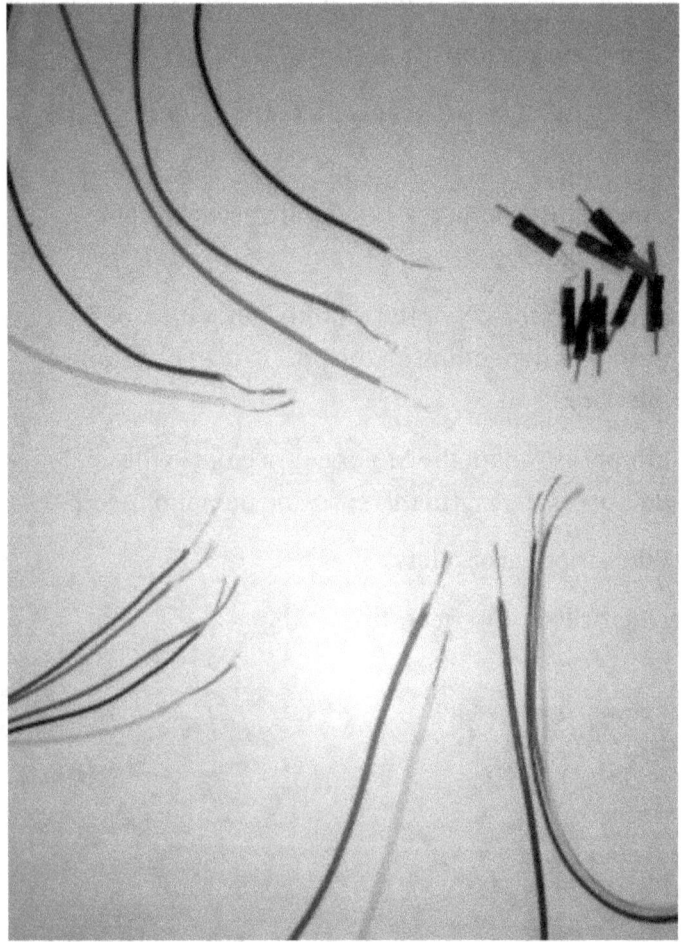

Figure 4-18. *Wire assembly for the Pixhawk ports 2*

As a final step, the exposed wire joints are covered with heat shrink tubing, and continuity is tested between the jumper terminals and the connector terminals, see Figure 4-19.

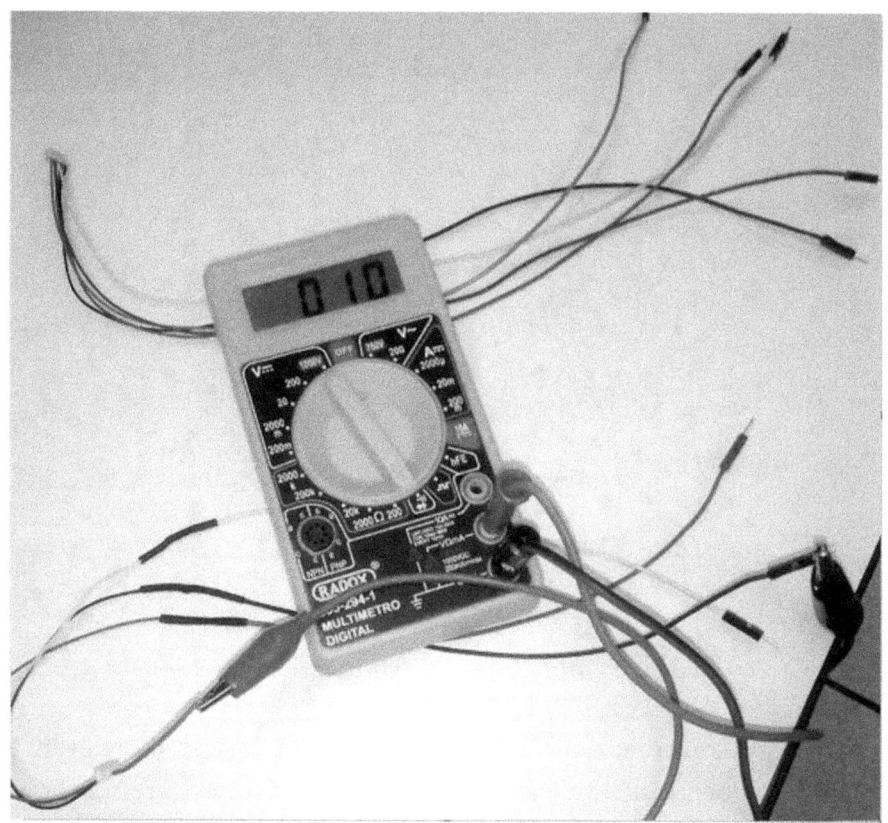

Figure 4-19. *Wire assembly for the Pixhawk ports 3*

In this way, the connectors that will be used between the Pixhawk ports and the analog or serial devices are ready, see Figure 4-20.

CHAPTER 4   AEROPENDULUM

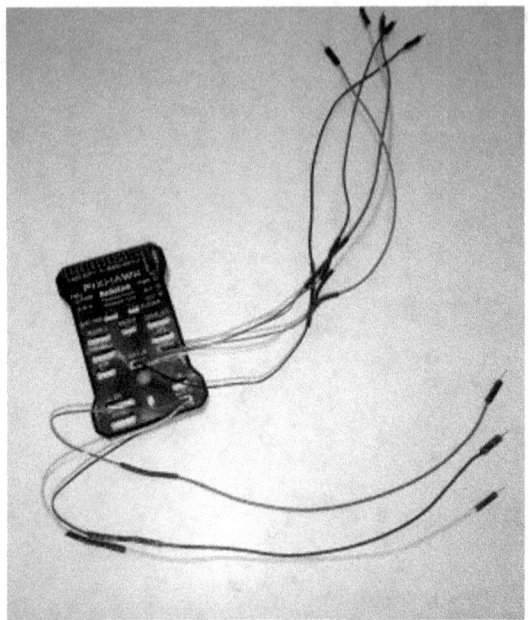

Figure 4-20.* Wire assembly for the Pixhawk ports 4*

Once you want to use the Pixhawk ports or your devices, it's relevant to verify the voltage values indicated online or in datasheets. Here, we show that although it's mentioned that there will be 5V output on the 6.6 analog input port, there are only 4.82V (see Figure 4-21), which may or may not be enough for the user's tests. However, it's the user's responsibility to confirm this.

CHAPTER 4   AEROPENDULUM

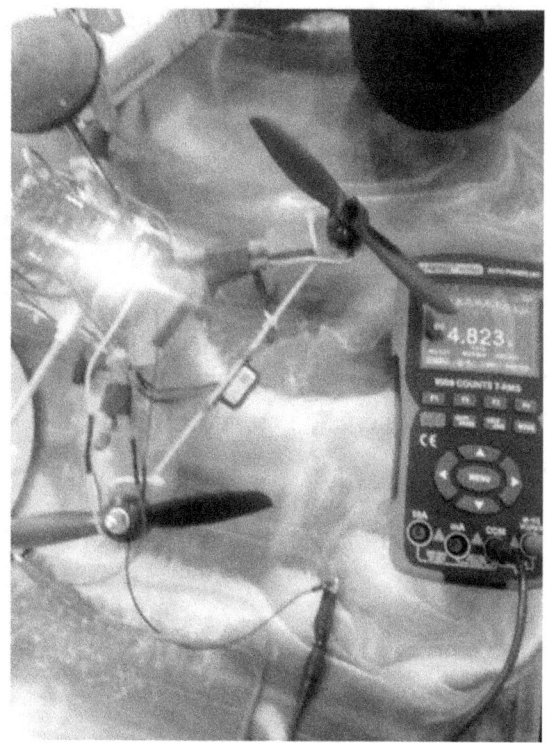

Figure 4-21. *Autopilot's available voltages verification*

Having said this, two utility programs are described below: Analog port test codes (6.6V ADC)

1. As shown in Listing 4-1, declare an object of type AnalogSource in the UserVariables.h file (although it can be in another file where it's needed, we recommend it to be in that one). Likewise, declare the variable where the analog reading will be stored in the same file.

Listing 4-1. Lines of code for declaring an analog source object in the UserVariables.h file

```
AP_HAL::AnalogSource* chan1;
float adc15;
// According to the Pixhawk online documentation, the
6.6V port is associated with channel 15
```

2. Define the channel to be read; this is only done once in the initialization task called USERHOOK_INIT within the UserCode.cpp file, as indicated in Listing 4-2:

Listing 4-2. Analog port inicialization in the UserCode.cpp file

```
#ifdef USERHOOK_INIT
void Copter::userhook_init()
{
    chan1 = hal.analogin->channel(15); // Here, channel 15 (6.6V) will be read
}
#endif
```

3. Get the analog reading where needed; for example, in a task within UserCode.cpp called USERHOOK_MEDIUMLOOP as illustrated in Listing 4-3 (although it can be used directly in the user's custom file, which in our case will be indicated later as mode_rolquad.cpp).

CHAPTER 4 AEROPENDULUM

Listing 4-3. Analog port reading wherever you need it; in this case in the UserCode.cpp file inside the USERHOOK_MEDIUMLOOP

```
#ifdef USERHOOK_MEDIUMLOOP
void Copter::userhook_MediumLoop()
{    // MediumLoop is a predefined cycle that runs at 10 Hz
     adc15=chan1->voltage_average();  // getting the average voltage
     hal.console->printf("%.3f\n",adc15);  // printing the voltage to the console
}
#endif
```

4. Finally, the code should be loaded onto the autopilot using MissionPlanner; connect the potentiometer or some other analog sensor to the 6.6V port, see Figure 4-22 (remember the pins facing you are: Vcc, Signal, GND), and observe the readings from a serial monitor (we've already explained how to use MissionPlanner as a serial monitor).

CHAPTER 4   AEROPENDULUM

Figure 4-22. *Connection of a potentiometer to the Pixhawk via the 6.6 analog port*

Note   The port number can be difficult to find in the scattered online documentation of ArduPilot; so it may be useful to open the demonstration files, such as AnalogIn.cpp (see Figure 4-23), and then compile and load it onto the autopilot through a target, as previously indicated, so that it displays with a small pause all the content of the available channels; evidently the one that varies will correspond to our potentiometer.

UserCode.cpp UserVariables.h Copter.cpp Copter.h AnalogIn.cpp

```
}

static int8_t pin;

void loop(void)
{
    float v  = chan->voltage_average();
    if (pin == 0) {
        hal.console->printf("\n");
    }
    hal.console->printf("[%u %.3f] ",
                (unsigned)pin, (double)v);
    pin = (pin+1) % 16;
    chan->set_pin(pin);
    hal.scheduler->delay(100);
}

AP_HAL_MAIN();
```

Figure 4-23. *File to test and identify the analog channel of interest on the Pixhawk in case its assigned number is unknown (AnalogIn.cpp)*

From the previous code, the dependence on predefined real-time tasks such as USERHOOK_MEDIUMLOOP, which runs at 10 Hz, is notable. As much as possible, and throughout the rest of the codes in this book, we will also use predefined tasks; but if you need to create your own tasks with the execution speed you need, you can make the following procedure (in this case, we will illustrate with two tasks, one running at 3Hz and the other at 7Hz):

CHAPTER 4　AEROPENDULUM

1. In the copter.h file, look for the following lines, see Figure 4-24.

```
const char* get_frame_string();
void allocate_motors(void);
bool is_tradheli() const;

// terrain.cpp
void terrain_update();
void terrain_logging();

// tuning.cpp
void tuning();
```

```
// UserCode.cpp
void userhook_init();
void userhook_FastLoop();
void userhook_50Hz();
void userhook_MediumLoop();
void userhook_SlowLoop();
void userhook_SuperSlowLoop();
void userhook_auxSwitch1(uint8_t ch_flag);
void userhook_auxSwitch2(uint8_t ch_flag);
void userhook_auxSwitch3(uint8_t ch_flag);
```

```
#if OSD_ENABLED == ENABLED
    void publish_osd_info();
#endif
```

Figure 4-24. *Example of custom task definition (analog and serial reading) in the Scheduler 1*

Once there, declare the following lines as indicated in Listing 4-4.

Listing 4-4. Adding real time tasks in the file copter.h

```
void mi_ciclo7();//this will run 7 times per second
void mi_ciclo3();//this will run 3 times per second
```

CHAPTER 4 AEROPENDULUM

2. Following the same approach as the tasks in UserCode.cpp, we will create a flag that allows activating or deactivating our custom cycles (they are activated or deactivated only by commenting or uncommenting). This is done within the APM_Config.h file; look for the block of code in Figure 4-25.

```
// User Hooks : For User Developed code that you wish to run
// Put your variable definitions into the UserVariables.h file
(or another file name and then change the #define below).
#define USERHOOK_VARIABLES "UserVariables.h"
// Put your custom code into the UserCode.cpp with function
names matching those listed below and ensure the appropriate
#define below is uncommented below
//#define USERHOOK_INIT userhook_init();                          //
for code to be run once at startup
#define USERHOOK_FASTLOOP userhook_FastLoop();                    // for
code to be run at 100hz
#define USERHOOK_50HZLOOP userhook_50Hz();                        //
for code to be run at 50hz
#define USERHOOK_MEDIUMLOOP userhook_MediumLoop();                // for
code to be run at 10hz
//#define USERHOOK_SLOWLOOP userhook_SlowLoop();                  //
for code to be run at 3.3hz
//#define USERHOOK_SUPERSLOWLOOP userhook_SuperSlowLoop();        //
for code to be run at 1hz
//#define USERHOOK_AUXSWITCH ENABLED                              //
for code to handle user aux switches
//#define USER_PARAMS_ENABLED ENABLED                             //
to enable user parameters
```

Figure 4-25. *Example of custom task definition (analog and serial reading) in the Scheduler 2*

And then define the enablers for your custom cycles as exemplified in Listing 4-5.

CHAPTER 4 AEROPENDULUM

Listing 4-5. Adding real time tasks in the file APM_Config.h

```
#define MI_CICLO7    mi_ciclo7(); // this runs 7 times per second
#define MI_CICLO3    mi_ciclo3(); // this runs 3 times per second
```

3. Locate the following lines within the copter.cpp file as a reference, see Figure 4-26.

```
#if GRIPPER_ENABLED == ENABLED
    SCHED_TASK_CLASS(AP_Gripper,              &copter.g2.gripper,
update,             10,    75),
#endif
#if WINCH_ENABLED == ENABLED
    SCHED_TASK_CLASS(AP_Winch,                &copter.g2.winch,
update,             50,    50),
#endif
#if GENERATOR_ENABLED
    SCHED_TASK_CLASS(AP_Generator_RichenPower,
&copter.generator,       update,     10,      50),
#endif
#ifdef USERHOOK_FASTLOOP
    SCHED_TASK(userhook_FastLoop,      100,       75),
#endif
#ifdef USERHOOK_50HZLOOP
    SCHED_TASK(userhook_50Hz,           50,       75),
#endif
#ifdef USERHOOK_MEDIUMLOOP
    SCHED_TASK(userhook_MediumLoop,     10,       75),
#endif
#ifdef USERHOOK_SLOWLOOP
    SCHED_TASK(userhook_SlowLoop,       3.3,      75),
#endif
#ifdef USERHOOK_SUPERSLOWLOOP
    SCHED_TASK(userhook_SuperSlowLoop,  1,        75),
#endif
#if BUTTON_ENABLED == ENABLED
    SCHED_TASK_CLASS(AP_Button,               &copter.button,
update,             5,    100),
```

Figure 4-26. *Example of custom task definition (analog and serial reading) in the Scheduler 3*

Add the following real-time tasks to the scheduler within that file, as shown in Listing 4-6; remember to respect the following syntax:

SCHED_TASK(task name, execution frequency in Hz, expected maximum duration in microseconds).

Listing 4-6. *Defining the real time tasks' properties also in the file APM_Config.h*

```
#ifdef MI_CICLO7
    SCHED_TASK(mi_ciclo7,   7,     50),
#endif
#ifdef MI_CICLO3
    SCHED_TASK(mi_ciclo3,   3,     20),
#endif
```

To determine the last parameter, i.e., the duration in microseconds, it's recommended to test the task separately and use a timestamp to determine its duration.

4. Finally, you should define what these custom tasks or cycles do. Since we created them within copter, they are part of the copter class and can be used in any .cpp file that belongs to copter, such as UserCode.cpp; and from there, they can be linked to some other user's custom file, which in our case will be indicated later as mode_rolquad.cpp.

As a reference, in UserCode.cpp, look for the lines in Figure 4-27.

CHAPTER 4   AEROPENDULUM

```
#include "Copter.h"


#ifdef USERHOOK_INIT
void Copter::userhook_init()
{
    // put your initialisation code here
    // this will be called once at start-up
}
#endif
```

```
#ifdef USERHOOK_FASTLOOP
```

Figure 4-27. *Example of custom task definition (analog and serial reading) in the Scheduler 4*

And before the definition of USERHOOK_FASTLOOP, place the code shown in Listing 4-7.

Listing 4-7. Defining the real time tasks functions in the file UserCode.cpp

```
#ifdef MI_CICLO3
void Copter::mi_ciclo3()
{
    // put your 3Hz code here
        // Here we could read the 6.6V ADC that we previously
           explained
        adc15=chan1->voltage_average();// getting the
        average voltage
        hal.console->printf("%.3f\n",adc15); // printing the
        voltage to the console
}
#endif
#ifdef MI_CICLO7
```

```
void Copter::mi_ciclo7()
{
    // put your 7Hz code here
        // for example, serial communication or some
            other task
}
#endif
```

To finish this part about the code, we will develop a useful program within the 7Hz cycle, although the reader can place it in the predefined cycles or any other custom cycle. We refer to a serial reading, which, as indicated in the appendices, can be very useful for receiving data from multiple external sensors to the autopilot or sending data from the autopilot to a companion computer.

First, we must clarify that in this code, both the Arduino and ArduPilot share a serial port with the computer; so to avoid any data conflict, other digital ports different from the predefined ones were used for Arduino's serial communication as exemplified in Listing 4-8.

Listing 4-8. Defining the 7 Hz real time task, the Arduino part of a serial communication (the transmitter)

```
#include <SoftwareSerial.h>
byte buff_tx[3]; // Very basic serial data bus, for more details read our previous book
// Advanced Robotic Vehicles Programming or extensive web documentation
// We remind you that Ardupilot libraries, unlike other code environments
// only receive serial data in unsigned integer format
int contador=0;
SoftwareSerial mySerial(2, 3); // serial RX, TX ports, they are different from the original serial ports
```

CHAPTER 4   AEROPENDULUM

```
void setup()
{
// when using Arduino, defining other serial pins is pretty simple
// instead of Serial.begin(57600), declare
mySerial.begin(57600);
}

void loop()
{
  // Here we assemble the data packet to send
  buff_tx[0]=82;  // start value
  buff_tx[1]=contador;  // data of interest
  buff_tx[2]='\n'; // end value
// Here we write to the virtual port we've created
  mySerial.write(buff_tx,3);
// In this case, our data of interest to be sent are the numbers from 0 to 9 indefinitely until
// the system is disconnected
 if(contador>=10)
{
    contador=0;
}
else
{
    contador++;
 }
  delay(143);
}
```

And the reception codes for ArduPilot are as follows:

We resume the 7Hz task we created; inside it we'll write the code described in Listing 4-9 (remember we defined this task in UserCode.cpp):

Listing 4-9. Defining the 7 Hz real time task, the Pixhawk part of a serial communication (the receiver)

```
#ifdef MI_CICLO7
void Copter::mi_ciclo7()
{
    // put your 7Hz code here
        while (hal.uartD->available())
        {
            buff_rx[0] = hal.uartD->read(); // reading the
            start of the data packet
            if (buff_rx[0] == 'R')
            { //R=82
                for (int i = 1; i < 3; i++)
                {
                    buff_rx[i] = hal.uartD->read();
                }
            }
        }
        hal.console->printf("%d\n",buff_rx[1]);
}
#endif
```

For the above, we need to declare a variable to store the read buffer coming from the Arduino in the userVariables.h file as specified in Listing 4-10.

Listing 4-10. Defining the 7 Hz real time task, the Pixhawk part of a serial communication, variable declaration in the file userVariables.h

```
uint8_t buff_rx[3]
```

CHAPTER 4 AEROPENDULUM

Since the Telem2 port (uartD) is not initialized by default, we need to initialize it in the UserCode.cpp file in the userhook_init() task as detailed in Listing 4-11.

Listing 4-11. Defining the 7 Hz real time task, the Pixhawk part of a serial communication, serial port initialization in the file UserCode.cpp

```
#ifdef USERHOOK_INIT
void Copter::userhook_init()
{
    // put your initialisation code here
        hal.uartD->begin(57600); // Initialize the Telem2 port
        to 57600 baud
}
#endif
```

How do we know that Telem2 corresponds to UARTD? We have the option to consult the documentation and codes directly as shown in Figure 4-28, in this case the HAL.h file.

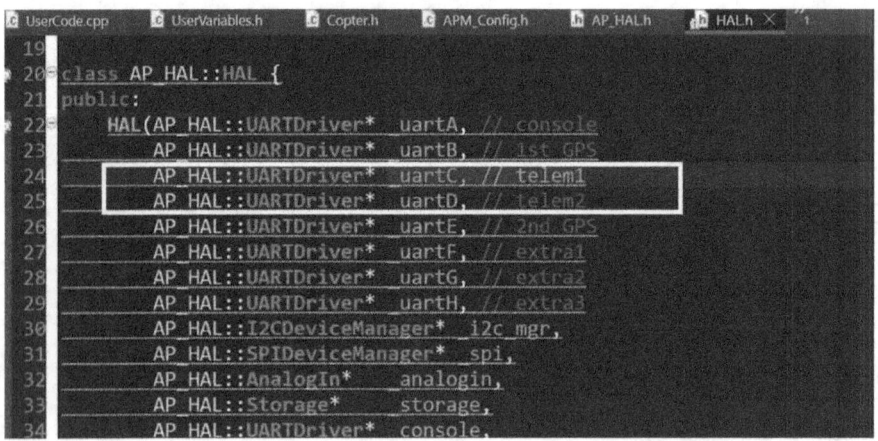

Figure 4-28. *Example of custom task definition (analog and serial reading) in the Scheduler 5*

224

CHAPTER 4 AEROPENDULUM

The next step is to configure the hardware from MissionPlanner as follows (note that we could have placed this description in the section on special uses of MissionPlanner, but given the importance of the topic, we decided to place it here):

To perform the configuration within MissionPlanner, the first step is to connect via MAVLink, see Figure 4-29.

Figure 4-29. *Example of custom task definition (analog and serial reading) in the Scheduler 6*

Then, go to the Config tab and then to the Full Parameter List option. In the search box, search for "Serial" in the case of UARTD Serial2, see Figure 4-30.

CHAPTER 4 AEROPENDULUM

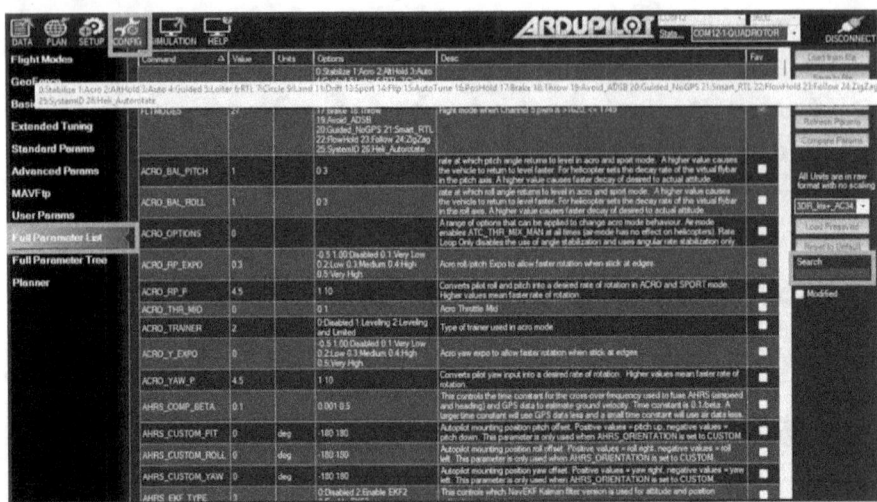

Figure 4-30. Example of custom task definition (analog and serial reading) in the Scheduler 7

Look for the Serial2_protocol option and use the "beacon" option, which is option 13. On the other hand, in serial2_baud, change it to 57 so that it's a speed of 57600, see Figure 4-31.

SERIAL2_BAUD	57	1:1200 2:2400 4:4800 9:9600 19:19200 38:38400 57:57600 111:111100 115:115200 256:256000 500:500000 921:921600 1500:1500000
SERIAL2_OPTIONS	0	
SERIAL2_PROTOCOL	13	-1:None 1:MAVLink1 2:MAVLink2 3:Frsky D 4:Frsky SPort 5:GPS 7:Alexmos Gimbal Serial 8:SToRM32 Gimbal Serial 9:Rangefinder 10:FrSky SPort Passthrough (OpenTX) 11:Lidar360 13:Beacon 14:Volz servo out 15:SBus servo out 16:ESC Telemetry 17:Devo Telemetry 18:OpticalFlow 19:RobotisServo 20:NMEA Output 21:WindVane 22:SLCAN 23:RCIN 24:MegaSquirt EFI 25:LTM 26:RunCam 27:HottTelem 28:Scripting 29:Crossfire 30:Generator 31:Winch

Figure 4-31. Example of custom task definition (analog and serial reading) in the Scheduler 8

CHAPTER 4   AEROPENDULUM

Finally, click "Write Params" and then "Refresh Params", see Figure 4-32.

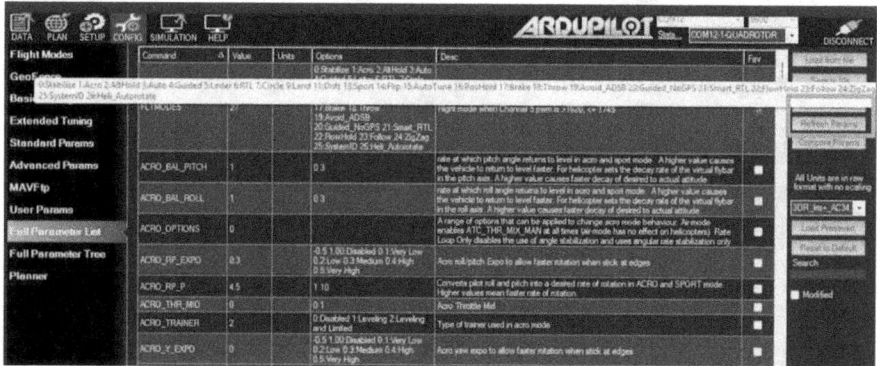

Figure 4-32. *Example of custom task definition (analog and serial reading) in the Scheduler 9*

Now, given the previous codes and the following connections: The Arduino connected to the UART of the Pixhawk, which can be TELEM1 or TELEM2, i.e., UARTC and UARTD, as well as a potentiometer to the 6.6 analog port, see Figures 4-33 and 4-34.

CHAPTER 4 AEROPENDULUM

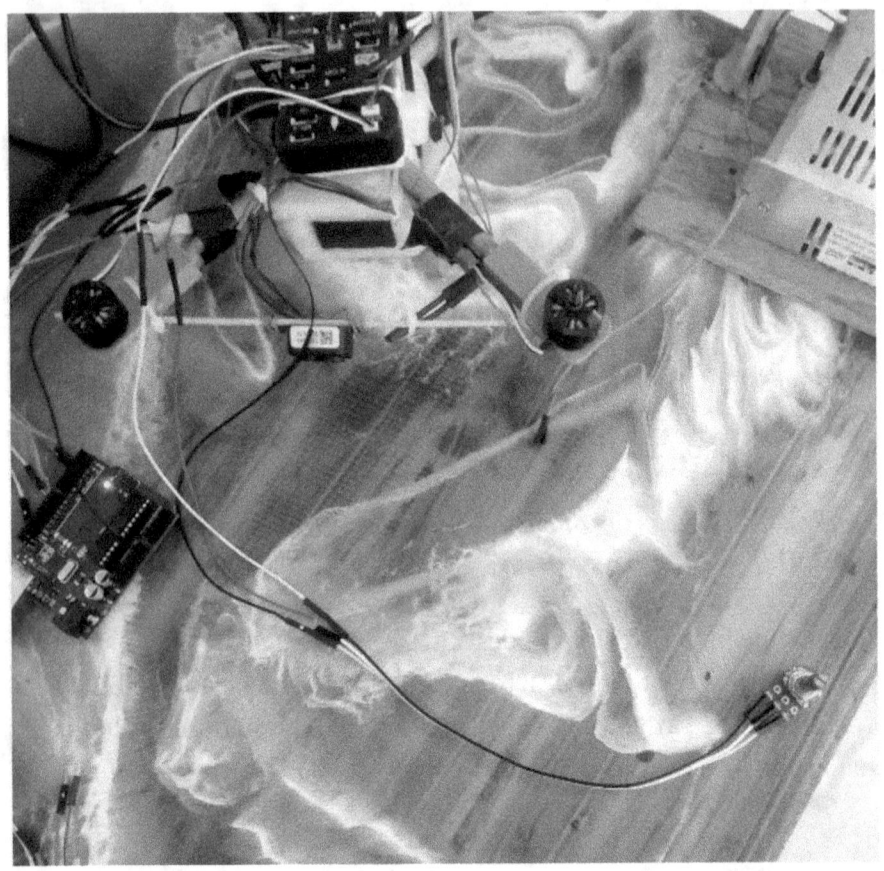

Figure 4-33. *Example of custom task definition (analog and serial reading) in the Scheduler 10*

CHAPTER 4 AEROPENDULUM

Figure 4-34. *Example of custom task definition (analog and serial reading) in the Scheduler 11*

The following will be displayed in MissionPlanner, see Figure 4-35. Remember that the numbers from 0 to 9 were sent via serial, and the analog port reads values from the potentiometer (they vary in voltage between 0 and 4.98).

It can also be noted that, as designed, the serial reading occurs at a higher frequency (7Hz) than the analog reading (3Hz). Finally, since we did a very basic serial reading, some corrupted characters are occasionally introduced due to the interaction with the laptop that runs MissionPlanner.

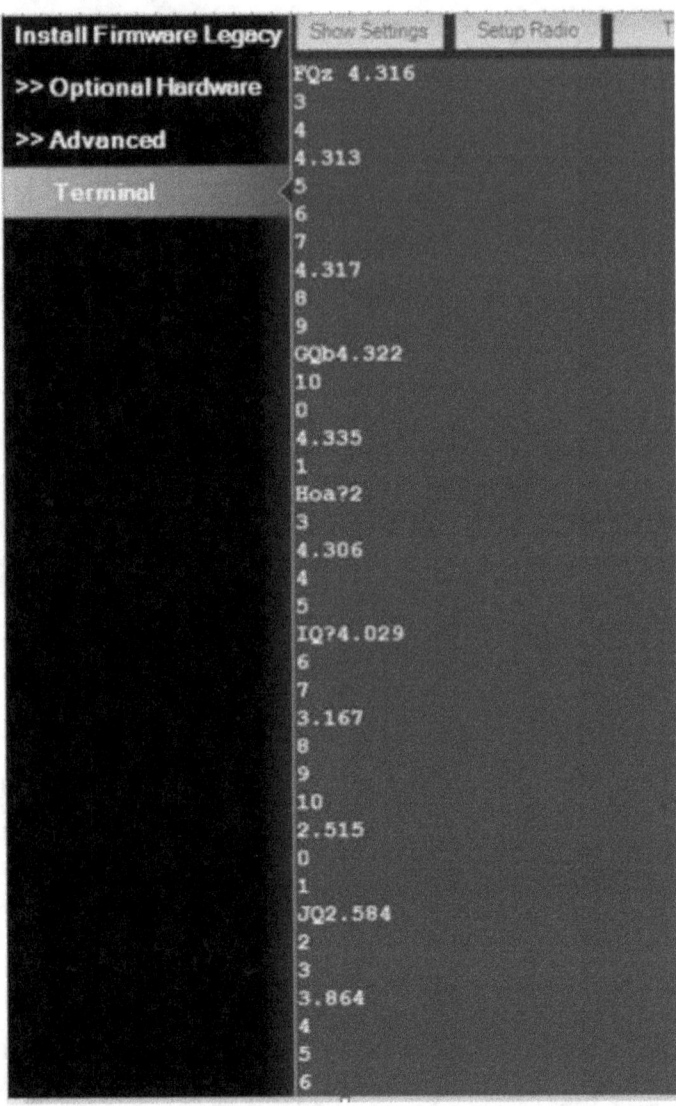

Figure 4-35. Example of custom task definition (analog and serial reading) in the Scheduler 12

Restoring the Autopilot to Its Factory Settings

In this code, we read the ADC and at the same time the serial port of the Pixhawk to communicate with an Arduino. In the first attempts (and also in the successful ones), we disabled the MAVLink protocol as it comes by default and used the beacon option (13). When we recorded the program, the Pixhawk did not initialize correctly and no longer allowed us to record the firmware again or display anything via MAVLink. The Pixhawk did not accept another firmware, the onboard LED no longer turned on, and many attempts to restart the autopilot were in vain. Specifically, it seemed that the autopilot had suffered irreparable damage.

As a solution, we used the "Install Firmware" tab instead of "Install Firmware Legacy" and we recorded a firmware completely different from Copter (we used the Rover firmware in this case), see Figure 4-36. This reset all the modified parameters and the Pixhawk became operational again.

If this happens to you, beyond worrying about the autopilot's functionality (which exists with the suggested recovery method), be cautious and remove the propellers or disconnect the motors, because in our case, they suddenly turned on when we recovered the Pixhawk.

CHAPTER 4   AEROPENDULUM

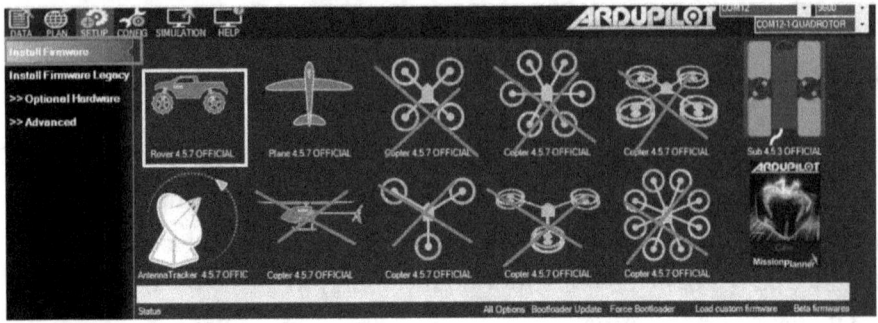

Figure 4-36. *Autopilot firmware recovery in case of failure*

In later attempts, the code worked successfully (we believe the TX and RX pins were misplaced while being connected), but beyond this error, the purpose of this paragraph is to illustrate possible recoveries in case of autopilot's failure.

Mechanical Analysis

An aeropendulum, like any other pendulum, has four critical mechanical elements, see Figure 4-37:

- Pivot or axis of rotation: The point around which the pendulum rotates or oscillates
- Mass: The amount of material that needs to be lifted
- Lever arm: The distance from the pivot to the end of the pendulum, which contributes to the inertial mass effect or torque to be overcome
- Motion limiter

A first critical point is that the pivot must be as well-aligned as possible and not have too much friction because it would increase the force required by the motor. For this reason, we selected a sensor with low friction anchored directly to the pivot with aligned pillow blocks and internal bearings.

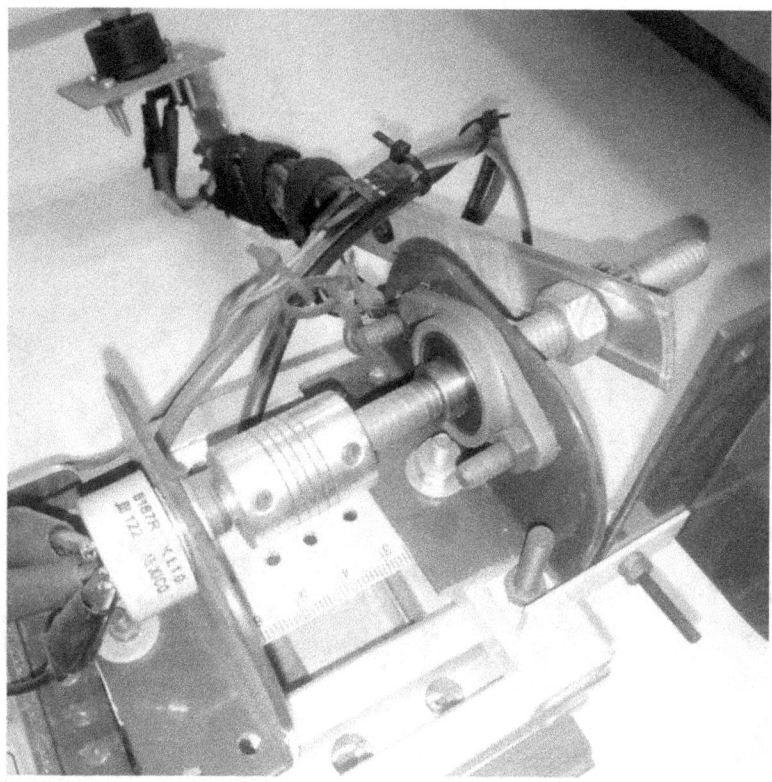

Figure 4-37. *Detail of the pivot, mass, lever arm, and motion limiter of the aeropendulum*

CHAPTER 4   AEROPENDULUM

In the case of the mass, it was crucial for selecting the motor. As we said, the mass is enhanced by the pendulum's radius, so we proceeded to weigh it using a scale, see Figure 4-38. The idea is that the motor had to have, according to its datasheet, enough force to lift itself and the lever arm.

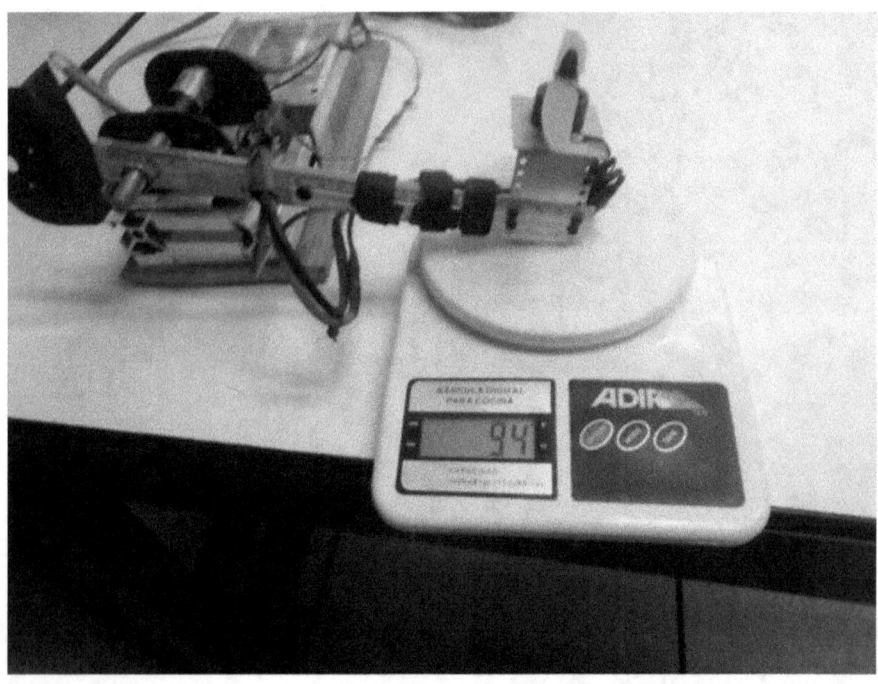

Figure 4-38. *Procedure for measuring the maximum hanging mass (inertial) and selecting the appropriate motor 1*

CHAPTER 4   AEROPENDULUM

The motor used in this case was an EMAX PM1806.

Testing Data:

Motor Type	Voltage (v)	Propeller	Current (A)	Thrust (G)	Power (W)	Efficient (G/W)
PM1806-2300KV	7.4	5030 Carbon Fiber Propeller	3.3	148	24.42	6.06
		GEMFAN 5030	3.5	150	25.9	5.79
		GEMFAN 6030	4.4	185	32.56	5.68
		5*4.5 (3 Blade Propeller)	4.8	188	35.52	5.29
	11.1	5030 Carbon Fiber Propeller	5.9	286	65.49	4.37
		GEMFAN 5030	5.7	290	63.27	4.58

https://emaxmodel.com/products/emax-platics-motor-for-multicopter-pm1806

Figure 4-39. *Procedure for measuring the maximum hanging mass (inertial) and selecting the appropriate motor 2 (taken from emax)*

According to the datasheet in Figure 4-39 and with the type of propeller used, as well as the power source employed, this motor provides 290 grams of thrust against the 94 grams of the pendulum mass.

Note Although these motors are already discontinued, the procedure for selecting an available motor is the same.

The motion limiter is necessary to avoid breaking the cables, which could be solved with a slip ring; this device allows communication between fixed and rotating elements, as illustrated in Figure 4-41. However, since the viable operating zone of the aeropendulum is only in the semi-plane indicated in Figure 4-40 (remember the single-propeller aeropendulum must have a propeller effect and a counter-effect of gravity in order to work, and this is only valid in that semi-plane), we decided to solve this problem by placing a barrier.

CHAPTER 4 AEROPENDULUM

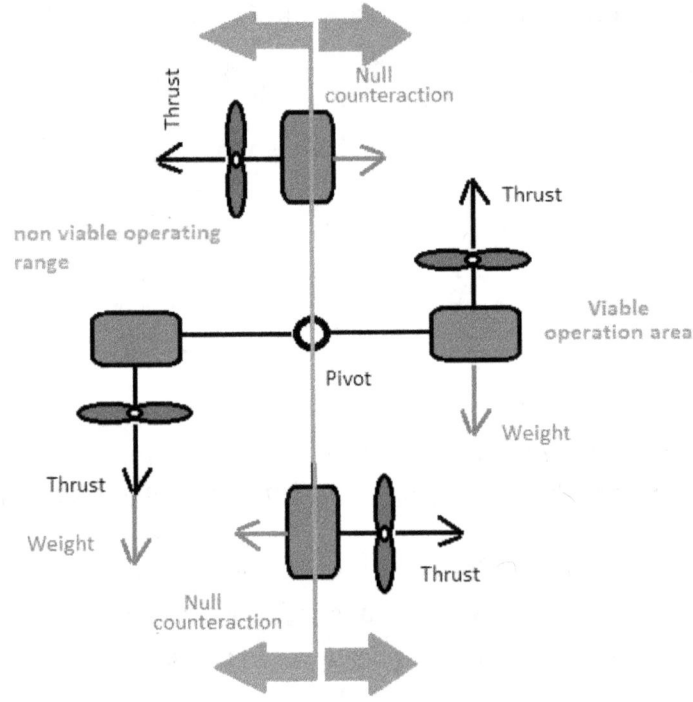

Figure 4-40. *Operating zone of the aeropendulum*

CHAPTER 4 AEROPENDULUM

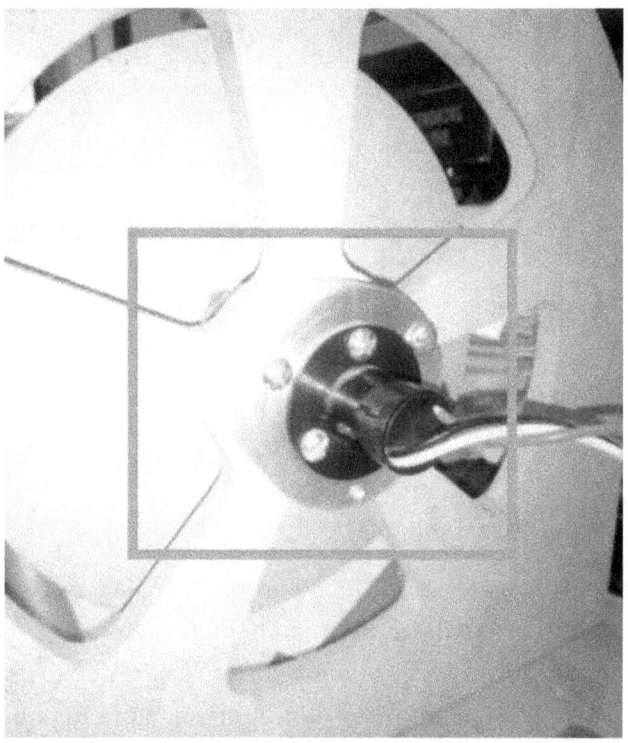

Figure 4-41. *A slip ring in case of working in the nonviable operating zone of the aeropendulum (by using a counter-propulsion motor)*

In the case of the lever arm, it had to meet two conditions: being light and resistant to possible impacts from the motor. As can be observed, this was achieved with a thin steel sheet (a metal ruler), and the resistance to possible impacts was solved by placing the ruler in its perpendicular position with respect to the main plane.

Observe in Figure 4-42 that, in addition to being less resistant to impacts, the main face of the ruler can produce oscillations like a trampoline or diving board, whereas on the perpendicular side, the ruler is practically a 5cm thick profile.

CHAPTER 4 AEROPENDULUM

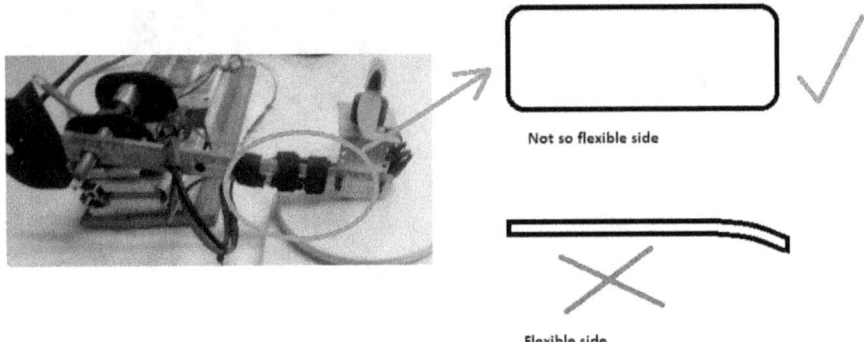

Figure 4-42. Details for selecting the lever arm

Control Analysis

How often to perform the closed-loop control, i.e., read and write sensors and actuators, and with what equipment to do it?

The control in our case was already chosen as PD due to its simplicity and functionality, but the following doubts arose: how often to apply it and which computer to use to program it?

The first question has to do with the type of signal accepted or taken from the fastest component; in this case, the BLDC motor in PWM RC mode, which requires values between 1000 and 2000 microseconds with integer increments (from microsecond to microsecond).

In the case of the programming platform, since it's a single motor, it's indistinct to use a Pixhawk or an Arduino (we actually used both for comparison purposes); in both cases, there's support for a BLDC motor with the previously indicated response times (in Arduino, depending on the model, it can support between 1 and 2 motors; in our case, we used the Uno version that only supports a single motor).

The next step is to describe the generic operation for both Arduino and Pixhawk, summarized in the flowchart in Figure 4-43.

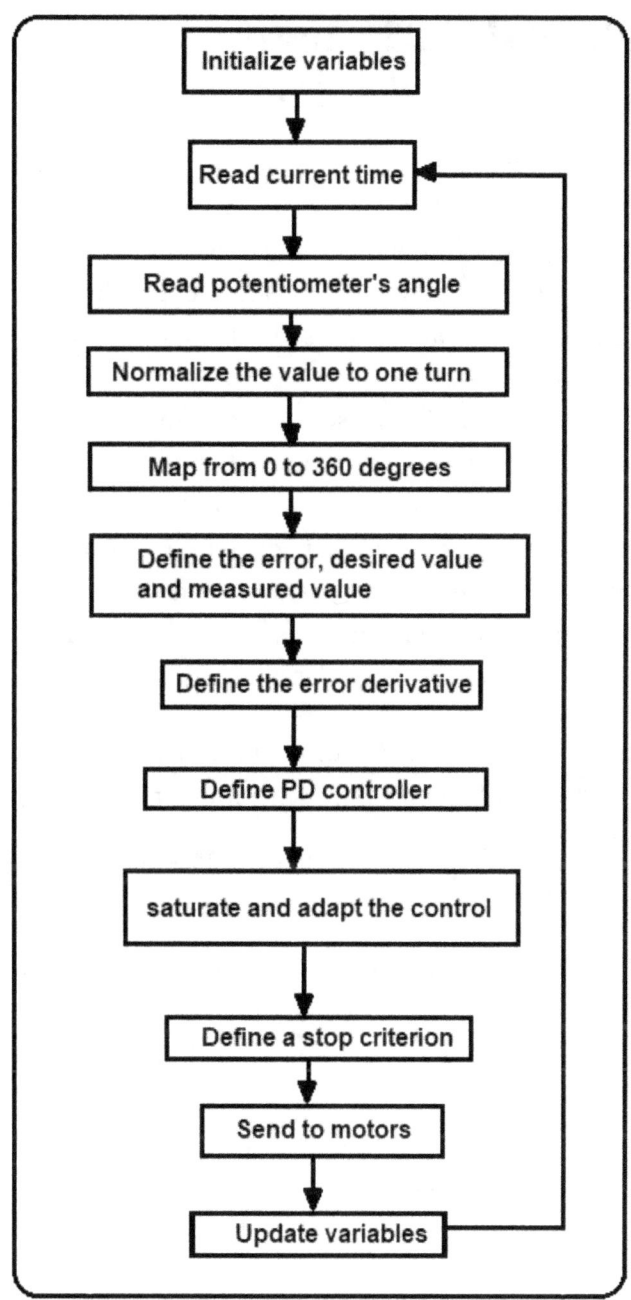

Figure 4-43. *Flowchart of the aeropendulum operation*

CHAPTER 4 AEROPENDULUM

Code Analysis Illustrated with the Arduino Version

In the Arduino code without OOP described in Listing 4-12, prior to the ArduPilot code but used in comparative mode, we must indicate that we use auxiliary mapping and saturation functions, whether using predefined versions found on the web (both of them are usual in standard Arduino libraries) or modified versions to be used with floating-point numbers as in the given example.

The first one allows scaling sensor values or any other value of interest to interpretable values in a different context of utility. In our example, our potentiometer obtains values between 0 and 1024, and it's desirable for our control that they be reinterpreted in degrees from 0 to 360.

On the part of the saturation function, it allows that the motor values do not exceed a safety value and also that the minimum motor value is such that it always keeps spinning (bias or startup value).

Listing 4-12. Our non-OOP Arduino version of the aeropendulum code used in this book to compare with the ArduPilot version

```
#include<Servo.h> // library to use RC PWM devices like servos
o BLDC motors

Servo ESC; //This will serve to work with our BLDC motor
(its ESC)
int velmo = 1100; //this value controls the motor speed (set to
its bias value)
int potPin = 0;  // this variable assigns an analog pin to the
potentiometer that measures the
// angle
int val = 0;     // this variable is assigned the value read
from the potentiometer
```

```
float grado; // this variable will contain the potentiometer
value converted to degrees
int time1=millis(); // the initial system time
float lastpos=0; // these variables will calculate the angular
velocity with dirty derivative
float lastErr;
float veloc=0;
float Referencia; // here the angle to be tracked by the
aeropendulum is indicated

void setup() {
  ESC.attach(9);   // the brushless control pin will be 9
  ESC.writeMicroseconds(1000); // the motor starts at 0 for
  safety reasons
  delay(5000);
  Serial.begin(9600); // to display the system behavior on the
  computer screen
}

void loop() {
  int time2=millis();// here the time delta is obtained in
  milliseconds
  float timeChange=time2-time1;
  val = analogRead(potPin);    // the potentiometer
                                  value is read
  val=abs(val%1024); // it has unlimited turns
                    // so it is normalized with respect to its
                       maximum value
  grado=mapo(val,0,1024,0,360); // then it is mapped to degrees
  grado=360-grado; // a small correction to make the pendulum
                      sense compatible (a mirror projection)
  Referencia=120; // the degree to be reached
```

CHAPTER 4   AEROPENDULUM

```
float error=Referencia-grado; // the control error

float dErr = (error - lastErr) / (timeChange/1000);
//the dirty derivative of the error
//remember it's calculated in milliseconds
float sinal=(4*error+0.2*dErr)+1300; // the control plus the
                                         motor bias
float motoro=satu(1400,1100,sinal); // control saturation
velmo=(int) motoro;   // the control becomes an integer, as
                    the PWM writing accepts this format

// this task has a stop by time, not by buttons or levers
if (time1>10000)  // after 10 seconds of operation, the motor
                    shuts down
{
velmo=1000;
}

// the reader can uncomment the following lines to see system
   information
// in this case, the code displays the measured degree and
   the injected control
//Serial.print(grado);
//Serial.print(" ");
//Serial.println (int(motoro));
//Serial.print("\n");

// writing to the motor
ESC.writeMicroseconds(velmo);
```

```
  // a small delay is added so the system doesn't collapse
  delay(2);

  // the initial time, initial position, and initial error
      are updated
  time1=time2;
  lastpos=grado;
  lastErr=error;
}
// mapping function
 float mapo(float x, float in_min, float in_max, float out_min,
 float out_max)
{
  return (x - in_min) * (out_max - out_min) / (in_max - in_min)
    + out_min;
}
// saturation function

float satu(float maxi,float mini,float sena)
{
  if (sena>=maxi)
  return maxi;
  if (sena<=mini)
  return mini;
  if (sena<maxi and sena >mini)
  return sena;
}
```

CHAPTER 4   AEROPENDULUM

Assembly and Testing with ArduPilot

The aeropendulum is assembled as indicated in the previous figures. The following modifications can be made (also involving adapting the code):

- Replace the potentiometer with an IMU on board the pendulum or an encoder instead of the potentiometer at its pivot.

- Although not recommended due to limitations in propeller thrust, this pendulum can have uninterrupted rotation if a slipring is placed to supply the ESC.

The following conditions must also be verified:

- Ensure that the cables allow the system to move within its full desired operating range (in our case, it was sufficient to leave a limit of approximately 180 degrees, so our adaptation with zip tie links is adequate). This is crucial for a good performance.

- Remember that the operating limit of this device is near to 180 degrees relative to its vertical position.

- Do not connect a mobile device power supply and leave it floating close to the aeropendulum (connected to the power supply but not to the mobile), as this can generate false logic levels that modifies Arduino/Autopilot operation.

- Add a coaxial motor with opposite propellers instead of a single motor; in this case, the aeropendulum will have a working range of 360 degrees (as long as it has a slipring).

- Prefer the use of lugs and specialized connectors instead of direct connection; this prevents cables from breaking or coming loose.

Here are the assembly instructions:

A

1. Form a chassis with the IPS structural elements (or your preferred choice).
2. Place the supports for the main axis or aeropendulum's pivot and the angular sensor (in our case, a potentiometer) on the previous structure. Using screws is recommended in this case.
3. Mount the pillow blocks on the supports.
4. Place the other side of the sensor and the main axis into an opposite pillow block.
5. Connect the sensor to the cantilever of the lever arm by using a coupling.

B

1. Attach the other side of the cantilever to one support.
2. Mount a BLDC motor to said support.
3. Fix the ESC and the motor power cables to the pendulum body (using Velcro for adjustments or later changes is recommended).

CHAPTER 4　AEROPENDULUM

C

1. Fix the main power source and Arduino/Autopilot to the main chassis, keeping them close to the mechanism.

2. Secure the power source input cables with connectors or lugs.

3. Fix the ESC cables connected to the power source output between the pendulum body and the main structure, twisting them (to reduce electrical noise) and securing with zip ties to prevent detachment. Carefully link these connections to allow mobility. Connect the ESC control cables to the Arduino/Autopilot by using extensions if necessary.

4. Connect the potentiometer cables to the Arduino/Autopilot.

D

1. Calibrate the sensor such that its zero point starts at the pendulum's rest position (this can be done by loosening the coupling and adjusting carefully). You can use Arduino or your autopilot in this step.

2. Tighten all other components and connections securely.

3. Secure the main structure to a table by using clamps.

4. Upload the previous code (for Arduino) or the codes described in Listings 4-13 through 4-17 (for ArduPilot-Pixhawk).

Listing 4-13. Our OOP ArduPilot version of the aeropendulum code: UserCode.cpp file modifications

```
/ *     FILE UserCode.cpp
This file is modified in specific lines for including the
previous customized methods (tasks) in order to be executed at
certain specific frequencies
*/

#include "Copter.h"

#ifdef USERHOOK_INIT
void Copter::userhook_init()
{
    chan1 = hal.analogin->channel(15); // Here, channel 15
(6.6) will be read
}
#endif

//      Inside this 100 Hz loop, the translation control
method is executed.
#ifdef USERHOOK_FASTLOOP
void Copter::userhook_FastLoop()
{
//         Remote control signal acquisition occurs here
    copter.mode_rolquad.captura_radio();
//         Retrieve current flight mode
    switch(copter.mode_rolquad.get_state())
    {
        case OFFPEND: // Stabilized control (only rotational
        control available)

            // Reset control on X, Y, Z axes for orientation"
```

```cpp
            copter.mode_rolquad.reset_controlxyz();
            break;
        case ONPEND:
            // Activate hovering control to maintain spatial
position (x, y, z)
            copter.mode_rolquad.ejecuta_controlxyz();
            break;
        default: // An undefined state, revert to default
translation control
            copter.mode_rolquad.reset_controlxyz();
            break;
    }
}
#endif

//           This code segment runs at 10 Hz
#ifdef USERHOOK_MEDIUMLOOP
void Copter::userhook_MediumLoop()
{
    //    The following block checks the status of the auxiliary
    //    2 remote control
    if(copter.mode_rolquad.get_rdaux2() > 1800)
    {
        // Assign set-points when remote control value
        //   surpasses 1800
        if(flag_ctrlxyz == false) // you can try different flag
        logics, this is one that works for us
        {
            // In this case Z set point is a constant that
            varies over time which specifically is the desired
            // angle of the pendulum
            //
```

```cpp
            If (AP_HAL::millis() < 15000)
            {
                    copter.mode_rolquad.set_spz(100);
            }
            If ( (AP_HAL::millis() >= 15000) && (AP_
            HAL::millis() < 25000))
            {
                    copter.mode_rolquad.set_spz(50);
            }
            If ( (AP_HAL::millis() >= 25000) && (AP_
            HAL::millis() < 34000))
            {
                    copter.mode_rolquad.set_spz(100);
            }
            If ( (AP_HAL::millis() >= 34000) )
            {
                    copter.mode_rolquad.set_spz(0);
            }
             flag_ctrlxyz = true; // Flag status is changed
         }
      //  Then switch to state 2 (hover control)
         copter.mode_rolquad.set_state(ONPEND); ////HOVER
    }
    else
    {
      // If remote control value is less than or equal to 1800,
         switch to state 1 (orientation control)
         copter.mode_rolquad.set_state(OFFPEND); /// ORIENTACION
         flag_ctrlxyz = false; // Reset the flag
    }
 }
#endif
```

CHAPTER 4 AEROPENDULUM

Listing 4-14. Our OOP ArduPilot version of the aeropendulum code: UserVariables.h file modifications

```
/ *      FILE UserVariables.h
This file is modified in order to declare certain variables for
changing our flightmodes
Those variables will be used in the file UserCode.cpp where
faster and slower tasks are declared
*/

AP_HAL::AnalogSource* chan1;
float adc15;
uint32_t lastime ;   //ATTENTION some systems require also a
                     static prefix
float deltatime ; //ATTENTION some systems require
                 also a static prefix
float lastpos;

#ifdef USERHOOK_VARIABLES
// the available flight modes off aeropendulum and on
aeropendulum
enum ModeVuelo {
    OFFPEND = 1,
    ONPEND = 2,
};
bool flag_ctrlxyz=false;
#endif  // USERHOOK_VARIABLES
```

Listing 4-15. Our OOP ArduPilot version of the aeropendulum code: Log.cpp file modifications

```
/ *     Log.cpp
This file is modified in specific lines for including the
customized data package in order to be executed by Copter.cpp
and other main files  and then saved into the autopilot memory
YOU COULD LEAVE THIS FILE IDENTICAL AS IN THE QUADCOPTER CASE,
YOU MUST REMEMBER THAT THE Z  setpoint and the Z MEASURED ARE
DEFINED AS INDICATED IN THE OTHER FILES
* /

//      as described in the book Advanced Robotic Vehicles
        Programming,
//      data logging has 3 sections: declaration, writing
        and header
//                  (1)  data package declaration
//                  this is done as a struct that contains all
                    the variables that
//                  we want to save
struct PACKED log_Control_Tuning
{
    LOG_PACKET_HEADER;
    uint64_t time_us;
    float    c_roll;
    float    control_z;
    uint8_t  estado;
    float    c_pitch;
    float    pos_x;
    float    altura;
    int32_t  baro_alt;
    float    ref_x;
```

CHAPTER 4   AEROPENDULUM

```
    float    ref_y;
    float    ref_z;
    float    pos_y;
    float    error_x;
};
//                (2)  data package SD writing function
void Copter::Log_Write_Control_Tuning()
{
    struct log_Control_Tuning pkt = {
        LOG_PACKET_HEADER_INIT(LOG_CONTROL_TUNING_MSG),
        time_us            : AP_HAL::micros64(),
        c_roll             : copter.mode_rolquad.get_tauphi(),
        control_z          : copter.mode_rolquad.get_ctrlz(),
        estado             : copter.mode_rolquad.get_state(),
        c_pitch            : copter.mode_rolquad.get_tauth(),
        pos_x              : copter.mode_rolquad.get_x(),
        altura             : copter.mode_rolquad.get_z(),
                           // HERE IS THE MEASURED ANGLE
        baro_alt           : baro_alt,
        ref_x              : copter.mode_rolquad.get_spx(),
        ref_y              : copter.mode_rolquad.get_spy(),
        ref_z              : copter.mode_rolquad.get_spz(),
                           //HERE IS the DESIRED ANGLE
        pos_y              : copter.mode_rolquad.get_y(),
        error_x            : copter.mode_rolquad.get_
                             errorx() //
    };
    logger.WriteBlock(&pkt, sizeof(pkt));
}
```

```
//         A second package declaration
struct PACKED log_Precland
{
    LOG_PACKET_HEADER;
    uint64_t time_us;
    float error_y;
    float error_z;
    float vel_x;
    float vel_y;
    float vel_z;
    float comodin1;
    float comodin2;
    float c_yaw;
    float comodin3;
    float comodin4;
    float comodin5;
    float comodin6;
};
//         The second package writing to the SD memory
void Copter::Log_Write_Precland()
{
    struct log_Precland pkt = {
        LOG_PACKET_HEADER_INIT(LOG_PRECLAND_MSG),
        time_us         : AP_HAL::micros64(),
        error_y         : copter.mode_rolquad.get_errory(),
        error_z         : copter.mode_rolquad.get_errorz(),
        vel_x           : copter.mode_rolquad.get_velx(),
        vel_y           : copter.mode_rolquad.get_vely(),
        vel_z           : copter.mode_rolquad.get_velz(),
        comodin1        : 0.0, // remember that you can save
                          other desired variables
```

CHAPTER 4   AEROPENDULUM

```
            comodin2           : 0.0,
            c_yaw              : copter.mode_rolquad.get_taupsi(),
            comodin3           : 0.0,
            comodin4           : 0.0,
            comodin5           : 0.0,
            comodin6           : 0.0
    };
    logger.WriteBlock(&pkt, sizeof(pkt));
}

/*  (3) header of the firts data package (the way you will
    find the first line of the texts files inside the SD
    memory),  consider the advice described in Advanced
    Robotic Vehicles Programming  concernig the data types of
    this headers       */

{ LOG_CONTROL_TUNING_MSG, sizeof(log_Control_Tuning),
      "CTUN", "QffBfffefffff", "TimeUS,c_ph,ctrlz,edo,c_th,posx,posz,BAlt,spx,spy,spz,posy,e_x", "s------------", "F------------" },

//       header of the second data package

 { LOG_PRECLAND_MSG, sizeof(log_Precland),
      "PL",    "Qfffffffffff",    "TimeUS,e_y,e_z,velx,vely,velz,cm1,cm2,c_psi,cm3,cm4,cm5,cm6", "s------------","F------------" },
```

CHAPTER 4 AEROPENDULUM

Listing 4-16. Our OOP ArduPilot version of the aeropendulum code: mode_rolquad.cpp file modifications

```
/ *     FILE   mode_rolquad.cpp (our customized code)
       In this file we define the class methods that are
declared on the file mode.h       */
#include "Copter.h"
#include "UserVariables.h"
//              RADIO SECTION
//        method for Reading the radio signals
void ModeRolQuad::captura_radio()
{
// auxiliar channels for changing the flight modes
    rd.aux1 = rc().get_radio_in(4);
    rd.aux2 = rc().get_radio_in(5);
}
//      radio getters
int ModeRolQuad::get_rdaux1()
{
    return rd.aux1;
}
int ModeRolQuad::get_rdaux2()
{
    return rd.aux2;
}
// getter for the available state, useful for changing the
flightmodes
uint8_t ModeRolQuad::get_state()
{
    return state;
}
```

CHAPTER 4   AEROPENDULUM

```cpp
// setter for the state, the previous method complement
void ModeRolQuad::set_state(uint8_t _state)
{
    state = _state;
}

//         ANGULAR POSITION SECTION

float ModeRolQuad::get_z()
{
    return pos.z;
}
float ModeRolQuad::get_velz()
{
    return vel.z;
}
//         CONTROL SECTION
//         set point setters XYZ
void ModeRolQuad::set_spz(float _spz)
{
    sp.z = _spz;
}

//         set-point getters
float ModeRolQuad::get_spz()
{
    return sp.z;
}
```

```
//         error getters
float ModeRolQuad::get_errorz()
{
    return err.z;
}

//         XYZ controller getters
float ModeRolQuad::get_ctrlz()
{
    return ctrlz;
}

// method for the XYZ control (Hover flight setpoint is
obtained in usercode.cpp when flight mode changes to: HOVER,
lines 66-68)

void ModeRolQuad::ejecuta_controlxyz()
{
    err.z = pos.z - sp.z;   // the Z error

    ctrlz = 1300 + (kp.z * err.z) + (kd.z * -vel.z); // Z
PD control
}

//         method for resetting the translation control
void ModeRolQuad::reset_controlxyz()
{
    ctrlz = 0;
}

//         MAIN CODE   (run) 400 Hz
void ModeRolQuad::run()
{
```

CHAPTER 4 AEROPENDULUM

```
// Updating positions and velocities
// for simplicity, the analog reading is done here, but in larger projects,
// it would be more efficient to handle it in a separate, slower loop
    uint32_t currtime = AP_HAL::millis();
    adc15=chan1->voltage_average();   // Getting the
                                        average voltage
    pos.z = adc15;
    pos.z=abs(pos.z % 4.82); // Normalizing with respect to the
                        maximum value (4.8V)
    pos.z= (pos.z - 0) * (360 - 0) / (4.82 - 0) + 0;
    pos.z=360-pos.z;

    deltatime = (float)(currtime - lastime) / 1000.0f;
    vel.z = (pos.z-lastpos) / deltatime;    // you can filter
                                              this signal
    lastime=curtirme;
    lastpos=pos.z;

    // Calculation of the signals to be sent to the motors
    float m1;
    m1 = ctrlz ;

// Saturating the signal to the motor's minimum and maximum limits
    if (m1>=1400)
        m1= 1400;
    if (m1<=1100)
        m1= 1100;
    if (m1<1400 and m1 >1100)
        m1=m1;
```

```
    // Writing the signal to the motors (just one motor in
this case)
    hal.rcout->write(0, uint16_t(m1));
}
```

Listing 4-17. Our OOP ArduPilot version of the aeropendulum code: mode.h file modifications

```
/ *    FILE mode.h
This file is modified in order to declare the class
ModeRolQuad, this is done before the line
#if MODE_AUTOROTATE_ENABLED == ENABLED
*/
class ModeRolQuad : public Mode
{ // class beginning
public:
    // this class inherits the base class constructor Mode
    using Mode::Mode;
    //              main method declaration
    // remember, this and most of the other customized methods
    // are defined in the file mode_rolquad.cpp
    virtual void run() override;
    // some sensor inicialization methods
    bool requires_GPS() const override { return false; }
    bool has_manual_throttle() const override { return true; }
    bool allows_arming(bool from_gcs) const override {
    return true; }
    bool is_autopilot() const override { return false; }
    //           declaration of the method for Reading
                the radio
    void captura_radio();
    //           radio getters declaration
```

CHAPTER 4   AEROPENDULUM

```cpp
    int get_rdaux1();
    int get_rdaux2();
    //          XY and Z positions and velocities getters
                declaration
    float get_z();
    float get_velz();

    //         declaration of the method for performing the XYZ
               translation control
    void ejecuta_controlxyz();
    //         state getter and setter declaration, useful for
               changing the flight modes
    uint8_t get_state();
    void set_state(uint8_t _state);
    //         declaration of the method for resetting the XYZ
               translation control
    void reset_controlxyz();
    //           Setpoint setters declaration (XYZ)
    void set_spz(float _spz);
    float get_ctrlz();  // Gets ctrl.z
    //              XYZ setpoint getters declaration
    float get_spz();//Gets z setpoint
    //              XYZ error getters declaration
    float get_errorz();
//   protected methods used for overwriting the Mode class
     with the user-customized ones
protected:
//       This method returns the name of the flight mode as
         a string.
```

CHAPTER 4 AEROPENDULUM

```
//          This method overrides the virtual method of the base
            class Mode.
    const char *name() const override { return "ROLQUAD"; }
//          This method eturns a shortened version of the flight
            mode name.
//          Also overrides the virtual method of the base
            class Mode.
    const char *name4() const override { return "ROQD"; }
//          Attributes declaration
private:
    uint8_t state = 1; //  Our flight mode initial state
//   the position, velocity, errors and setpoints have a roll,
pitch, yaw, XY and Z components
//  in this case just the z components will be used, the others
are assigned to zero by default
//  but remember that certain compilers dont do this assignment
    struct pose {
        float phi; // Roll
        float th;  // Pitch
        float psi; // Yaw
        float x;   // X
        float y;   // Y
        float z;   // Z
    } pos, vel, err, sp;
    float ctrlz;   // control  declaration
 //  PD gains declaration and inicialization, for phi,theta, psi
and XYZ, only the Z components
//  will be used, this code was recycled from the quadcopter
    const struct ganancias {
```

CHAPTER 4 AEROPENDULUM

```
        float phi;
        float th;
        float psi;
        float x;
        float y;
        float z;
    } kp{0, 0, 0, 0, 0, 120}, kd{0, 0, 0, 0, 0, 70}; //in this
case just the Z-gain components are set up
    //          radio struct declaration with roll, pitch, yaw,
throttle and auxiliar channels
    struct radio {
        int roll;
        int pitch;
        int thr;
        int yaw;
        int aux1;
        int aux2;
    } rd;
};   // end of the class
```

The following shows the results of the previous code for tracking different values over time (a step trajectory in this case). Notice a time lag at the beginning; this is because the task execution was dependent on the Pixhawk activation (the operator took around three seconds to arm the autopilot).

CHAPTER 4   AEROPENDULUM

As described in the previous code, the purpose of this test was to send a step signal such that the pendulum would follow a reference of 100 degrees during the first 15 seconds, then 50 degrees until the 25th second, and from that second to the 34th second, again 100 degrees, before shutting off, see Figures 4-44 and 4-45.

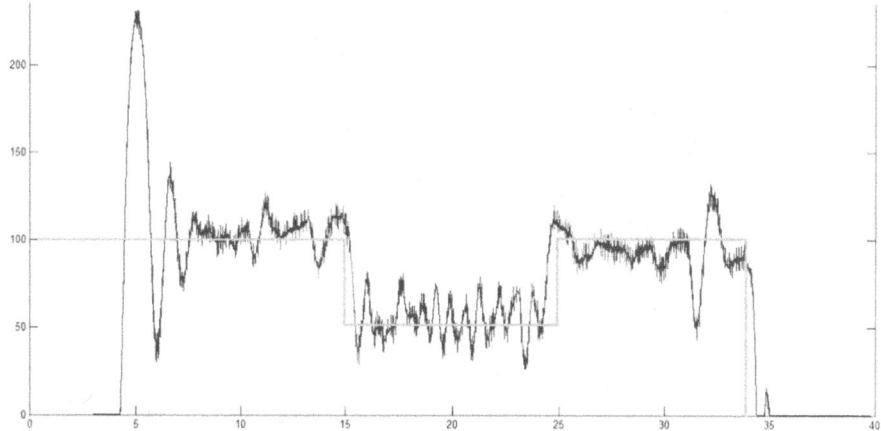

Figure 4-44. *Graph of our trajectory tracking test for the aeropendulum using the ArduPilot code*

CHAPTER 4   AEROPENDULUM

Figure 4-45. *A picture of the previous experiment with the aeropendulum in operation*

CHAPTER 4 AEROPENDULUM

Although the performance is not ideal, the overshoots were intentionally placed for demonstration purposes (these can be reduced by increasing the differential gain). Additionally, note that the pendulum slightly deviates from its reference due to not having an integral value in its control and also due to motor vibrations and sensor noise.

Note In the previous experiment, a Pixhawk was used as the processor for the aeropendulum, and it was externally mounted on a drone for our convenience. The primary PWM output of the Pixhawk was connected directly to the BLDC ESC (only the control pin and ground), and the potentiometer used as a sensor was connected directly to the autopilot's analog input, see Figures 4-46, 4-47, and 4-48.

CHAPTER 4 AEROPENDULUM

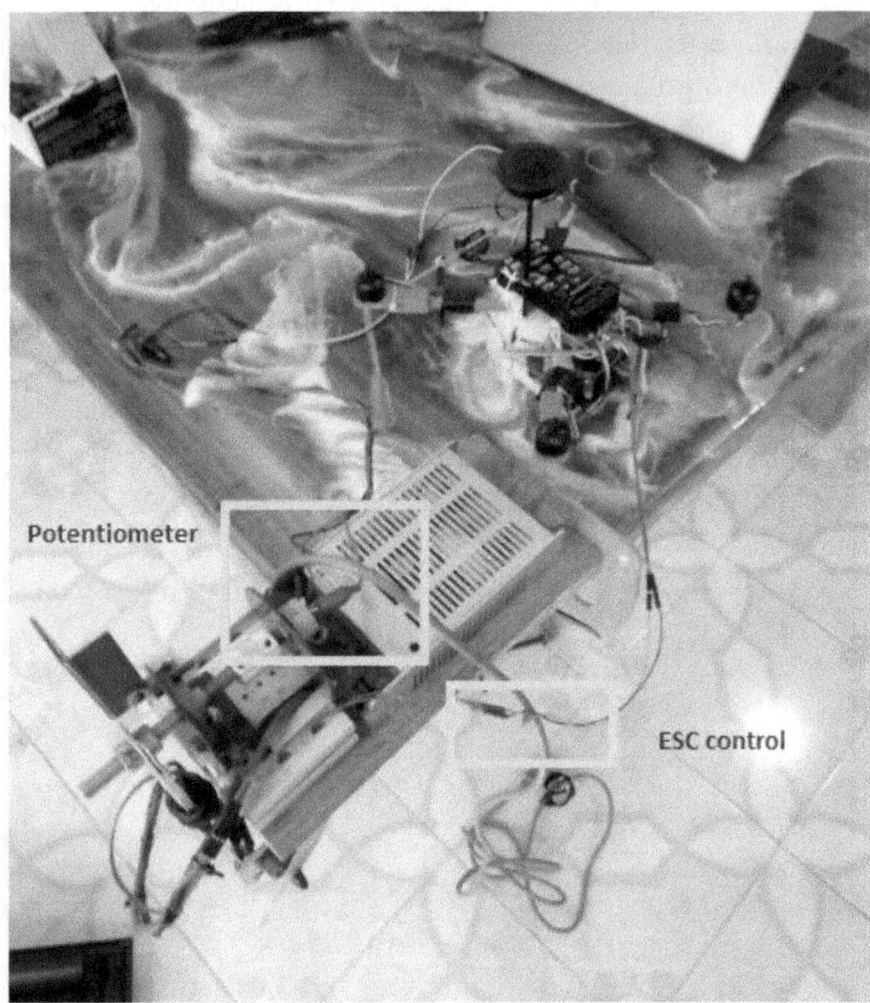

Figure 4-46. *Details on the autopilot configuration for the aeropendulum test 1*

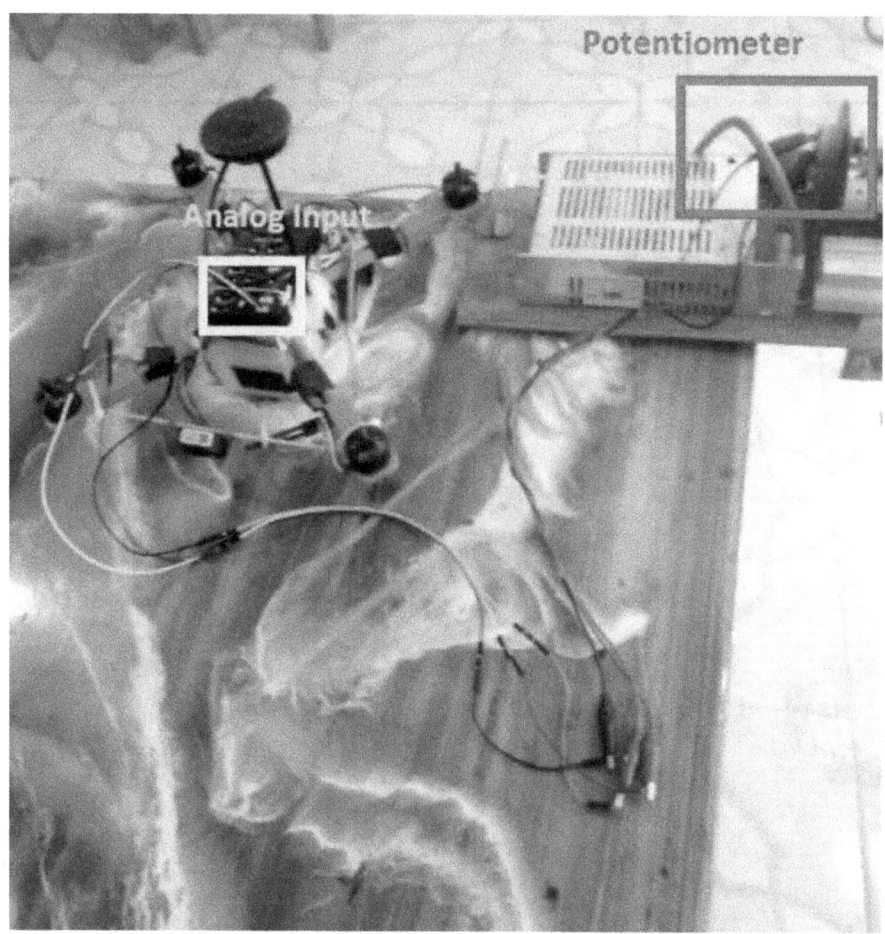

Figure 4-47. *Details on the autopilot configuration for the aeropendulum test 2*

CHAPTER 4　AEROPENDULUM

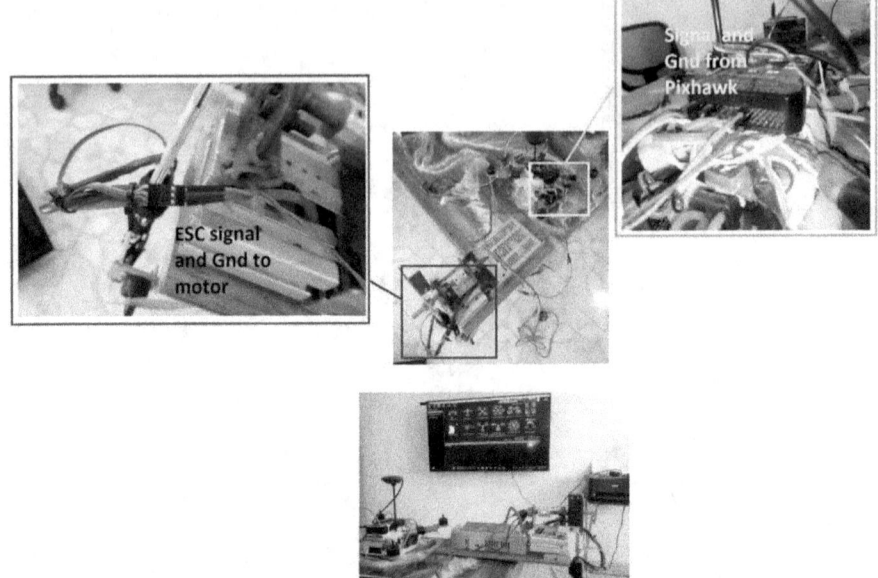

Figure 4-48. Details on the autopilot configuration for the aeropendulum test 3

CHAPTER 4   AEROPENDULUM

Note   The electrical and physical connections were as shown in Figure 4-49.

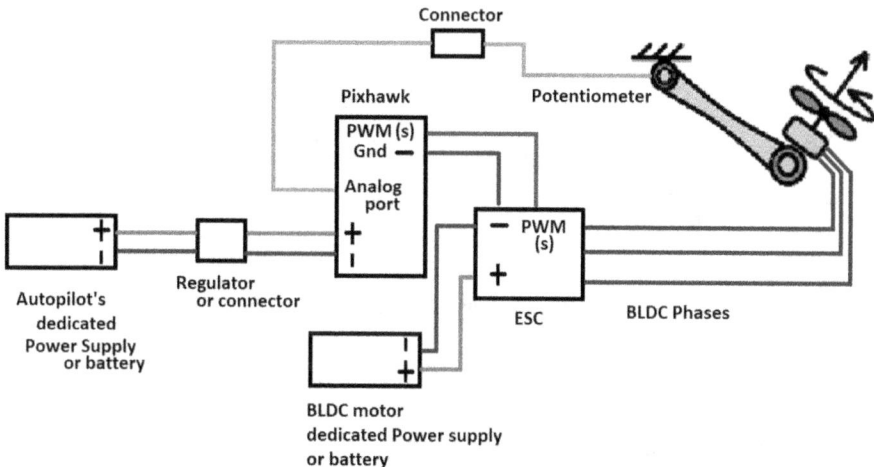

Figure 4-49. *Pixhawk-controlled aeropendulum diagram*

An onboard version of the aeropendulum could also be used, as indicated in Figure 4-50. The recommendation here is to use the autopilot's own IMU. In this case, the best approach is to place the autopilot on the pendulum's pivot (the autopilot must rotate along with the pivot). Clearly, the code would change since an external analog sensor like the potentiometer would no longer be used, but rather the autopilot's embedded orientation sensors.

CHAPTER 4 AEROPENDULUM

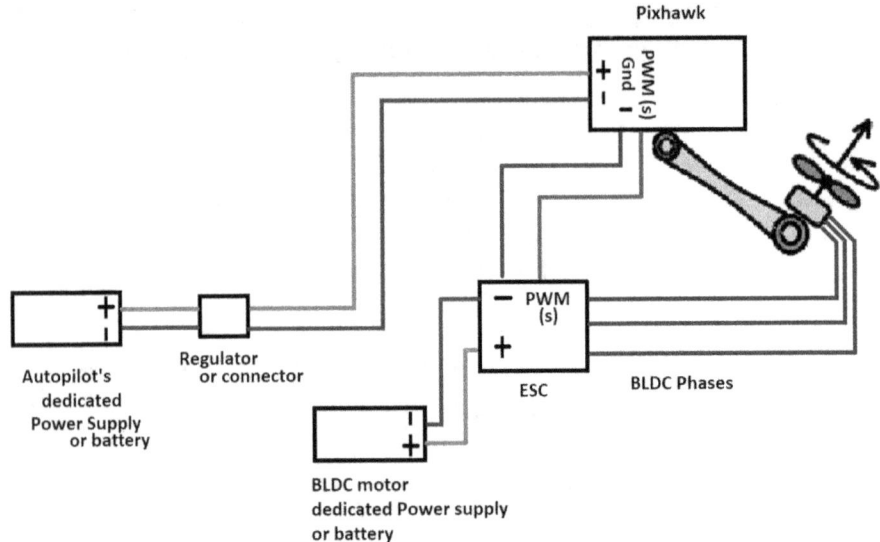

Figure 4-50. Pixhawk-controlled aeropendulum diagram using the autopilot as a sensor

Chapter Summary

In this chapter, we described the design of the aeropendulum, showing extensive mechatronic and code details, since it is the base project for the other two prototypes in this book. We also described two working code versions for comparison, one in sequential mode typical of the Arduino environment and the other in modular ArduPilot 2023 OOP mode.

In the next chapter, we will continue with the following part of our sequential robotic design—again an anchored device: a quadcopter mounted on a test stand.

CHAPTER 5

Quadcopter Mounted on a Test Stand

This chapter extensively covers the second guided project: the quadcopter mounted on a test stand, starting with its definition, uses, and variants that are complemented in the theoretical context by references at the end of the book. Following this subject, we describe the prototype assembly, covering a suggested list of components and required knowledge, a mechatronic design, and finally we conclude with the full code using ArduPilot 2023 libraries in modular OOP mode and its experimental results.

Additionally, and for comparative purposes, an operational code using ArduPilot 2018 libraries in its semi-sequential style or template version is also presented.

Description and Applications of the Quadcopter Mounted on a Test Stand

This chapter uses a quadcopter mounted on a ball joint or a 3D rotational structure, see Figure 5-1. Unlike the previous chapter, the balance must be achieved not in one but in three angles.

CHAPTER 5   QUADCOPTER MOUNTED ON A TEST STAND

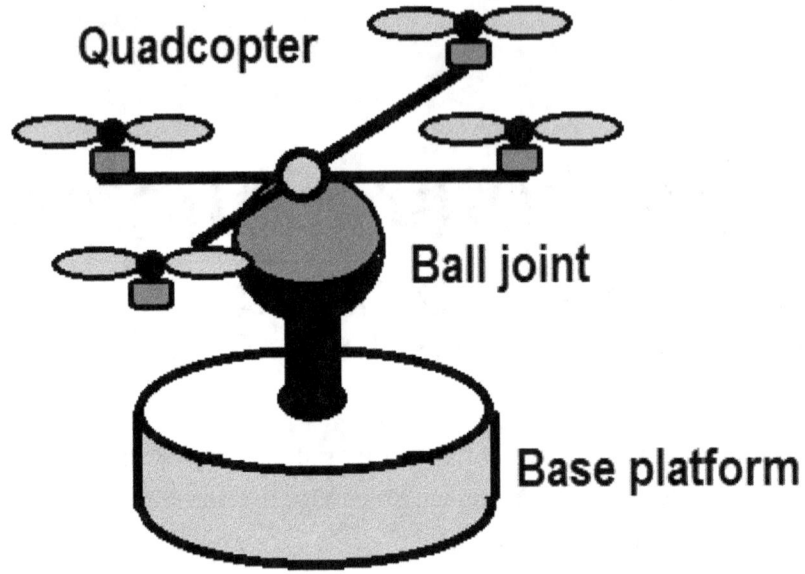

Figure 5-1. Quadcopter mounted on a test stand diagram

Prior to vehicle flight, achieving dynamic rotational balance is desirable. If this is not done, the drone would tend to perform unwanted planar movements when taking off.

The quadcopter mounted on a test stand is designed exclusively to move in its roll, pitch, and yaw angles on a three-dimensional mechanism—typically a gimbal or ball joint, with its translational movements in X, Y, and Z blocked by the anchorage.

The anchored quadcopter has dual utility. The first is the stabilization of the vehicle regarding its orientation. A poorly balanced vehicle will have unstable flight and, even if achieved, will consume more energy to function.

In the second case, the anchored quadcopter is a scalable design version of a mechanical vectorizer, a widely used system to modify the position and orientation of an aerial vehicle. Other good examples of vectorizers are the nozzles of a fighter jet or the cyclic and collective plates of a helicopter.

As an illustration, Figure 5-2 shows, in an exaggerated way, an anchored quadcopter but as a means of deviating the main propulsion of a rocket.

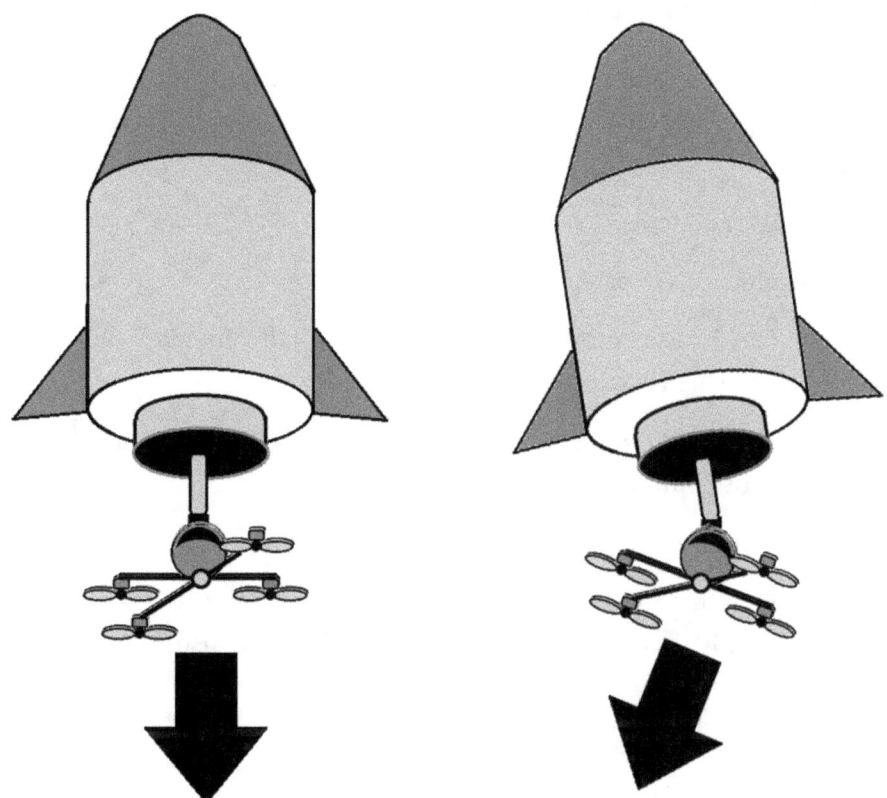

Figure 5-2. *Possible use of an anchored quadcopter as a thrust vectoring element of an aircraft (even of itself)*

For further details, including its extensive mathematical models and more applications and control modes, we recommend reading the selected references section at the end of this book.

CHAPTER 5 QUADCOPTER MOUNTED ON A TEST STAND

List of Materials and Minimum Knowledge Required to Build a Quadcopter Mounted on a Test Stand

Regarding the materials, tools, and knowledge for the embedded drone, the following is required:

Mechanics

Materials and tools:

- One 3-DOF ball joint
- One bearing for yaw movement, as the ball joint may have high friction
- Lubricant for the ball joint, preferably WD40, as oils can cause bumps when dried
- One quadcopter
- One shock absorber to deal with vehicle vibration on the GPS sensor or a pedestal to separate the sensor from the vehicle
- IPS profile or any other available to assemble a T-shaped or L-shaped pedestal
- One clamp to fix the pedestal to a table or heavy furniture
- Fasteners for IPS profiles or generic Nylock fasteners
- If necessary, dies and taps to make threads on the pedestal
- A thin screw or stud to improvise the union of the profile with the ball joint

CHAPTER 5 QUADCOPTER MOUNTED ON A TEST STAND

- Wood, plastic, or foam to join the drone body with the ball joint
- Straps or plastic ties to facilitate the previous union without affecting the vehicle's weight
- One cheap compass to locate the vehicle relative to the global magnetic north
- One metal plate to facilitate the union of the system to the T-structure
- If using a fixed power source, add a dead weight to emulate the effect of an onboard battery

Previous knowledge:

- Manual machining operations to create threads using dies or taps
- Assembling a quadcopter and locating ports on the Pixhawk (or your preferred autopilot)

Electronics

Materials and tools:

- The required instrumentation and power elements of a drone
- One GPS sensor for autopilot's setup
- Power source for the drone, either fixed for long-term use or an onboard LiPo battery for a more realistic operation
- Remote control with PPM receiver and at least four channels for manual operation
- If using batteries, a compatible charger and a sound monitor to alert when batteries have low level

CHAPTER 5 QUADCOPTER MOUNTED ON A TEST STAND

Previous knowledge:

- Electronic and electrical assembly of drone components (described in our previous books *Advanced Robotic Vehicles Programming* and *Drones to Go*)

Programming
Materials and tools:

- A Computer with ArduPilot libraries and Mission Planner installed
- A compatible USB cable between the autopilot and the computer

Previous knowledge:

- Understanding matrix allocation concept
- Reading remote control data
- Reading orientation and position data on the autopilot
- Writing data to drone BLDC motors using the autopilot

Control
Materials and tools:

- One Pixhawk autopilot

Previous knowledge:

- Understanding PD control algorithm
- Understanding the differences and dependencies between position control and orientation control

CHAPTER 5 QUADCOPTER MOUNTED ON A TEST STAND

- Understanding gravitational compensation or bias concept
- Understanding state machine concepts in order to define drone actions via remote control

Previous Designs

A previous nonfunctional design of our test stand is shown in Figures 5-3 and 5-4. Although it was not entirely useful, it serves to illustrate the necessary components in an exaggerated way.

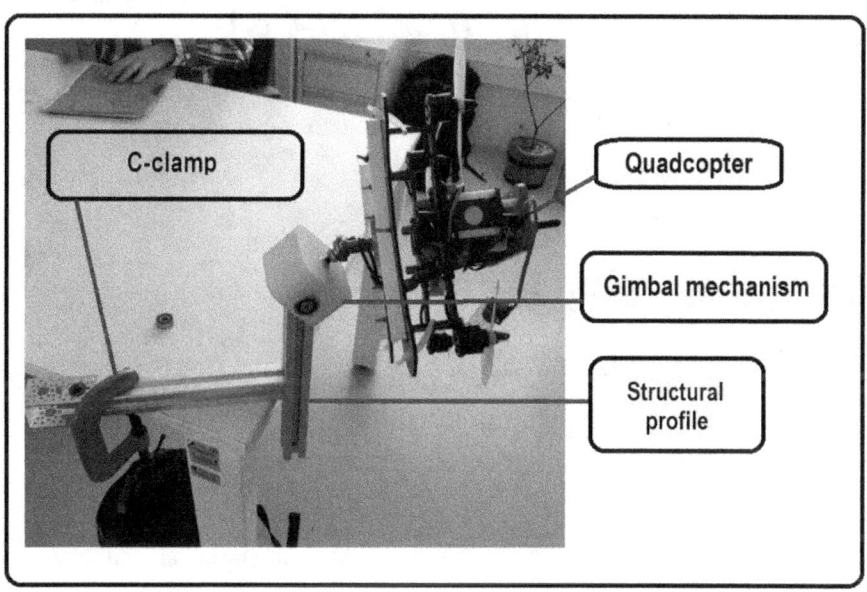

Figure 5-3. *Details of our original test stand 1 (shown as a comparative view of the final version)*

CHAPTER 5 QUADCOPTER MOUNTED ON A TEST STAND

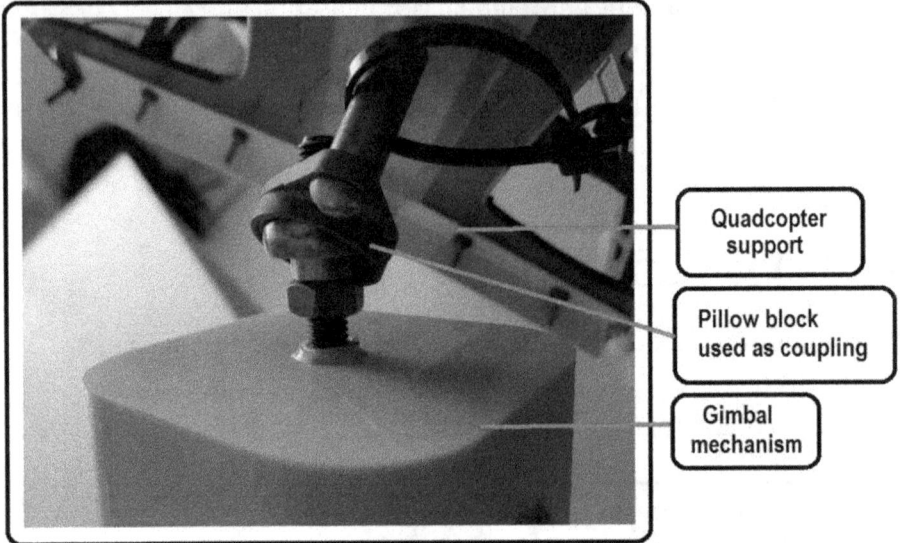

Figure 5-4. *Details of our original test stand 2 (shown as a comparative view of the final version)*

Some Assembly Details

- The coupling between the vehicle and the joint must be strong enough to support the vehicle's weight and various jerks, and light enough not to influence the drone's movement.

- The ball joint, in addition to having three-dimensional angular mobility, must have low friction to avoid influencing the drone's movement.

- It is recommended to leave a battery onboard, allowing the vehicle to operate in real-world conditions. However, it is also viable to power the drone from an external source that allows for longer operation times, such as a DC power supply or a car battery.

- It is recommended to ensure that the vehicle does not collide with tables or the structural support in any position. To achieve this, it is suggested to build a T-shaped or L-shaped structural profile considering acceptable distances to place the drone.

Electrical and Electronic Analysis

The electrical and electronic part is divided into two: that of the vehicle, indicated in our previous book *Advanced Robotic Vehicles Programming*, and the other one of the support or pedestal, which refers to wiring and selection of the power source.

In this case, with 4 BLDC motors, even the smallest ones required a high-amperage power source or an onboard battery. This led us to the same case presented in the comparative table between power sources for the aeropendulum and, in general, all the projects in this book. In this case, we opted to use an onboard battery, which finally is the expected real situation for the vehicle's flight.

Mechanical Analysis

To the basic design of an aeropendulum plus the description from our previous book, *Advanced Robotic Vehicles Programming*, the following mechanical design considerations are added:

Since three-dimensional rotational movement was required, a mechanism or transmission with the least possible friction was needed so that this effect would interfere as little as possible with the drone's performance. There were several options (see Figure 5-5); for example, a gimbal with bearings having three perpendicular axes, a flexible spring embedded in a bearing, or simply a ball joint, which is what we ended up using. Table 5-1 provides a comparison between them.

CHAPTER 5 QUADCOPTER MOUNTED ON A TEST STAND

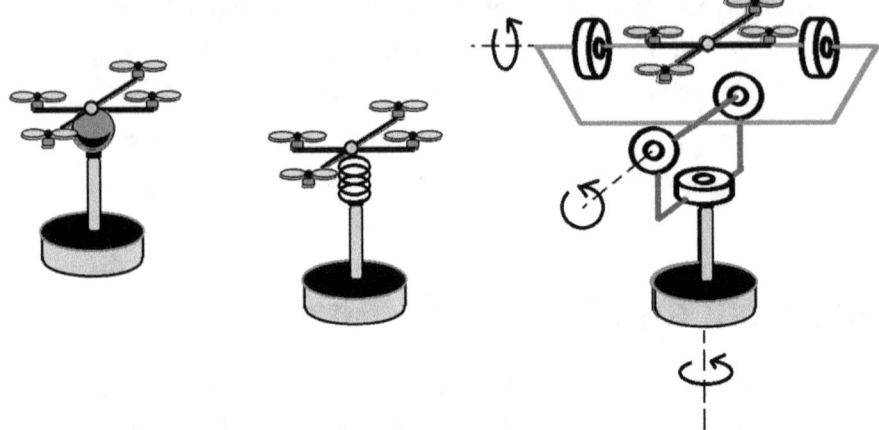

Figure 5-5. *Drone mounted on test stand variants (illustrating the cases of a ball joint, a flexible spring, and a gimbal mechanism)*

Table 5-1. *Comparison between three rotational mechanisms for fixing the quadcopter mounted on a test stand*

Three-dimensional rotation mechanism	Gimbal with three bearings perpendicular to each other	Flexible spring embedded in a bearing	Ball joint
Size	The least compact	Intermediate	Compact
Main problem	Gimbal lock	Eccentric radius	Needs lubrication to avoid scratching and can dislocate like a human joint
Components	Three bearings, housings or pillow blocks, and perpendicular joints between them	One bearing, a pillow block or housing, a spring, the union between the spring and the bearing	Pedestal with a spherical interior, a ball joint, a nut for joining the pedestal and the ball joint

(*continued*)

Table 5-1. (*continued*)

Three-dimensional rotation mechanism	Gimbal with three bearings perpendicular to each other	Flexible spring embedded in a bearing	Ball joint
Availability	High, but the user must perform machining or 3D printing	High, but the user must join the spring to the bearing	Low, only a few companies sell the device, e.g., Norelem
Machinability	Moderate, the complicated part is making the housings or pillow blocks and ensuring orthogonality between them	Moderate, generally, the spring must be joined to the bearing by some method like press-fitting or welding	Low, it's recommended to buy it, since making it with a lathe doesn't guarantee good sliding, and doing it with CNC requires at least a 4-axis machine; even then, a finishing process is necessary, which can destroy the sphericity
Usage characteristics	It's difficult to set a mobility limit, and this implies starting the vehicle from a position close to equilibrium; it's also easy to get stuck in certain positions	The spring's radius produces an additional eccentric translational movement besides the expected roll, pitch, and yaw rotations	The mobility limit is the ball joint's own geometry; there are no eccentric distances or they are very small

Another issue is the use of small versus wide platforms. It's true that a longer lever arm generates inertial mass effects, but in this case, being a symmetrical structure, one arm compensates for the other like a counterweight. What we can indicate is that small platforms require much faster control since they generate overshoots much more easily than medium or large designs. Therefore, we recommend you use 450 frames instead of 250 structures.

Control Analysis

In this case, interchangeable use between Arduino and Pixhawk was no longer possible due to Arduino's limitations (at least in its basic versions) to operate four BLDC motors at high speeds and also process control calculations, sensors, and communication and data storage much faster or simultaneously. Therefore, it was done purely with Pixhawk. On the other hand, as indicated in the mechanical analysis of this device, we preferred the use of larger platforms due to their ease of control; a large aircraft has more stability than a small one due to its inertial resistance to overshoots and vibrations.

Figure 5-6 describes the flowchart.

CHAPTER 5 QUADCOPTER MOUNTED ON A TEST STAND

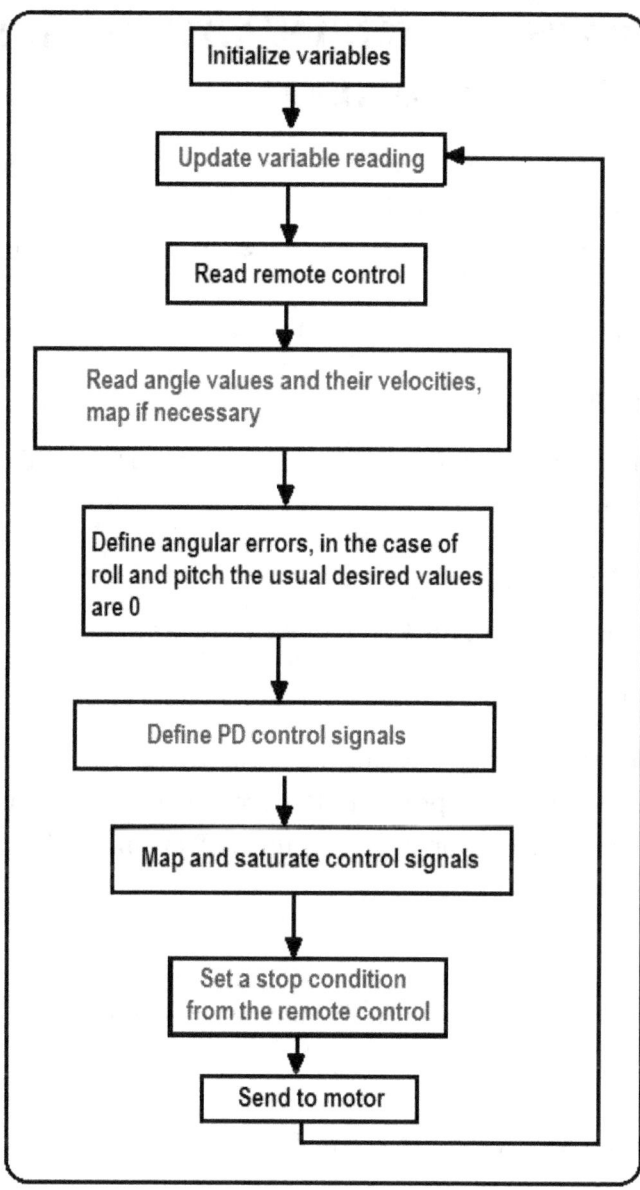

Figure 5-6. *Quadcopter mounted on a test stand flowchart*

CHAPTER 5   QUADCOPTER MOUNTED ON A TEST STAND

Code Analysis Illustrated with Old ArduPilot Libraries for Comparison

For comparison purposes, in this section we show the code in the old ArduPilot libraries and later in the new ones.

Required commands to write this project using the old ArduPilot libraries

The ArduPilot commands used in this prototype are

`hal.rcout->enable_ch:`

This command was used to enable or activate the PWM RC output channels to the motors.

`hal.rcout->write:`

This command writes the PWM RC signal to the motors.

`hal.rcin->read:`

This command allowed reading the PWM RC signal from the remote control, which is useful for programming emergency stops or events such as opening or closing a gripper, turning on or off an onboard LED, starting a flight routine, etc.

`ahrs.update:`

This command updated the angular measurements.

`ahrs.roll:`

After the above, this line allowed taking the roll component

`ahrs.pitch:`

After the above, this line allowed taking the pitch component

`ahrs.yaw:`

After the above, this line allowed taking the yaw component

`ins.get_gyro:`

This command allowed obtaining the angular velocity components; remember that to program a PD control, the velocities or derivatives must be obtained or calculated. Since the angles were already obtained, it's also necessary to obtain the angular velocities (in the previous chapter these derivatives are calculated, in this one they are measured directly from the onboard sensors)

`gyro.x:`

This line took the X component of the angular velocity

`gyro.y:`

This line took the Y component of the angular velocity

`gyro.z:`

This line took the Z component of the angular velocity

`hal.scheduler->delay:`

This is one of the ways for time handling that the ArduPilot libraries had; in this case, it's used to generate pauses.

Given the above, the following modifications can be made (this may involve modifying the code or retuning the control gains):

- Test with small, medium, or large drone platforms to deal with a greater or lesser degree of natural stability.
- Adjust the limit angles of the ball joint so that it is farther or closer to the unstable equilibrium position (with the drone parallel to the ground); this can be achieved with a kind of collar around the ball joint or by using posts that block the drone's mobility.

CHAPTER 5   QUADCOPTER MOUNTED ON A TEST STAND

- Conduct tests with an onboard battery or without it; although the first case is an ideal flight condition, this can be emulated with dead weight with the same dimensions and weight as the onboard battery (even the battery itself without connecting) while having unlimited testing time through a tethered connection to a power source.

The following conditions should also be verified:

- Ensure that the cables allow the system to move within its operating range. This is crucial for correct operation.

- Verify that the ball joint is properly lubricated and avoid scratching it or loading it beyond the manufacturer's recommended weight.

- Do not connect a BEC (Battery Eliminator Circuit) or a mobile device power source and leave it floating on the same electrical supply that will power the drone (i.e., the BEC connected to the electrical supply but not to the mobile device); this can generate false logic levels that modifies the autopilot's operation.

- Prefer using specialized connectors and lugs instead of direct connections to avoid cables breaking or coming loose.

Assembly and usage instructions:

A

1. Build a pedestal with IPS elements (or your preferred choice), either in an L or T shape.

2. Place the supports for the ball joint on the pedestal using screws.

3. Place the drone supports on the ball joint.

4. Secure a previously assembled drone to the ball joint using elements that do not alter its weight, such as ropes or straps, and secure the ball joint to the support and the support to the pedestal.

5. Secure the pedestal to a heavy table using clamps.

B

1. If using an onboard battery, verify that it is properly charged, preferably using suitable connectors. If using a tethered power supply, secure its cables with connectors or lugs.

C

1. Tighten the propellers appropriately.

2. Verify the motor numbering and its correspondence with the autopilot.

3. Use a compass to orient the drone's yaw relative to the world's magnetic north.

4. Load the code from the following pages and modify it according to the designer's preference. The drone or code should have a safety arming mechanism to prevent false starts with the propellers attached. It is suggested that, in addition to the physical arming, a remote control be used to switch between safe operating modes and the user-defined modes.

CHAPTER 5 QUADCOPTER MOUNTED ON A TEST STAND

5. Verify the expected drone behavior. If it doesn't work as expected, modify the code or the control and its allocation matrix. Remember the previous safety guidelines regarding the use of goggles or long sleeves.

6. If using a battery, have an alarm to prevent it from discharging below its minimum allowed value.

For comparative purposes regarding the old libraries, we describe the code in Listing 5-1. It is basically a modified template of the copter file.

Listing 5-1. Our old ArduPilot version of the quadcopter mounted on a test stand used in this book to compare with the new ArduPilot version

```
///////////////////////////// DECLARATION /////////////////////
//              Paste the header code here
//          See Advanced Robotic Vehicles Programming appendix

// verify or add this line
static AP_InertialNav_NavEKF inertial_nav(ahrs);

////////////////////////// place here your code////////////////

//      verify or add this lines
static Vector3f pos_gps;
static Vector3f vel_gps;
static AP_GPS   gps;
static Compass compass;

static float refx,refy,refz,ref_px,ref_py,ref_pz,errorx,errory,
errorz,posx,posy,posz;
static float roll,pitch,yaw,err_yaw,gyrox,gyroy,gyroz,velx,
vely,velz;
```

```
static float kp_roll, kd_roll,kp_pitch,kd_pitch,kp_yaw,kd_yaw;
static float p_x,d_x,p_y,d_y,p_z,d_z;

// the reader should add the rest of the necessary variables
(see writing to engines
//   and see radio reading)
///////////////////////////// INITIALIZATION /////////////////////
void setup(){
//         verify or add those lines
    gps.init(NULL,serial_manager);
    ahrs.set_compass(&compass);
    hal.rcout->enable_ch(0);
    hal.rcout->enable_ch(1);
    hal.rcout->enable_ch(2);
    hal.rcout->enable_ch(3);
    hal.rcout->set_freq( 15, 490);
// resetting all the engines
    hal.rcout->write(0,0);
    hal.rcout->write(1,0);
    hal.rcout->write(2,0);
    hal.rcout->write(3,0);
}
///////////////////////////// EXECUTION /////////////////////////
void loop(){
// the required radio channels are read for semi-automatic
operation
    radio[4] = hal.rcin->read(4);
    aux_1 = radio[4];
```

CHAPTER 5   QUADCOPTER MOUNTED ON A TEST STAND

```
// this channel replaces the fact to add the term mg
    radio[2] = hal.rcin->read(2);
    radio_throttle = radio[2];
    refalt=radio_throttle;

    ahrs.update();
    barometer.update();
// angular values of orientation and speed
    roll  = ahrs.roll;
    pitch = ahrs.pitch;
    yaw   = ahrs.yaw;

    gyro  = ins.get_gyro();

    gyrox = gyro.x;
    gyroy = gyro.y;
    gyroz = gyro.z;
// gains of the controllers CAUTION, the readers are responsible for their own
// and correct tuning

    kp_roll=800;
    kd_roll=350;
    kp_pitch=800;
    kd_pitch=350;
    kp_yaw=85/2;
    kd_yaw=100/2;

// PD controllers

    err_yaw=yaw-0;
    c_roll  = kp_roll  * roll    + kd_roll  * gyrox;
    c_pitch = kp_pitch * pitch   + kd_pitch * gyroy;
    c_yaw   = kp_yaw   * err_yaw + kd_yaw   * gyroz;
```

```
// manual bias
   c_gas=refalt;

   // BEWARE the signs of roll, X, pitch and Y, can vary according to the
   // sense of the remote control (the lever can be reversed)
// saturated propulsion matrix so that the motors never turn off
// and at the same time do not reach the maximum value of operation, this also
// is the responsibility of the reader, see also the section of the propulsion matrix
   m1_c=satu((-c_roll  + c_pitch  + c_yaw + cgas),1700,1100);
   m2_c=satu(( c_roll  - c_pitch  + c_yaw + cgas),1700,1100);
   m3_c=satu(( c_roll  + c_pitch  - c_yaw + cgas),1700,1100);
   m4_c=satu((-c_roll  - c_pitch  - c_yaw + cgas),1700,1100);
// writing to the motors if the auxiliary lever that serves as emergency stop
// is activated, otherwise, stop the motors
   if (aux_1<1500)
   {
       hal.rcout->write(0,uint16_t(m1_c));
       hal.rcout->write(1,uint16_t(m2_c));
       hal.rcout->write(2,uint16_t(m3_c));
       hal.rcout->write(3,uint16_t(m4_c));
   }
   else
   {
       hal.rcout->write(0,900);
       hal.rcout->write(1,900);
```

```
        hal.rcout->write(2,900);
        hal.rcout->write(3,900);
    }
    hal.scheduler->delay(50);
}
// auxiliary functions including the AP_HAL_MAIN
// saturation function
static float satu(float nu, float ma, float mi){
    if(nu>=ma) nu=ma;
        else nu=nu;
        if(nu <= mi) nu=mi;
        else nu=nu;
    return nu;
}
AP_HAL_MAIN(); // Ardupilot function call
```

Redesign and Results with the New ArduPilot Libraries

To redesign the system, additional operating conditions were done:

- The vehicle needed assistance to start and be balanced near its equilibrium point, especially if it's a small drone, because in such dimensions, changes are more abrupt than in larger drones.

- The best mechanism we opted to use was an industrial ball joint (apparently designed for automotive purposes), as other attempts lacked the necessary sphericity to move properly.

CHAPTER 5   QUADCOPTER MOUNTED ON A TEST STAND

- Despite the sphericity of the ball joint used, it was necessary to add an extra bearing as redundancy to help improve the quadcopter's movement and prevent the ball joint from getting scratched and stuck, similar to what happens with roll-on deodorants as they dry out.

First, a Norelem ball joint is used, which is shown in the following figure. To prevent ball joint blocking and help the drone's performance, a bearing was placed at its end, see Figure 5-7.

Figure 5-7. *Details of the quadcopter mounted on the commercially available ball joint 1*

The ball joint was placed on a pedestal, see Figure 5-8.

CHAPTER 5 QUADCOPTER MOUNTED ON A TEST STAND

Figure 5-8. *Details of the quadcopter mounted on the commercially available ball joint 2*

Then, a positioning element was added to mount the drone (a wood piece), see Figures 5-9 and 5-10.

CHAPTER 5 QUADCOPTER MOUNTED ON A TEST STAND

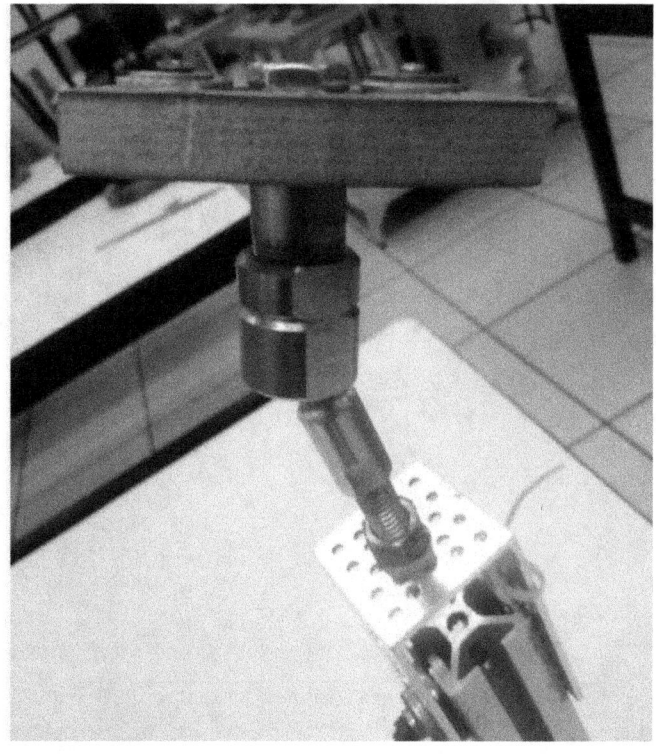

Figure 5-9. *Details of the quadcopter mounted on the commercially available ball joint 3*

CHAPTER 5   QUADCOPTER MOUNTED ON A TEST STAND

Figure 5-10. *Details of the quadcopter mounted on the commercially available ball joint 4*

Finally, the quadcopter was coupled to the previous system using ropes and a C-clamp, see Figures 5-11 and 5-12.

CHAPTER 5   QUADCOPTER MOUNTED ON A TEST STAND

Figure 5-11. *Details of the quadcopter mounted on the commercially available ball joint 5*

CHAPTER 5 QUADCOPTER MOUNTED ON A TEST STAND

Figure 5-12. *Details of the quadcopter mounted on the commercially available ball joint 6*

Figures 5-13 and 5-14 show the results of the tethered flight or balance tests of the vehicle. The compass is used to determine the drone's orientation relative to the magnetic north before its use. Additionally, it's notable that we manually assisted the vehicle in reaching the balanced position at startup.

Figure 5-13. Picture of the tethered drone in operation 1

CHAPTER 5   QUADCOPTER MOUNTED ON A TEST STAND

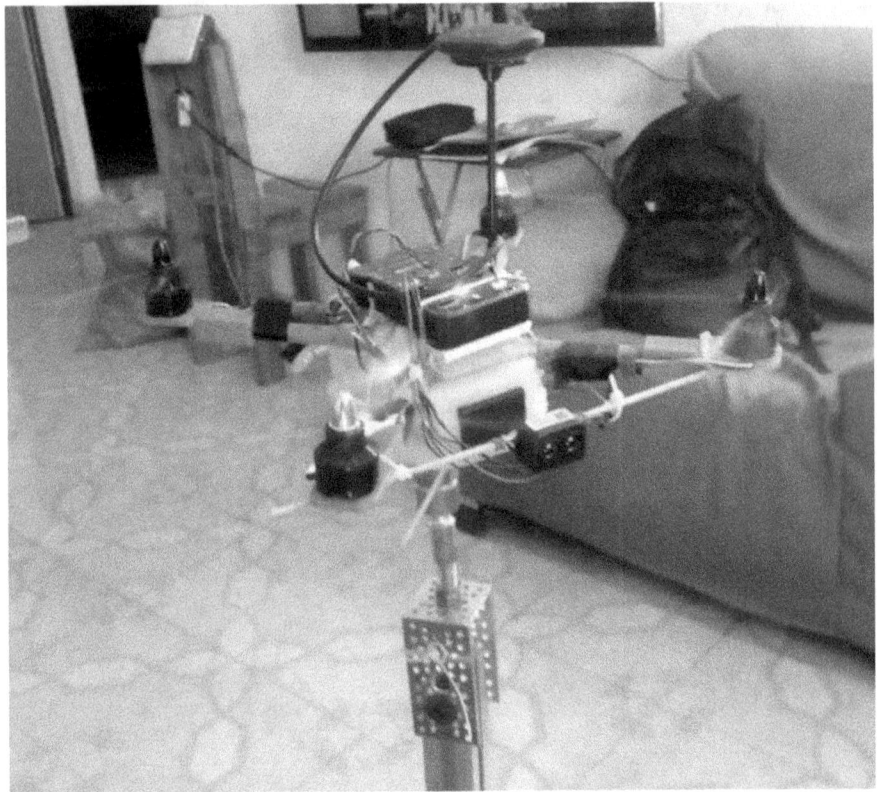

Figure 5-14. *Picture of the tethered drone in operation 2*

In addition, Figure 5-15 presents a version designed by our students, which aims to not only balance the vehicle but also control each angle at specific non-zero values.

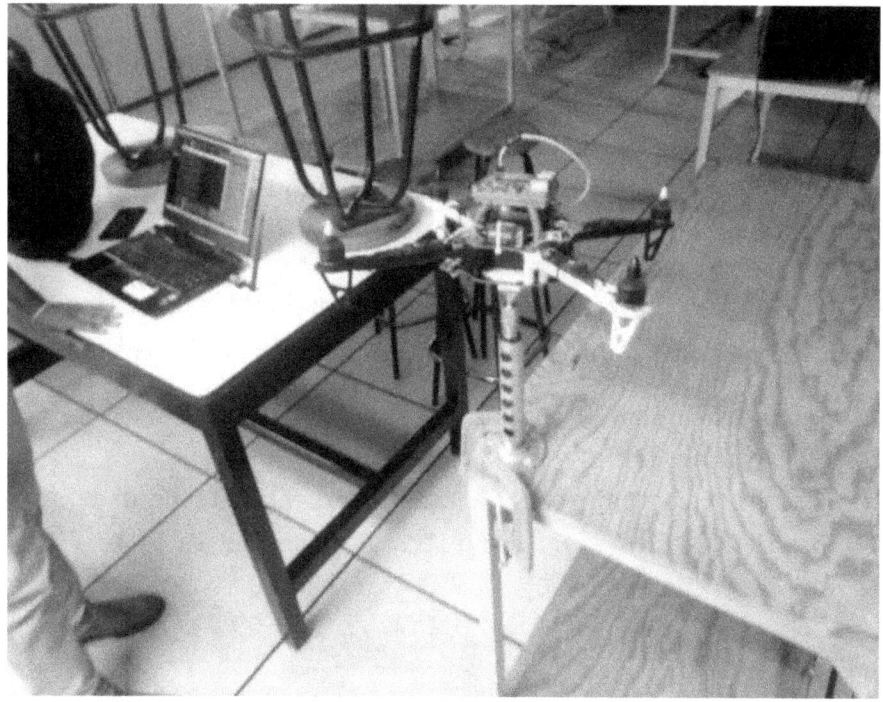

Figure 5-15. *An alternative version of the tethered drone, designed and implemented by our students at UPIITA*

Now, we will discuss the code modifications implemented in our experiment; they were based on the free-flight vehicle codes described in the following chapter, this time using the new ArduPilot libraries and OOP methodology as described in Listings 5-1 through 5-7.

Attention The codes shown below are a special modification of the programs corresponding to the chapter on the free-flight quadcopter, so it is necessary to read the next chapter to fully understand them.

CHAPTER 5 QUADCOPTER MOUNTED ON A TEST STAND

They are illustrated in this way because the book has a focus on a staggered mechatronic design (first the quadcopter mounted on a test stand and then the free-flight one) and the code has a reverse design sequence (first the free-flight quadcopter and then the anchored one).

In the file mode_rolquad.cpp, in the orientation section, search the following lines:

Listing 5-2. Our new full OOP ArduPilot version of the quadcopter mounted on a test stand: mode_rolquad.cpp file modifications

```
// Orientation PD control
// Angular errors
err.phi = pos.phi - 0; // Roll is expected to be 0
err.th = pos.th - 0;   // Pitch is expected to be 0
err.psi = pos.psi - 0; // Yaw is expected to be 0
```

And modified this line:

```
err.phi = pos.phi - 0;
```

To the following (even when balanced on the ball joint, it is expected that the drone can spin around its own axis):

```
err.psi = pos.psi - sp.psi; // Now the yaw angle will vary
err.th = pos.th - 0;   // Pitch is expected to be 0
err.phi = pos.phi - 0; // Roll is expected to be 0
```

Regarding planar errors, although the drone is fixed on the ball joint, two options are available:

Leave the following lines unchanged

```
// Calculation of motors' signals
    float m1, m2, m3, m4, m1a, m2a, m3a, m4a;
    m1 = rd.thr + tau.phi - tau.th - tau.psi - rd.roll +
    rd.pitch + rd.yaw + ctrl.x + ctrl.y + ctrl.z;
```

```
    m2 = rd.thr - tau.phi + tau.th - tau.psi + rd.roll -
    rd.pitch + rd.yaw - ctrl.x - ctrl.y + ctrl.z;
    m3 = rd.thr - tau.phi - tau.th + tau.psi + rd.roll +
    rd.pitch - rd.yaw + ctrl.x - ctrl.y + ctrl.z;
    m4 = rd.thr + tau.phi + tau.th + tau.psi - rd.roll -
    rd.pitch - rd.yaw - ctrl.x + ctrl.y + ctrl.z;
// remember to see the free flight quadcopter chapter order to
understand the following block
    m1a = rd.thr + tau.phi - tau.th - tau.psi - rd.roll +
    rd.pitch + ctrl.x + ctrl.y + ctrl.z;
    m2a = rd.thr - tau.phi + tau.th - tau.psi + rd.roll -
    rd.pitch - ctrl.x - ctrl.y + ctrl.z;
    m3a = rd.thr - tau.phi - tau.th + tau.psi + rd.roll +
    rd.pitch + ctrl.x - ctrl.y + ctrl.z;
    m4a = rd.thr + tau.phi + tau.th + tau.psi - rd.roll -
    rd.pitch - ctrl.x + ctrl.y + ctrl.z;
```

This is because the XY and Z set-points are assigned to the drone's current position and in a certain way contribute to balancing the drone fixed on the ball joint.

Or modify them as follows:

```
// Calculation of motors' signals
    float m1, m2, m3, m4, m1a, m2a, m3a, m4a;
    m1 = rd.thr + tau.phi - tau.th - tau.psi - rd.roll +
    rd.pitch + rd.yaw;
    m2 = rd.thr - tau.phi + tau.th - tau.psi + rd.roll -
    rd.pitch + rd.yaw;
    m3 = rd.thr - tau.phi - tau.th + tau.psi + rd.roll +
    rd.pitch - rd.yaw;
    m4 = rd.thr + tau.phi + tau.th + tau.psi - rd.roll -
    rd.pitch - rd.yaw;
```

```
m1a = rd.thr + tau.phi - tau.th - tau.psi - rd.roll +
rd.pitch;
m2a = rd.thr - tau.phi + tau.th - tau.psi + rd.roll -
rd.pitch;
m3a = rd.thr - tau.phi - tau.th + tau.psi + rd.roll +
rd.pitch;
m4a = rd.thr + tau.phi + tau.th + tau.psi - rd.roll -
rd.pitch;
```

In the last case, a purely orientation control is injected but the first case is convenient because the drone, once in its free flight mode (decoupled from the ball joint), can be pushed by the wind even if it floats balanced, so there must be a planar control that counteracts the wind interaction.

In our opinion, both options are valid to achieve a balance, but the one that preserves planar control gives a more reliable behavior of what the vehicle can expect in a real-life situation.

Given the above, the following modifications must also be made:

Search in the file mode.h for the following lines.

Listing 5-3. Our new full OOP ArduPilot version of the fixed quadcopter: mode.h file modifications

```
//              Setpoint setters declaration (XYZ)
void set_spx(float _spx);
void set_spy(float _spy);
void set_spz(float _spz);
```

Add the yaw setter.

```
void set_refYaw(float _ang);
```

Then describe its behavior in our customized class; in the mode_rolquad.cpp file.

Listing 5-4. *Our new full OOP ArduPilot version of the fixed quadcopter: mode_rolquad.cpp file modifications*

```
void ModeRolQuad::set_refYaw(float _ang){
    sp.psi=_ang;
}
```

Add this new flight mode and the following variables in the UserVariables.h file.

Listing 5-5. *Our new full OOP ArduPilot version of the fixed quadcopter: UserVariables.h file modifications*

```
float refYaw = 0.0; // Yaw reference in radians
float tasa_yaw = 10 * M_PI / 180; // Yaw change rate: 10 degrees/s converted to radians/s
int ciclos_por_direccion = (90 / 10) * 3.3; // // Calculate the necessary cycles to scan 90 degrees
int contador_yaw = 0;
```

Then we add yaw tracking in the existing state machine

```
enum ModeVuelo {
    ORIENTACION = 1,           // Orientation control only
    HOVER = 2,                 // Hover control (stationary)
SEGUIMIENTO_TRAYECTORIAS = 3,  // Trajectory tracking
ESCANEAYAW= 4 // Here we create a new state to track the yaw angle
};
```

Finally, we add the necessary code to generate the yaw reference within the existing state machine in UserCode.cpp. (This can be a constant value or generating a back-and-forth movement as in this case.)

Listing 5-6. Our new full OOP ArduPilot version of the fixed quadcopter: UserCode.cpp file modifications

```
case ESCANEAYAW: // Code for the yaw back-and-forth, yaw is
restricted to n cycles by direction
            if (contador_yaw < ciclos_por_direccion)
            // Turn from 0 to -90 degrees (left)
            {
                refYaw = -tasa_yaw * contador_yaw / 3.3;
            }
            else if (contador_yaw < 2 * ciclos_por_
            direccion)
            // Turn from -90 to 0 degrees (back to center)
            {
                refYaw = -tasa_yaw * (2 * ciclos_por_
                direccion - contador_yaw) / 3.3;
            }
            else if (contador_yaw < 3 * ciclos_por_
            direccion)
            // Turn from 0 to 90 degrees (right)
            {
                refYaw = tasa_yaw * (contador_yaw - 2 *
                ciclos_por_direccion) / 3.3;
            }
            else if (contador_yaw < 4 * ciclos_por_
            direccion)
            // Turn 90 degrees back to 0 (center)
            {
                refYaw = tasa_yaw * (4 * ciclos_por_
                direccion - contador_yaw) / 3.3;
            }
            else
```

CHAPTER 5   QUADCOPTER MOUNTED ON A TEST STAND

```
// End of the sequence
{
    contador_yaw = 0; // Reset the scan counter
    break;
}

copter.mode_rolquad.set_refYaw(refYaw); // Pass
the yaw reference to the drone
contador_yaw++; // Increment the cycle counter
break;
```

Finally in the same UserCode.cpp file, search for the following line:

```
//    The following block checks the status of the auxiliary 2
remote control
```

And make the following modification: "ESCANEAYAW" will be selected instead of "HOVER", as shown below.

Listing 5-7. Our new full OOP ArduPilot version of the fixed quadcopter: UserCode.cpp file second modification

```
// The following block checks the status of the auxiliary 2
remote control
if(copter.mode_rolquad.get_rdaux2() > 1800)
{
    // If the remote control value is greater than 1800,
    the set-points are assigned
    if(flag_ctrlxyz == false)
      {
        copter.mode_rolquad.set_spx(copter.mode_rolquad.
        get_x()); // X set-point
        copter.mode_rolquad.set_spy(copter.mode_rolquad.
        get_y()); // Y set-point
```

CHAPTER 5　QUADCOPTER MOUNTED ON A TEST STAND

```
                copter.mode_rolquad.set_spz(copter.mode_rolquad.
                    get_z()); // Z set-point
                flag_ctrlxyz = true; // Change the flag state
            }
            // Change to state 2 (here it was previously a hover
                mode, now it is YAW mode)
            copter.mode_rolquad.set_state(ESCANEAYAW);
        }
      else
      {
    // If the remote control value is less than or equal to 1800,
    change the state to 1 (orientation control)
            copter.mode_rolquad.set_state(ORIENTACION);
            flag_ctrlxyz = false; // Reset the control flag
      }
```

Below are the performance graphs of the previous experiment; the data was taken from the SD card.

We start with a constant yaw position different from the magnetic zero and roll and pitch angles equal to 0 (drone balanced on the ball joint), see Figure 5-16; for this, we help the vehicle a bit by starting it in a nearby position and with the aid of our compass.

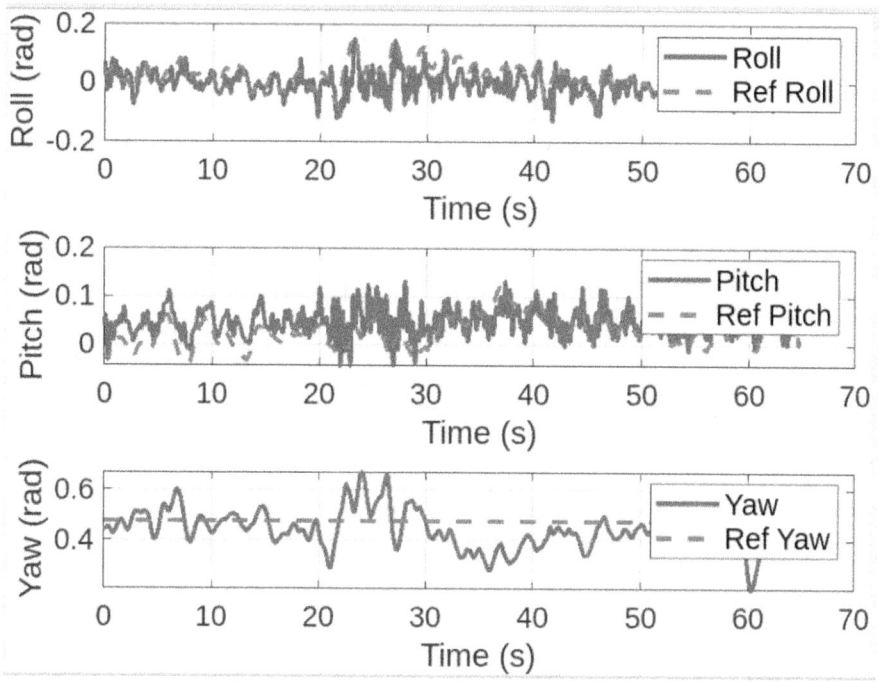

Figure 5-16. *Graphs of the angular performance of the fixed drone in balance mode (all desired angles are equal to 0 except for the yaw).*

In the position (see Figure 5-17), we see that Z remains around the anchored point with respect to the chair (0,0,1 meter).

CHAPTER 5   QUADCOPTER MOUNTED ON A TEST STAND

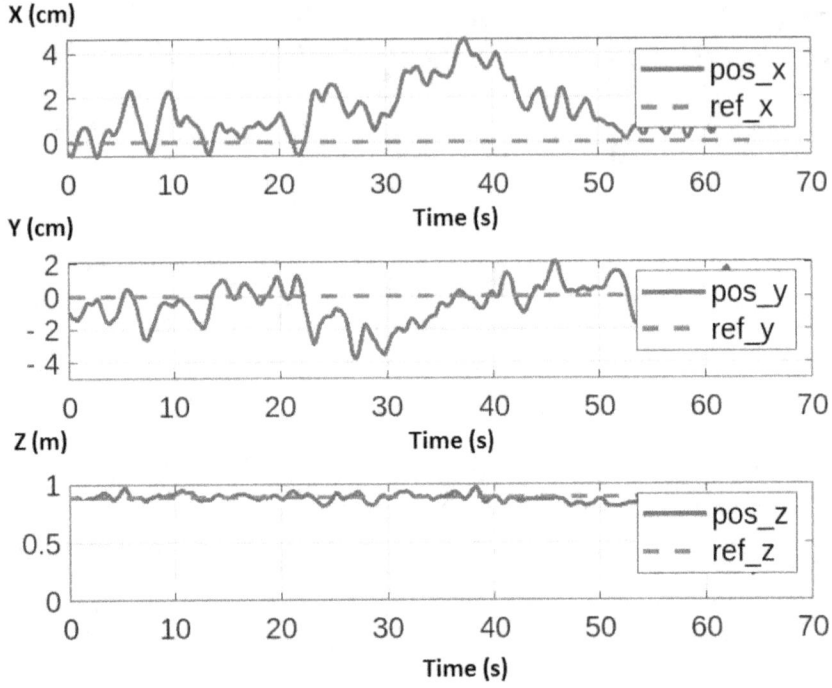

Figure 5-17. *Graphs of the translational performance of the fixed drone in balance mode, (0,0,1) meters with respect to the chair where the vehicle was fixed*

And finally, the forces applied to the center of the vehicle are shown in Figure 5-18. Remember that these forces are also mounted on an identical offset applied to the four motors. The reader should observe that these forces and offset propagate to the motors through the allocation matrix defined in the code (for more information on this matrix, see our previous book, *Advanced Robotic Vehicles Programming*).

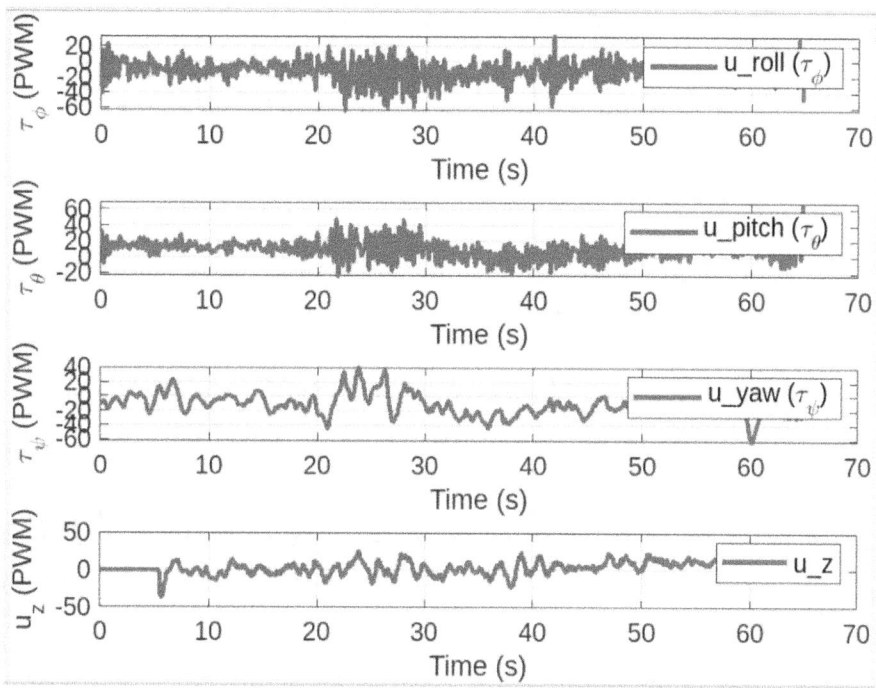

Figure 5-18. *An estimate of the force and torques at the center of the vehicle to keep its balance (obtained as a proportion of the allocation matrix).*

The offset is relative to the user's drone—and some vehicles may require a smaller or larger one—and is included to ensure that all motors maintain an operating speed on which to mount the control negative values.

Similarly, the vehicle was programmed to follow an oscillating trajectory around its own axis (yaw). Below is its performance in Figure 5-19; note that the actual graph was filtered for educational purposes but actually has more noise due to the nature of the vehicle and its sensors.

CHAPTER 5 QUADCOPTER MOUNTED ON A TEST STAND

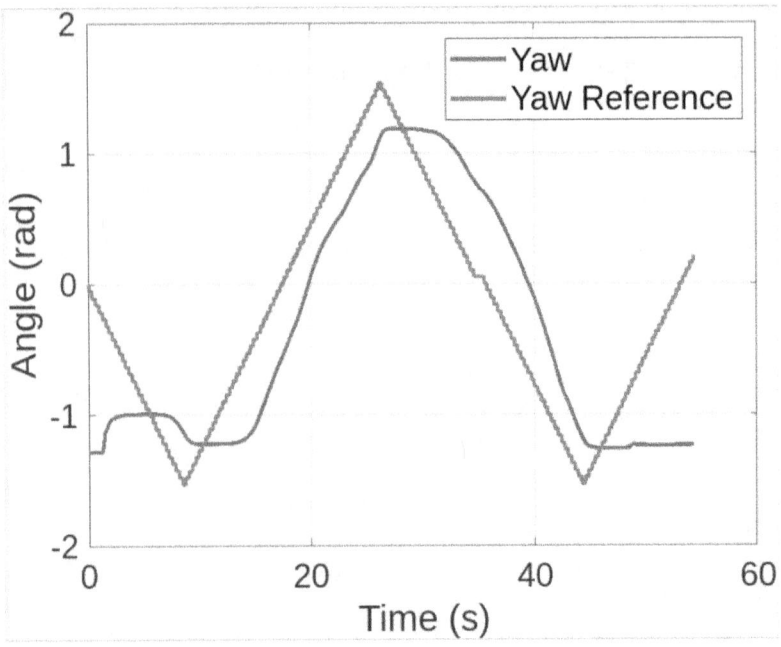

Figure 5-19. *Filtered graph (the original noise does not allow it to be appreciated) of a variant of the previous example with variable angular performance in yaw (all other desired angles are equal to 0)*

Chapter Summary

In this chapter, we described the design of a quadcopter mounted on a test stand, presenting mechatronic details of both a preliminary and a definitive version. We also described two operational versions of code for comparative purposes, both from the ArduPilot libraries, but one in its sequential or template version from 2018 and the other in modular OOP mode from 2023. For the latter case, the code from the next chapter was modified only in specific blocks or lines.

In the next chapter, we will continue with the final part of our staged robotic design, allowing the quadcopter full range of motion (free flight mode).

CHAPTER 6

Free Flight Quadcopter, Altitude, Planar Position, and Orientation Control

In this final chapter, the third guided project is addressed: the free-flight quadcopter. It begins with its definition, uses, and variants, which in the theoretical context are complemented by references to the device at the end of the book.

After that, we follow with the prototype development, covering a suggested list of components and knowledge, assembly instructions, and a mechatronic design, to finally conclude with the complete code using ArduPilot 2023 libraries in modular OOP mode and its experimental results.

CHAPTER 6   FREE FLIGHT QUADCOPTER, ALTITUDE, PLANAR POSITION, AND ORIENTATION CONTROL

Description and Applications of the Free Flight Quadcopter

The quadcopter dates back to the early 1900s, but it had a boom by 2012. Beyond being a favorite among hobbyists, it also saw a boom in research due to being relatively simple and economical compared to other flight platforms, allowing for a more direct approach to concepts of movement and control of three-dimensional vehicles, including acrobatics.

Since then, a wide range of applications and derivative works have emerged, such as the development of new aircraft, including snake aerial manipulators, new thrust vectoring technologies, various control devices like Pixhawk autopilot, and coding libraries like ArduPilot. Quadcopter uses range from academia to movies, building scanning, pest monitoring and control, automatic seeding, and even scaring ducks in polluted lagoons. We can affirm that, although the quadcopter itself is a simple design with seemingly limited utility to the entertainment industry, a large number of technologies and new sciences have flourished around it, or have facilitated the approach to more complex disciplines.

The authors of this book, in particular with Apress-Springer, already have two texts related to this platform, and the one you are reading now.

Its operation is as follows: two generally rigid, perpendicular, and invariant bars with a pair of fixed propellers at their ends and coplanar to each other regulate—in a differential manner—four possible independent movements: elevation, and roll, pitch, and yaw angles, with the remaining planar translations in X and Y being dependent on the roll and pitch angles.

For this section, the vehicle was assembled as extensively described in our previous book, *Advanced Robotic Vehicles Programming*. In Figure 6-1, most of the mechanical, electronic, and control hardware components (Pixhawk autopilot) are shown. For greater safety, we recommend that you (like us) attach the propellers only when you're ready to flight and

CHAPTER 6   FREE FLIGHT QUADCOPTER, ALTITUDE, PLANAR POSITION, AND
              ORIENTATION CONTROL

once that the programmed control follows an acceptable motor logic (remember, if the vehicle's altitude exceeds the reference, all four motors should shut off or reduce their speed simultaneously; if the vehicle's altitude is below the reference, all four motors should increase their speed simultaneously; if the X or Y error increases, one diagonal pair of motors should increase their speed relative to the other, and so on).

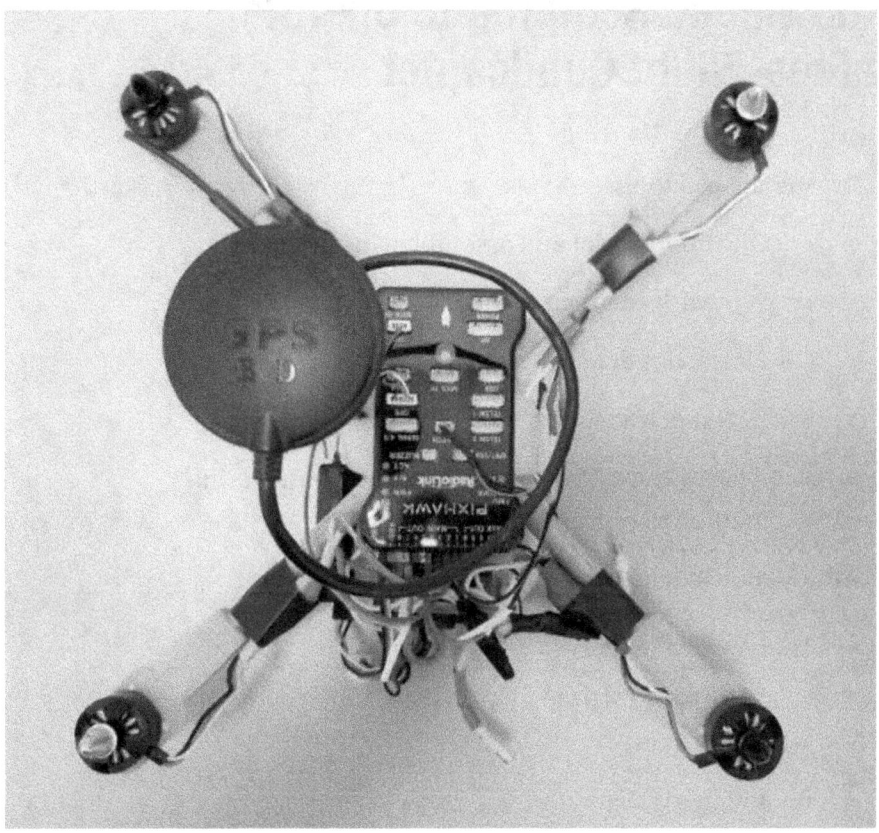

Figure 6-1. *Aerial view of one of our quadcopters assembled with its Pixhawk autopilot*

CHAPTER 6 FREE FLIGHT QUADCOPTER, ALTITUDE, PLANAR POSITION, AND ORIENTATION CONTROL

For further information, including detailed mathematical models and additional applications and control modes, we recommend reading the selected references section of this book.

List of Materials and Minimum Knowledge Required to Operate a Free-Flight Quadcopter

Mechanics

Materials and tools:

- One operational and assembled quadcopter
- Screwdrivers or wrenches
- Plastic ties or adhesive tape
- GPS shock absorber
- A safety net or rope can be used as an anchoring method to prevent damage or loss

Prior knowledge:

- Drone assembly
- Basic repairs (propellers or arms replacement)

Electronics

Tools and materials:

- Remote control with PPM receiver (at least with six channels: four channels dedicated to manual control, with two additional channels for switching between flight modes)
- GPS

CHAPTER 6 FREE FLIGHT QUADCOPTER, ALTITUDE, PLANAR POSITION, AND ORIENTATION CONTROL

- Batteries or tethered connection
- Battery charger
- Battery level indicator
- Micro SD adapter in order to retrieve flight data
- A compatible USB data cable

Prior knowledge:

- Drone electronic components (BLDC motors, ESCs, etc.)
- Basic operation of multimeters and oscilloscopes

Programming
Tools and materials:

- ArduPilot and Mission Planner libraries installed

Prior knowledge:

- General use of ArduPilot libraries (current and previous versions)

Control
Materials and tools:

- An autopilot (we use a Pixhawk)

Prior knowledge:

- The difference between position and orientation control
- A basic arithmetic control (PD)
- A basic logic control (a state machine)

CHAPTER 6 FREE FLIGHT QUADCOPTER, ALTITUDE, PLANAR POSITION, AND
            ORIENTATION CONTROL

Electrical and Electronic Analysis

Here the problem is that, unlike the quadcopter mounted on a test stand, the free flight drone is no longer being anchored; in this way, a system with greater range is required for data transmission. This is solved in two ways: one is through the use of telemetry modules, which demands knowledge of serial communications, and the simpler one is having a good remote control. As will be noted in the code lines later in this chapter, this remote control has several operating modes depending on the position of its switches, and this allows us to quickly switch to a safe operating mode if our customized mode fails. The remaining electronic issues are covered in our two preceding books or are the same as those described in the previous chapters.

Mechanical Analysis

In addition to ensuring a dynamic balance through the previous test platforms, it was also necessary to achieve a static balance. Let's remember that while automatic control can make something perform a task for which it was not designed, such as a bumblebee flying or an overweight animal running, it will end up consuming much more energy than a device with an optimized design, and in our case, this implies a shorter battery life. So, the first thing to do before flying is to ensure that both the propellers and the vehicle itself present static balance to guarantee that the vehicle does not try to move undesirably due to its unbalanced structure.

CHAPTER 6   FREE FLIGHT QUADCOPTER, ALTITUDE, PLANAR POSITION, AND ORIENTATION CONTROL

This is achieved relatively simply by using a balancer. In our case, we simply used our test stand for the fixed drone, but you can perform balance tests with a commercial balancer like the one in the figure and compensate in additive way (adding more material on the side with insufficient weight) or subtractive way (removing weight from where it is excessive). This balancer usually consists of two parallel plates with a rotating axis between them and a mounting surface to place the propellers or a complete drone, see Figure 6-2. In balance, the element to be tested does not rotate; in imbalance, the element to be tested will rotate toward the side that has more weight.

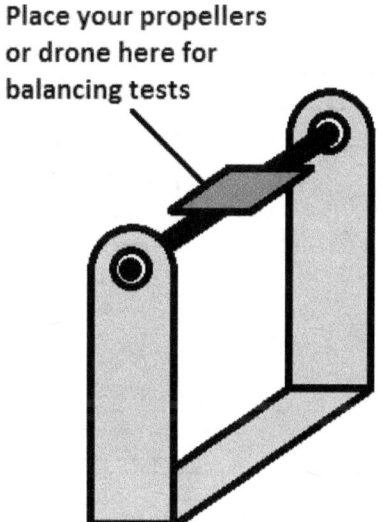

Figure 6-2. *The general design of a drone or propeller balancer*

CHAPTER 6 FREE FLIGHT QUADCOPTER, ALTITUDE, PLANAR POSITION, AND
            ORIENTATION CONTROL

Control Analysis

The flowchart is shown in Figure 6-3.

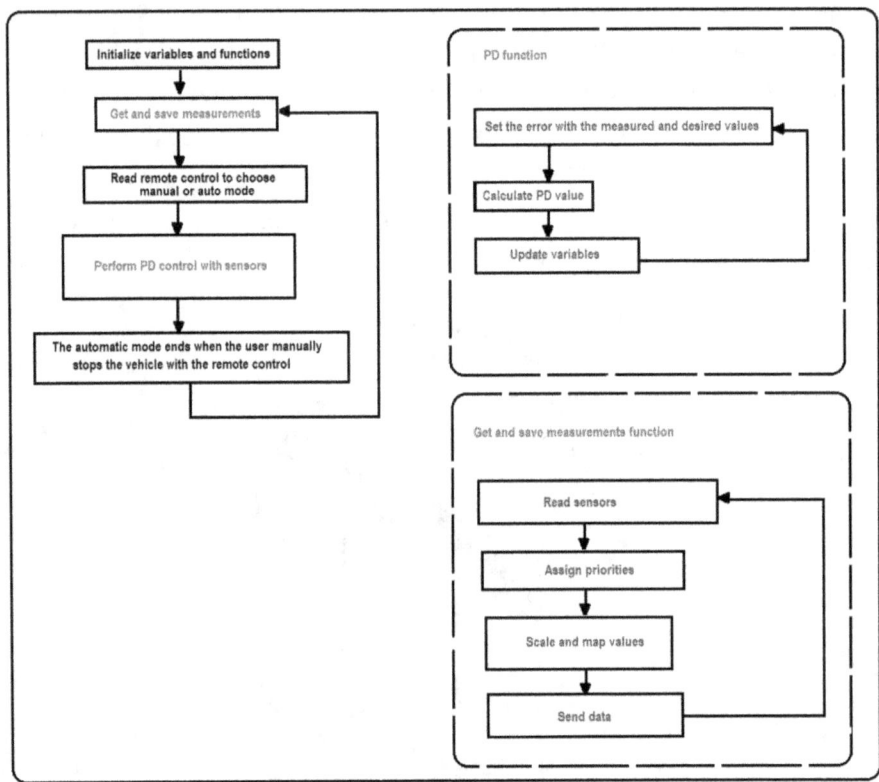

Figure 6-3. *Free-flight quadcopter flowchart*

Code Analysis

In this case, as we indicated in the previous chapter on the quadcopter mounted on a test stand, Arduino is no longer an option for so many operations, especially high-frequency ones; this is why the use of Pixhawk autopilots was essential.

CHAPTER 6　FREE FLIGHT QUADCOPTER, ALTITUDE, PLANAR POSITION, AND ORIENTATION CONTROL

Also, as will be noted in the subsequent codes, there are priority levels for the controllers, see Figure 6-4.

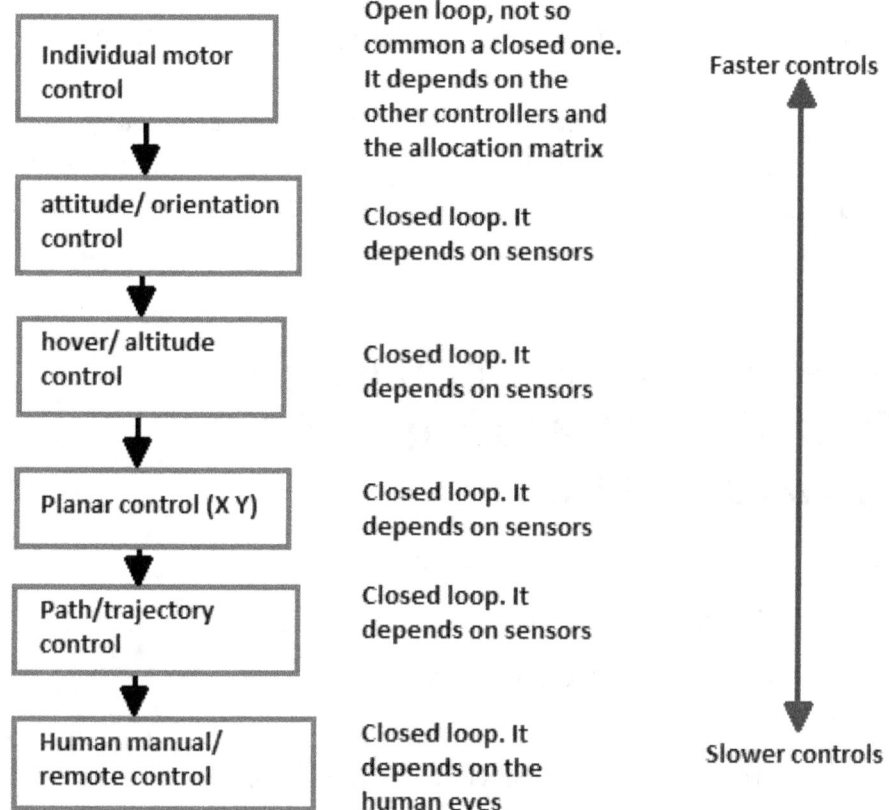

Figure 6-4. *Control hierarchy in terms of the execution speed for a free-flight drone*

The fastest is the orientation control.

The next is the altitude control.

The next is the XY positioning control.

The next level is the trajectory tracking control.

Finally, the slowest is the human command or remote control

CHAPTER 6   FREE FLIGHT QUADCOPTER, ALTITUDE, PLANAR POSITION, AND ORIENTATION CONTROL

For a more embedded designer, there is an even faster level, which is the individual control of the motors, but we opted, as most do, to rely on the speed and stability of the ESC manufacturer. However, we remind you that there are drone researchers that design the speed profile of each motor in closed loop.

It is also advisable to have a security return mode or at least a low battery warning for long-duration operations (which was not our case in the described codes). This mode obviously considers that a vehicle with low battery levels can collapse.

Assembly and Testing of the Free Flight Quadcopter Using the New ArduPilot Libraries

Regarding modifications, the user can simply

1. Try different drone sizes.
2. Retune their allocation matrix for + or X configurations.
3. Use some safety harness or net in preliminary flights, such that it prevents the drone from getting lost or damaging something or someone.

It's convenient to verify the following:

1. The numbering and distribution of the motors for which the control and allocation matrix of the drone were designed match the autopilot's connection ports.
2. The battery for both the drone and remote control are adequate and fully charged.

CHAPTER 6 FREE FLIGHT QUADCOPTER, ALTITUDE, PLANAR POSITION, AND ORIENTATION CONTROL

3. There are no loose connections or short circuits.

4. Drone components are properly secured and won't come loose.

5. Propellers, if used, are tightly secured.

Below are the assembly and usage instructions:

A

1. Verify the previous points.

2. Ensure that there are no people, living beings, buildings, or anything that could be damaged in the surroundings.

3. Load the code to the vehicle's autopilot, ensuring that there is a physical system for arming the motors or, alternatively, through software with remote control by switching between safe operation modes and the one defined by the user.

4. Verify the expected operation, preferably starting without propellers.

B

1. Verify that the battery does not approach to values below its safety limits.

2. In the opposite case, or when you wish, switch with the remote control (or using timers or based on the battery discharge) to manual or autonomous landing.

The codes to be created or modified are described in Listings 6-1 through 6-5 as follows:

CHAPTER 6 FREE FLIGHT QUADCOPTER, ALTITUDE, PLANAR POSITION, AND
           ORIENTATION CONTROL

Listing 6-1. Our new full OOP ArduPilot version of the free flight quadcopter: mode_rolquad.cpp file modifications

```cpp
/*      FILE   mode_rolquad.cpp (our customized code)
     In this file we define the class methods that are
declared on the file mode.h      */
#include "Copter.h"
#include "UserVariables.h"
//              RADIO SECTION
//         method for Reading the radio signals
void ModeRolQuad::captura_radio()
{
 // the following mapping depends on your radio, in this case,
only roll, pitch and yaw are mapped
    rd.roll = (copter.channel_roll->get_radio_in() - 1500) / 3;
    rd.pitch = (copter.channel_pitch->get_radio_in() - 1500) / 3;
    rd.thr = copter.channel_throttle->get_radio_in();
    rd.yaw = (copter.channel_yaw->get_radio_in() - 1500) / 2;
// auxiliar channels for changing the flight mode
    rd.aux1 = rc().get_radio_in(4);
    rd.aux2 = rc().get_radio_in(5);

}
//        radio getters
int ModeRolQuad::get_rdroll()
{
    return rd.roll;
}
int ModeRolQuad::get_rdpitch()
{
    return rd.pitch;
}
```

CHAPTER 6 FREE FLIGHT QUADCOPTER, ALTITUDE, PLANAR POSITION, AND
           ORIENTATION CONTROL

```
int ModeRolQuad::get_rdthr()
{
    return rd.thr;
}
int ModeRolQuad::get_rdyaw()
{
    return rd.yaw;
}
int ModeRolQuad::get_rdaux1()
{
    return rd.aux1;
}
int ModeRolQuad::get_rdaux2()
{
    return rd.aux2;
}
// state getter, it's used to switch between flight modes
uint8_t ModeRolQuad::get_state()
{
    return state;
}
// state setter, this complements the previous method
void ModeRolQuad::set_state(uint8_t _state)
{
    state = _state;
}
//              ATTITUDE AND POSITION SECTION
//              attitude getters
```

CHAPTER 6   FREE FLIGHT QUADCOPTER, ALTITUDE, PLANAR POSITION, AND
            ORIENTATION CONTROL

```
float ModeRolQuad::get_phi()
{
    return pos.phi;
}
float ModeRolQuad::get_theta()
{
    return pos.th;
}
float ModeRolQuad::get_psi()
{
    return pos.psi;
}

//         XY and Z positions and velocities getters
float ModeRolQuad::get_x()
{
    return pos.x;
}
float ModeRolQuad::get_y()
{
    return pos.y;
}
float ModeRolQuad::get_z()
{
    return pos.z;
}
float ModeRolQuad::get_velx()
{
    return vel.x;
}
```

CHAPTER 6 FREE FLIGHT QUADCOPTER, ALTITUDE, PLANAR POSITION, AND ORIENTATION CONTROL

```
float ModeRolQuad::get_vely()
{
    return vel.y;
}
float ModeRolQuad::get_velz()
{
    return vel.z;
}
//       CONTROL SECTION
//       XY and Z set point setters
void ModeRolQuad::set_spx(float _spx)
{
    sp.x = _spx;
}
void ModeRolQuad::set_spy(float _spy)
{
    sp.y = _spy;
}
void ModeRolQuad::set_spz(float _spz)
{
    sp.z = _spz;
}

//       set-point getters
float ModeRolQuad::get_spx()
{
    return sp.x;
}
float ModeRolQuad::get_spy()
{
    return sp.y;
}
```

CHAPTER 6   FREE FLIGHT QUADCOPTER, ALTITUDE, PLANAR POSITION, AND
              ORIENTATION CONTROL

```
float ModeRolQuad::get_spz()
{
    return sp.z;
}
//      error getters
float ModeRolQuad::get_errorx()
{
    return err.x;
}
float ModeRolQuad::get_errory()
{
    return err.y;
}
float ModeRolQuad::get_errorz()
{
    return err.z;
}
//    attitude control getters
float ModeRolQuad::get_tauphi()
{
    return tau.phi;
}
float ModeRolQuad::get_tauth()
{
    return tau.th;
}
float ModeRolQuad::get_taupsi()
{
    return tau.psi;
}
```

CHAPTER 6 FREE FLIGHT QUADCOPTER, ALTITUDE, PLANAR POSITION, AND ORIENTATION CONTROL

```
//          XYZ control getters
float ModeRolQuad::get_ctrlx()
{
    return ctrl.x;
}
float ModeRolQuad::get_ctrly()
{
    return ctrl.y;
}
float ModeRolQuad::get_ctrlz()
{
    return ctrl.z;
}

// XYZ control method (Altitude setpoint is obtained in
usercode.cpp when the flight mode changes to HOVER)
void ModeRolQuad::ejecuta_controlxyz()
{
    err.x = pos.x - sp.x;   // X error,  sp: setpoint
    err.y = pos.y - sp.y;   // Y error
    err.z = sp.z - pos.z;   // Z error
    ctrl.x = kp.x * err.x + kd.x * vel.x; // X PD control
    ctrl.y = kp.y * err.y + kd.y * vel.y; // Y PD control
    ctrl.z = kp.z * err.z + kd.z * -vel.z; // Z PD control
}

//    Translation control reset method
void ModeRolQuad::reset_controlxyz()
{
    ctrl.x = 0;
    ctrl.y = 0;
    ctrl.z = 0;
}
```

CHAPTER 6 FREE FLIGHT QUADCOPTER, ALTITUDE, PLANAR POSITION, AND ORIENTATION CONTROL

```cpp
//           MAIN CODE    (run)   operating at 400 Hz
void ModeRolQuad::run()
{
// Get the inertial sensor reference for orientation data
const AP_InertialSensor &ins = AP::ins();
// Read gyroscope data for rotation rates (roll, pitch, yaw).
const Vector3f &gyro = ins.get_gyro();
// Calculate translational position (x, y, z) in meters (scaled
by dividing by 100)
  Vector3f position = (inertial_nav.get_position() / 100);
// Calculate translational velocity
  Vector3f velocity = (inertial_nav.get_velocity() / 100);

// Update both rotational and translational positions and
velocities
    pos.phi = ahrs.roll;
    pos.th  = ahrs.pitch;
    pos.psi = ahrs.yaw;
    vel.phi = gyro.x;
    vel.th  = gyro.y;
    vel.psi = gyro.z;
    pos.x = position.x;
    pos.y = position.y;
    pos.z = position.z;
    vel.x = velocity.x;
    vel.y = velocity.y;
    vel.z = velocity.z;

    // Orientation PD control
    // Calculate angular errors (desired roll, pitch, yaw = 0)
    err.phi = pos.phi - 0;
    err.th  = pos.th  - 0;
```

CHAPTER 6 FREE FLIGHT QUADCOPTER, ALTITUDE, PLANAR POSITION, AND
           ORIENTATION CONTROL

```
err.psi = pos.psi - 0;

// Compute orientation controllers
tau.phi = kp.phi * err.phi + kd.phi * vel.phi;
tau.th = kp.th * err.th + kd.th * vel.th;
tau.psi = kp.psi * err.psi + kd.psi * vel.psi;

// Calculate motor signals
float m1, m2, m3, m4, m1a, m2a, m3a, m4a;
m1 = rd.thr + tau.phi - tau.th - tau.psi - rd.roll +
  rd.pitch + rd.yaw + ctrl.x + ctrl.y + ctrl.z;
m2 = rd.thr - tau.phi + tau.th - tau.psi + rd.roll -
  rd.pitch + rd.yaw - ctrl.x - ctrl.y + ctrl.z;
m3 = rd.thr - tau.phi - tau.th + tau.psi + rd.roll +
  rd.pitch - rd.yaw + ctrl.x - ctrl.y + ctrl.z;
m4 = rd.thr + tau.phi + tau.th + tau.psi - rd.roll -
  rd.pitch - rd.yaw - ctrl.x + ctrl.y + ctrl.z;
// safety feature explained in the upcoming fail safe check
  m1a = rd.thr + tau.phi - tau.th - tau.psi - rd.roll +
  rd.pitch + ctrl.x + ctrl.y + ctrl.z;
  m2a = rd.thr - tau.phi + tau.th - tau.psi + rd.roll -
  rd.pitch - ctrl.x - ctrl.y + ctrl.z;
  m3a = rd.thr - tau.phi - tau.th + tau.psi + rd.roll +
  rd.pitch + ctrl.x - ctrl.y + ctrl.z;
  m4a = rd.thr + tau.phi + tau.th + tau.psi - rd.roll -
  rd.pitch - ctrl.x + ctrl.y + ctrl.z;

  // Apply the previous allocation matrix (mixer) to
     each motor
  // Failsafe check: this prevents the motors from activating
     if radio throttle is below the threshold
```

CHAPTER 6 FREE FLIGHT QUADCOPTER, ALTITUDE, PLANAR POSITION, AND
         ORIENTATION CONTROL

```
    if(rd.thr > 1025)
        {
        hal.rcout->write(0, uint16_t(m1));
        hal.rcout->write(1, uint16_t(m2));
        hal.rcout->write(2, uint16_t(m3));
        hal.rcout->write(3, uint16_t(m4));
        }
    else
     {
        // Safety feature: this prevents the motors from
        activating if radio yaw is initialized to the right
        hal.rcout->write(0, uint16_t(m1a));
        hal.rcout->write(1, uint16_t(m2a));
        hal.rcout->write(2, uint16_t(m3a));
        hal.rcout->write(3, uint16_t(m4a));
     }
}
```

Listing 6-2. Our new full OOP ArduPilot version of the free flight quadcopter: mode.h file modifications

```
/ *    FILE mode.h
This file is modified in order to declare the class
ModeRolQuad, this is done before the line
#if MODE_AUTOROTATE_ENABLED == ENABLED
*/
class ModeRolQuad : public Mode
{  // class beginning
public:
    // this class inherits the base class constructor Mode
    using Mode::Mode;
    //              main method declaration
```

CHAPTER 6 FREE FLIGHT QUADCOPTER, ALTITUDE, PLANAR POSITION, AND
           ORIENTATION CONTROL

```
// remember, this and most of the other customized methods
// are defined in the file mode_rolquad.cpp
virtual void run() override;
// Flight mode configuration methods
bool requires_GPS() const override { return false; }
bool has_manual_throttle() const override { return true; }
bool allows_arming(bool from_gcs) const override {
return true; }
bool is_autopilot() const override { return false; }
//          attitude getters declaration
float get_phi();
float get_theta();
float get_psi();
//          declaration of the method for reading
            the radio
void captura_radio();
//          radio getters declaration
int get_rdroll();
int get_rdpitch();
int get_rdthr();
int get_rdyaw();
int get_rdaux1();
int get_rdaux2();
//          XY and Z positions and velocities getters
            declaration
float get_x();
float get_y();
float get_z();
float get_velx();
float get_vely();
float get_velz();
```

CHAPTER 6 FREE FLIGHT QUADCOPTER, ALTITUDE, PLANAR POSITION, AND ORIENTATION CONTROL

```
//         declaration of the method for performing the XYZ
           translation control
void ejecuta_controlxyz();
//    state getter and setter declaration, remember this is
      useful for changing the flight mode
uint8_t get_state();
void set_state(uint8_t _state);
//         declaration of the method for resetting the XYZ
           translation control
void reset_controlxyz();
//            Setpoint setters declaration (XYZ)
void set_spx(float _spx);
void set_spy(float _spy);
void set_spz(float _spz);
//         attitude controllers getters declaration (phi,
           theta, psi)
float get_tauphi();
float get_tauth();
float get_taupsi();
//         XYZ controllers getters declaration (X, Y, Z)
float get_ctrlx();  // this returns ctrl.x
float get_ctrly();  // this returns ctrl.y
float get_ctrlz();  // this returns ctrl.z
//              XYZ setpoint getters declaration
float get_spx(); //X setpoint
float get_spy();//Y setpoint
float get_spz();//Z setpoint
//              XYZ error getters declaration
float get_errorx();
float get_errory();
float get_errorz();
```

CHAPTER 6 FREE FLIGHT QUADCOPTER, ALTITUDE, PLANAR POSITION, AND ORIENTATION CONTROL

```
//    protected methods used for overwriting the Mode class to
      the customized one
protected:

//          This method returns the name of the flight mode as
            a string.
//          This method overrides the virtual method of the base
            class Mode.
    const char *name() const override { return "ROLQUAD"; }
//          This method returns a shortened version of the flight
            mode name.
//          Also overrides the virtual method of the base
            class Mode.
    const char *name4() const override { return "ROQD"; }
//              Attributes declaration
private:
    uint8_t state = 1; //  Our flight modes initial state
// Each position, velocity, error and setpoint has a roll,
// pitch, yaw, XY and Z components
    struct pose {
        float phi; // Roll
        float th;  // Pitch
        float psi; // Yaw
        float x;   // X
        float y;   // Y
        float z;   // Z
    } pos, vel, err, sp;
//              control vector declaration
    Vector3f ctrl;
//          attitude-control struct declaration, it has phi, psi
            and theta components
    struct controles {    // attitude control structure
```

```
        float phi; // roll
        float psi; // yaw
        float th;  // pitch
    } tau;
    //      phi, theta, psi, X, Y and Z PD gains declaration
            and inicialization
    const struct ganancias {
        float phi;
        float th;
        float psi;
        float x;
        float y;
        float z;
    } kp{230, 220, 130, 50, 50, 170}, kd{33, 30, 80, 58, 58, 80};
    //      radio-struct declaration it has roll, pitch, yaw,
            throttle and 2 auxiliar channels
    struct radio {
        int roll;
        int pitch;
        int thr;
        int yaw;
        int aux1;
        int aux2;
    } rd;
};  // end of the class
```

Listing 6-3. Our new full OOP ArduPilot version of the free flight quadcopter: UserVariables.h file modifications

```
/ *    FILE UserVariables.h
This file is modified in order to declare certain variables for
changing our flightmodes
```

Those variables will be used in the file UserCode.cpp where faster and slower tasks are declared
*/

```
#ifdef USERHOOK_VARIABLES

enum ModeVuelo {
    ORIENTACION = 1,                  // orientation control
    HOVER = 2,                        // Hover control
    SEGUIMIENTO_TRAYECTORIAS = 3      // Trajectory tracking
};
bool flag_ctrlxyz=false;
#endif   // USERHOOK_VARIABLES
```

Listing 6-4. Our new full OOP ArduPilot version of the free flight quadcopter: UserCode.cpp file modifications

```
/ *    FILE UserCode.cpp
This file is modified in specific lines for including the previous customized methods (tasks) in order to be executed at certain specific frequencies
*/

#include "Copter.h"

//      Inside this 100 Hz loop, the XYZ control method is executed (the translational part).
#ifdef USERHOOK_FASTLOOP
void Copter::userhook_FastLoop()
{
//              Remote control input is read here
    copter.mode_rolquad.captura_radio();
//              Then, the current flight mode is obtained
    switch(copter.mode_rolquad.get_state())
```

CHAPTER 6 FREE FLIGHT QUADCOPTER, ALTITUDE, PLANAR POSITION, AND ORIENTATION CONTROL

```
    {
        case ORIENTACION: // Stabilized control (only the rotational part)
            // X, Y and Z control is reset
            copter.mode_rolquad.reset_controlxyz();
            break;
        case HOVER:
            // The XY and Z part is activated for hovering
            copter.mode_rolquad.ejecuta_controlxyz();
            break;
        case SEGUIMIENTO_TRAYECTORIAS:
            // If you want insert your code here to follow a specific trajectory
            // Otherwise, comment this case or assign it to the previous actions
            break;
        default: // If undefined, reset or perform another action.
                    // In this case is identical to orientation control
            copter.mode_rolquad.reset_controlxyz();
            break;
    }
}
#endif

//          This code segment runs at 10 Hz
#ifdef USERHOOK_MEDIUMLOOP
void Copter::userhook_MediumLoop()
{
    // This commented block is an EXAMPLE used to print drone coordinates and velocities to the
```

CHAPTER 6   FREE FLIGHT QUADCOPTER, ALTITUDE, PLANAR POSITION, AND
            ORIENTATION CONTROL

```
// console
  // hal.console->printf("%.2f\t %.2f\t %.2f\t %.2f\t %.2f\t
    %.2f\n",
  //     copter.mode_rolquad.get_x(),
  //     copter.mode_rolquad.get_velx(),
  //     copter.mode_rolquad.get_y(),
  //     copter.mode_rolquad.get_vely(),
  //     copter.mode_rolquad.get_z(),
  //     copter.mode_rolquad.get_velz());

  //    The following block checks the status of the aux 2
       remote control channel
  if(copter.mode_rolquad.get_rdaux2() > 1800)
  {
      // when the channel surpasses 1800, set-points are
         assigned
      if(flag_ctrlxyz == false)
      {
          // In this case, the set-points are assigned to the
             drone's current position
          copter.mode_rolquad.set_spx(copter.mode_rolquad.
          get_x()); // X set-point at current X
          copter.mode_rolquad.set_spy(copter.mode_rolquad.
          get_y()); // Y set-point at current Y
          copter.mode_rolquad.set_spz(copter.mode_rolquad.
          get_z()); // Z set-point at current Z
          flag_ctrlxyz = true; // Flag status is changed
      }
      //  Then flight mode is switched to state 2 (hover
         control)
       copter.mode_rolquad.set_state(HOVER);
  }
```

CHAPTER 6   FREE FLIGHT QUADCOPTER, ALTITUDE, PLANAR POSITION, AND
            ORIENTATION CONTROL

```
    else
    {
       // If aux channel 2 value is less than or equal to 1800,
       flight mode is switched to state 1
       // (orientation control)
          copter.mode_rolquad.set_state(ORIENTACION);
          flag_ctrlxyz = false; // Reset the flag
    }
}
#endif
```

Listing 6-5. Our new full OOP ArduPilot version of the free flight quadcopter: Log.cpp file modifications

```
/ *    Log.cpp
This file is modified in specific lines for including the
customized data package in order to be executed by Copter.cpp
and other main files and then saved into the autopilot memory
* /

//    as described in the previous book Advanced Robotic
Vehicles Programming,
//    data logging has 3 sections: declaration, writing
and header
//              (1)  data package declaration
//                   this is done as a struct that contains all
                     the variables that
//                   we want to save
struct PACKED log_Control_Tuning
{
    LOG_PACKET_HEADER;
    uint64_t time_us;
    float    c_roll;
```

CHAPTER 6 FREE FLIGHT QUADCOPTER, ALTITUDE, PLANAR POSITION, AND ORIENTATION CONTROL

```
    float    control_z;
    uint8_t  estado;
    float    c_pitch;
    float    pos_x;
    float    altura;
    int32_t  baro_alt;
    float    ref_x;
    float    ref_y;
    float    ref_z;
    float    pos_y;
    float    error_x;
};

//                   (2)   data package SD writing function
void Copter::Log_Write_Control_Tuning()
{
    struct log_Control_Tuning pkt = {
        LOG_PACKET_HEADER_INIT(LOG_CONTROL_TUNING_MSG),
        time_us             : AP_HAL::micros64(),
        c_roll              : copter.mode_rolquad.get_tauphi(),
        control_z           : copter.mode_rolquad.get_ctrlz(),
        estado              : copter.mode_rolquad.get_state(),
        c_pitch             : copter.mode_rolquad.get_tauth(),
        pos_x               : copter.mode_rolquad.get_x(),
        altura              : copter.mode_rolquad.get_z(),
        baro_alt            : baro_alt,
        ref_x               : copter.mode_rolquad.get_spx(),
        ref_y               : copter.mode_rolquad.get_spy(),
        ref_z               : copter.mode_rolquad.get_spz(),
        pos_y               : copter.mode_rolquad.get_y(),
        error_x             : copter.mode_rolquad.get_
                              errorx() //
```

CHAPTER 6 FREE FLIGHT QUADCOPTER, ALTITUDE, PLANAR POSITION, AND ORIENTATION CONTROL

```
    };
    logger.WriteBlock(&pkt, sizeof(pkt));
}

//       A second package declaration
struct PACKED log_Precland
{
    LOG_PACKET_HEADER;
    uint64_t time_us;
    float error_y;
    float error_z;
    float vel_x;
    float vel_y;
    float vel_z;
    float comodin1;
    float comodin2;
    float c_yaw;
    float comodin3;
    float comodin4;
    float comodin5;
    float comodin6;
};

//       The second package writing to the SD memory
void Copter::Log_Write_Precland()
{
    struct log_Precland pkt = {
        LOG_PACKET_HEADER_INIT(LOG_PRECLAND_MSG),
        time_us         : AP_HAL::micros64(),
        error_y         : copter.mode_rolquad.get_errory(),
        error_z         : copter.mode_rolquad.get_errorz(),
        vel_x           : copter.mode_rolquad.get_velx(),
```

CHAPTER 6 FREE FLIGHT QUADCOPTER, ALTITUDE, PLANAR POSITION, AND ORIENTATION CONTROL

```
        vel_y              : copter.mode_rolquad.get_vely(),
        vel_z              : copter.mode_rolquad.get_velz(),
        comodin1           : 0.0, // remember that you can save
                             other desired variables
        comodin2           : 0.0,
        c_yaw              : copter.mode_rolquad.get_taupsi(),
        comodin3           : 0.0,
        comodin4           : 0.0,
        comodin5           : 0.0,
        comodin6           : 0.0
    };
    logger.WriteBlock(&pkt, sizeof(pkt));
}

/*  (3) header of the firts data package (the way you will
    find the first line of the text files inside the SD
    memory),  consider the advice described in Advanced
    Robotic Vehicles Programming  concerning the data types
    headers     */

{ LOG_CONTROL_TUNING_MSG, sizeof(log_Control_Tuning),
    "CTUN", "QffBfffefffff", "TimeUS,c_ph,ctrlz,edo,c_th,po
sx,posz,BAlt,spx,spy,spz,posy,e_x", "s------------", "F-----------" },

//      header of the second data package

  { LOG_PRECLAND_MSG, sizeof(log_Precland),
      "PL",    "Qffffffffffff",   "TimeUS,e_y,e_z,velx,vely,ve
lz,cm1,cm2,c_psi,cm3,cm4,cm5,cm6", "s------------",
"F------------" },
```

CHAPTER 6   FREE FLIGHT QUADCOPTER, ALTITUDE, PLANAR POSITION, AND
            ORIENTATION CONTROL

The results of taking off and once at the desired altitude performing a lobe or droplet trajectory (around 18 seconds after starting the autonomous flight)—see Figure 6-5—and then landing again (90 seconds after starting the autonomous flight) are presented.

Figure 6-5. *Another of our quadcopters performing an autonomous flight (except for its manual takeoff and landing)*

Figure 6-6 shows the XY and Z variables measured on board the vehicle as well as the desired or reference values.

CHAPTER 6 FREE FLIGHT QUADCOPTER, ALTITUDE, PLANAR POSITION, AND ORIENTATION CONTROL

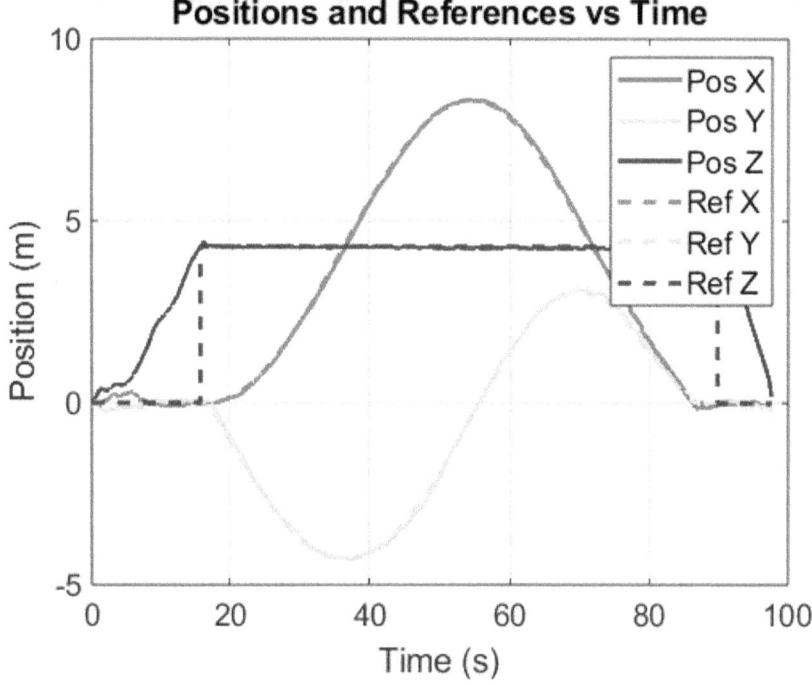

Figure 6-6. *Filtered graph of our trajectory tracking against time*

CHAPTER 6   FREE FLIGHT QUADCOPTER, ALTITUDE, PLANAR POSITION, AND
            ORIENTATION CONTROL

Next, the isolated planar X and Y positions is shown in Figure 6-7.

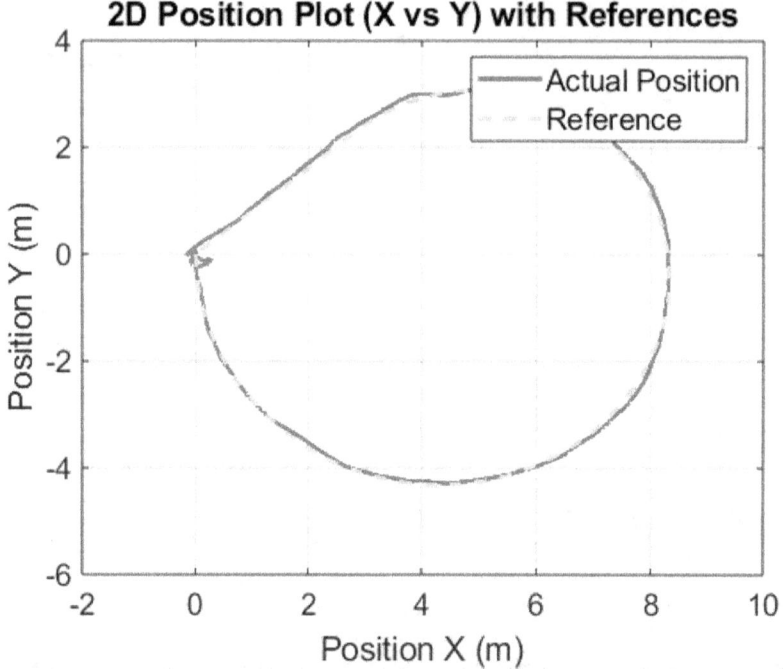

Figure 6-7. *Graph of the planar trajectory, also filtered to improve image details*

CHAPTER 6 FREE FLIGHT QUADCOPTER, ALTITUDE, PLANAR POSITION, AND ORIENTATION CONTROL

Similarly, the 3D tracking is shown in Figure 6-8.

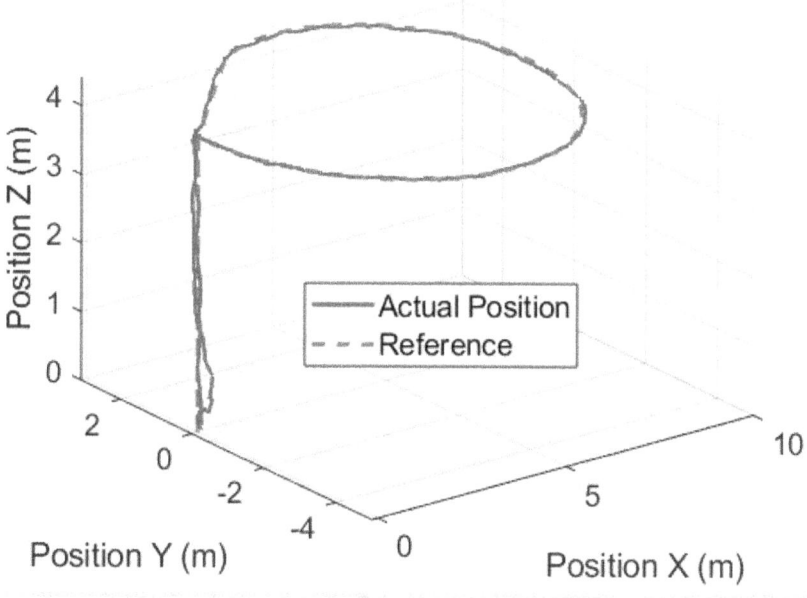

Figure 6-8. *Three-dimensional view of our trajectory tracking*

And finally, the isolated vehicle's orientation is shown in Figure 6-9. Remember, as this is a smooth flight, the desired behavior was simply to move the quadcopter while keeping its attitude or orientations at zero (airplane-type flight). Just before landing, a sudden change in orientations is noticeable because the vehicle does not land smoothly. To achieve this, a damped landing gear (passive protection) or a better landing control (active protection) needs to be added.

CHAPTER 6 FREE FLIGHT QUADCOPTER, ALTITUDE, PLANAR POSITION, AND ORIENTATION CONTROL

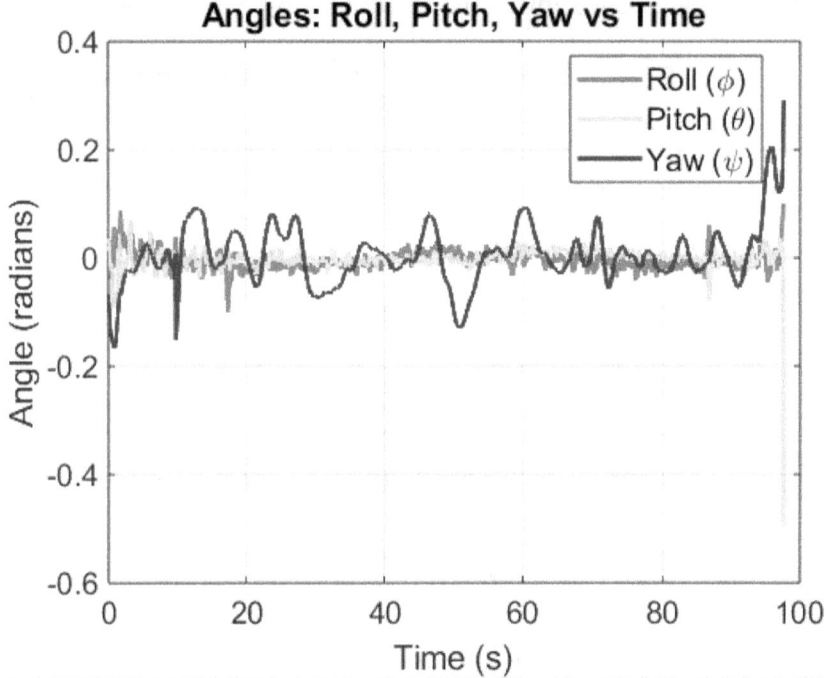

Figure 6-9. *Graphs of the angular performance of the free flight drone (despite following a special trajectory, the drone's angles are required to be around 0 or smooth flight). The sudden jump at the end implies a non-smooth manual landing*

Regarding flight quality, the following graphs show its performance in angular velocities as well as torques and applied forces.

Figure 6-10 shows how, at the angular velocity level, the vehicle maintained a fairly smooth performance.

CHAPTER 6 FREE FLIGHT QUADCOPTER, ALTITUDE, PLANAR POSITION, AND ORIENTATION CONTROL

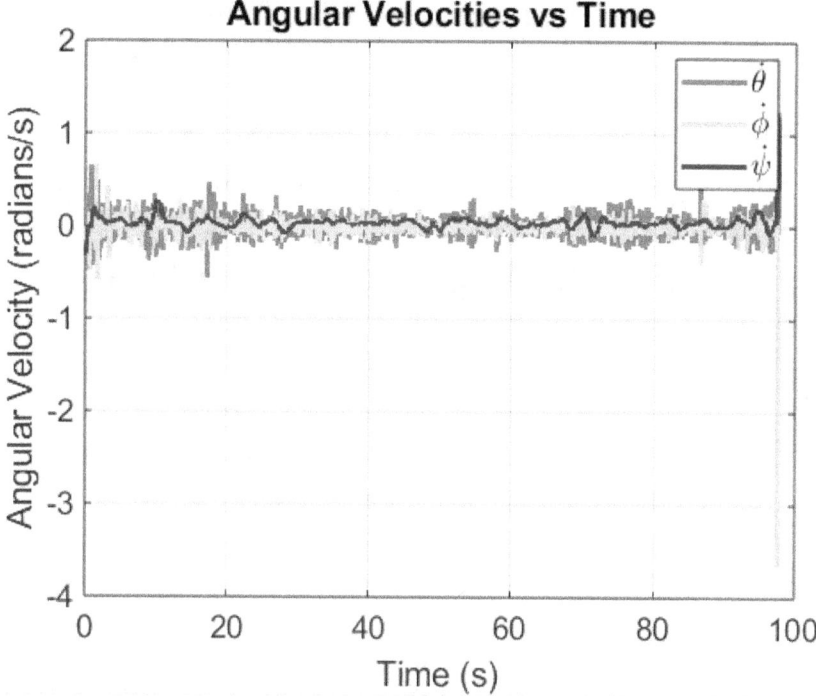

Figure 6-10. *Angular velocity performance of the free flight drone related to its flight smoothness (the chattering is due to the motos' induced noise)*

However, as the reader might deduce, keeping such dynamic smoothness implies injecting greater torques (relatively speaking) in roll, pitch, and yaw, as proven by Figure 6-11.

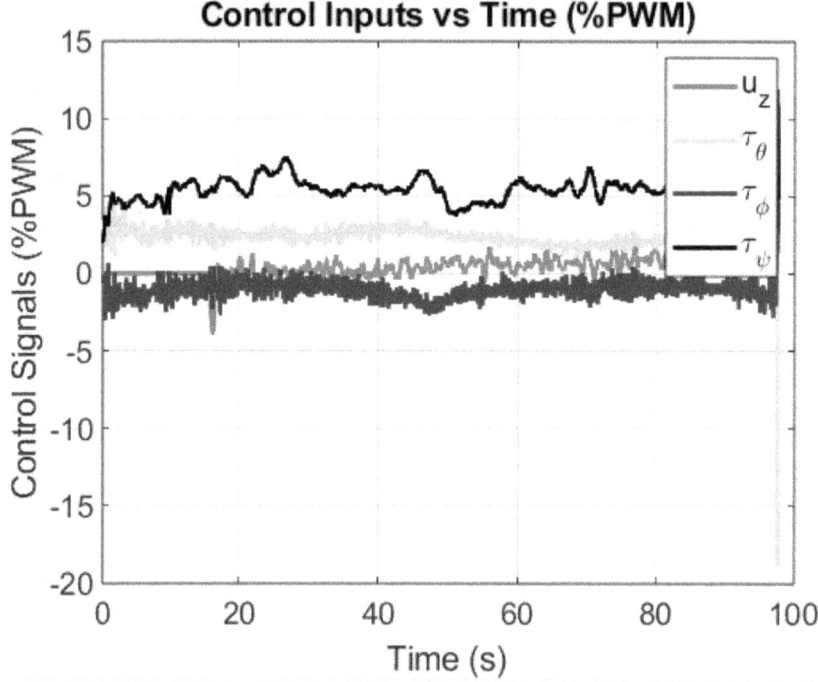

Figure 6-11. *Torques and force of the free flight drone as an estimate of its motors' allocation matrix. The sudden jump again is due to a non-smooth manual landing*

Chapter Summary

In this chapter, we described the design of the free flight quadcopter, with greater emphasis on the modular OOP code of the ArduPilot libraries. The extensive mechatronic details can be found in our previous books *Drones To Go* and *Advanced Robotic Vehicles Programming*; for this reason, only a few specific features were shown (mainly code).

We suggest reading the appendices, where we present a few comprehensive projects without code (leaving the implementation as an exercise for you), as well as some key details about managing input and output ports with the autopilot.

REFERENCES

Selected References

Selected References on Mechatronic Design

- The framework of all methodologies applied by any thinking being (scientific method)

    Descartes Rene, *Discourse on the Method of Rightly Conducting One's Reason and of Seeking Truth in the Sciences*, 1637

    Mario Bunge, La Ciencia, su metodo y su filosofía, Ed. Siglo XX, 1972 (in Spanish)

- One classic book with a general engineering approach

    Gerhard Pahl et al, *Engineering Design: A Systematic Approach*, 1984, Springer

- Two classic books with a mechatronic approach

    Bolton, *Mechatronics: Electronic Control Systems in Mechanical Engineering*, 2015, Pearson

    Sabri Cetinkunt, *Mechatronics with Experiments*, 2015, Wiley

- Complementary technological project development methodologies

    TRL: ISO 16290:2013 Space systems—Definition of the Technology Readiness Levels (TRLs) and their criteria of assessment

    SWEBOK: ISO/IEC TR 19759:2015 Software Engineering – Guide to the software engineering body of knowledge (SWEBOK)

    TRIZ: Nishiyama Juan, Los 40 principios de inventiva de TRIZ. UTN, 2019 (in Spanish)

Selected References on Object-Oriented Programming

- Two classic, well-developed didactic books on C/C++ and OOP published by Apress, the first one with an approach applied to Arduino

    Jack Purdum, *Beginning C for Arduino*, Second Edition, 2015, Springer-Apress

    Slobodan Dmitrovic, *Modern C++ for Absolute Beginners*, 2023, Springer-Apress

- The books and courses by Jean Cedric Chappelier (in French)

    https://www.coursera.org/learn/programmation-orientee-objet-cpp

    Jean Cedric Chappelier et al, C++ par la pratique: Recueil d'exercices corrigés et aide-mémoire, 2018, EPFL

- Another classic, quite didactic and extensive book (in Spanish)

    Joyanes, Programacion en C++, algoritmos, estructuras de datos y objetos, 2000, McGraw-Hill

Selected References on ArduPilot Libraries and Pixhawk Autopilots

- Our previous book on the old ArduPilot libraries and other complements to the current book

    Mendoza-Mendoza et al, *Advanced Robotic Vehicles Programming*, 2020, Springer-Apress

- Historical document about the original Pixhawk

    Lorenz Meier, Petri Tanskanen, Lionel Heng, Gim Hee Lee, Friedrich Fraundorfer, an d Marc Pollefeys, Pixhawk: A micro aerial vehicle design for autonomous flight using onboard computer vision, Autonomous Robots 33 (2012), no. 1-2, 21–39.

- Other documents such as theses and web reports on classic ArduPilot libraries

    https://blog.owenson.me/build-your-own-quadcopter-flight-controller/

    Alejandro Romero Galan, Revision y modificacion del firmware de libre acceso arducopter para su uso en el proyecto airwhale, Thesis, Universidad de Sevilla, 2015. (in Spanish)

REFERENCES   SELECTED REFERENCES

- Similar projects with wide use and also with ArduPilot support

    Dronekit (Python)

    https://dronekit.io

    MissionPlanner (GUI)

    https://ardupilot.org/planner/

    PX4 (C++)

    https://px4.io

    https://404warehouse.net/2015/12/20/autopilot-offboard-control-using-mavros-package-on-ros/

    Ty Audronis, Designing Purpose-Built Drones for ArduPilot Pixhawk 2.1, 2017

    Online search terms: ArduPilot libraries, Pixhawk autopilot

Selected References on the Aeropendulum

- Currently, the following pair of control courses with the aeropendulum as a testbed on EDX are no longer available, but they are indicated for readers to search for material derived from the instructors Jacob White and Joe Steinmeyer

    https://www.edx.org/es/course/introduction-control-system-design-first-mitx-6-302-0x

    https://www.edx.org/es/course/introduction-state-space-control-mitx-6-302-1x

REFERENCES   SELECTED REFERENCES

- Basic bibliography on the device

    Mechatronic aeropendulum: Demonstration of linear and nonlinear feedback control principles with matlab/simulink real-time windows target, ET Enikov et al, IEEE, 2012

    Nonlinear Model-Based Parameter Estimation and Stability Analysis of an Aero-Pendulum Subject to Digital Delayed Control, Giuseppe Habib et al, Springer, 2017

    Observer based fuzzy LMI regulator for stabilization and tracking control of an aeropendulum, Farooq et al, IEEE, 2015

    AERO-beam: An open-architecture test-bed for research and education in cyber-physical systems, O Lawlor et al, IEEE, 2015

    Modeling and control of mechatronic aeropendulum, MM Job et al, IEEE, 2015

    Pendulum Positioning System Actuated by Dual Motorized Propellers, Y Gultekin et al, 2011

    An Aeropendulum-Based Didactic Platform for the Learning of Control Engineering, Rafael C Neto et al, 2023

- Details on its assembly and operation

    http://aeropendulum.arizona.edu/

    https://www.linkedin.com/pulse/aero-pendulum-system-modeling-control-software-waleed-el-shemy

REFERENCES   SELECTED REFERENCES

- Its detailed control from a classic and frequency domain perspective, including parametric variation (mass, length, and viscosity)

  Modeling and Control of Mechatronic Aeropendulum, Arash Marashian, 2021

- Advanced projects based on the aeropendulum

  Snake aerial manipulators: A review, Mendoza-Mendoza et al, 2020, Springer

- Keywords for web search

  Aeropendulum, Propeller pendulum

Selected References on the Quadcopter Mounted on a Test Stand

- Select publications on the quadcopter mounted on a test stand, including its modeling and control

  N xuan et al, A Multicopter ground testbed for the evaluation of attitude and position controller, 2018, Int. J. Eng. Technol

  https://www.youtube.com/watch?v=Nju5yUpFetU

  Fernando dosSantos Barbosa, 4DOF Quadcopter: development, modeling and control, Thesis, 2017 (in Portuguese)

  https://www.youtube.com/watch?v=xUg1NO_sbRE

REFERENCES   SELECTED REFERENCES

- The following are based on a gimbal mechanism:

    Jaehyun Jin, A Test Bench with Six Degrees of Freedom of Motion for Development of Small Quadrotor Drones, 2017, Journal of Aerospace System Engineering (in Korean)

    Adam Bondyra, Experimental Test Bench for Multirotor UAVs, ICA 2017, Springer

    Vasfi Emre Omurlu, An experimental stationary quadrotor with variable DOF, 2013, Indian Academy of Sciences

- A magnetic test platform (in Korean)

    https://koreascience.kr/article/JAKO201732060955284.pdf

    Position and Attitude Control System Design of Magnetic Suspension and Balance System for Wind Tunnel Test Using Iterative Feedback Tuning and L1 Adaptive Control Scheme, Dong-Kyu Lee, 2017

- Cable-based test platform (like a marionette)

    Development of a 6-DOF Testing Platform for Multirotor Flying Vehicles with Suspended Loads, Saad M. S. Mukras et al, 2021

- Platform based on delta or Stewart mechanisms

    Further Results on Modeling and Control of a 3-DOF Platform for Driving Simulator Using Rotatory Actuators, Ivan Cañedo Farfan et al, 2021

- Argentine "anchored" platform (with centimetric elevation and support of walker-type wheels), Cicare company

    https://www.youtube.com/watch?v=vDnzpRVPCM4

    Online search terms: ball joint quadrotor, ball joint, quadcopter, fixed quadrotor, fixed quadcopter

Selected References on the Free Flight Quadcopter

- Texts with greater mathematical formality for quadcopter modeling and control, including our previous book

    Drones to go, Mendoza-Mendoza et al, 2021, Apress, Springer

    Luis Rodolfo Garcia Carrillo, Alejandro Enrique Dzul Lopez, Rogelio Lozano, Claude Pegard, Quad rotorcraft control: vision-based hovering and navigation, Springer Science & Business Media, 2012.

    Pedro Castillo, Rogelio Lozano, Alejandro E Dzul, Modelling and control of mini-flying machines, Physica-Verlag, 2006.

    Jinhyun Kim, Min-Sung Kang, and Sangdeok Park, Accurate modeling and robust hovering control for a quad-rotor vtol aircraft, Selected papers from the 2nd International Symposium on UAVs, Reno, Nevada, USA June 8–10, 2009, Springer, 2009, pp. 9–26.

Quan Quan, Introduction to multicopter design and control, Springer, 2017.

- MOOC de Vijay Kumar

    https://www.mooc-list.com/course/robotics-aerial-robotics-coursera

    Online search terms: quadcopter, quadrotor, drone, multirotor, multicopter

Selected References on the Zeppelin, Propeller-Driven Car, Hovercraft, Submarine, and Boat

- First, a bit of history

    Chris Chant, Zeppelin: The History of German Airships 1900-1937, 2019

- Academic and commercial robotic uses of medium to small-scale zeppelins (toys)

    Jack Jones, Inflatable robotics for planetary applications, 2001

    Nano blimp

    https://www.youtube.com/watch?v=17dV2B1M1dU

- Extensive mathematical modeling of the zeppelin

    Hao Cheng et al, RGBlimp: Robotic Gliding Blimp - Design, Modeling, Development, and Aerodynamics Analysis, 2023

REFERENCES   SELECTED REFERENCES

- A couple of operational zeppelin versions compatible with the one described in the appendix of this book

    Ning-shi Yao et al, Autonomous flying blimp interaction with human in an indoor space, 2019

    H Zhang et al, Visual servoing with dynamics: Control of an unmanned blimp, 1999

- Robotic submarine project with ArduPilot (quite popular)

    https://www.ardusub.com/

- Ideas for assembling a propeller-driven car (in this case, not differential or programmable, but useful for extending and understanding the prototype)

    https://www.youtube.com/watch?v=2A72h9epe-E

- Guided example for building a programmable propeller-driven boat (also capable of submerging)

    https://www.youtube.com/watch?v=wRco4tGXrzw

- This project proposes a terrestrial vehicle driven by propellers that can also be converted into a quadcopter

    https://roboticworx.substack.com/p/build-a-rc-car-that-can-fly-part

- Quite understandable and complete book on underwater robotics

    Gianluca Antonelli, *Underwater Robots*, 2018, Springer

Selected References on Differential Wheeled Robots and Manipulator Arms

- Classics of manipulator robotics

    Robot Dynamics and Control, Spong, 2004

    Robotics, Vision and Control, Corke, 2017, Springer

    Control of Robot Manipulators in Joint Space, Kelly et al, 2005, Springer

    Robotics: Modelling, Planning and Control, Siciliano et al, 2010, Springer

- Peter Corke's massive online course

    https://robotacademy.net.au

- Classics of mobile and wheeled robotics

    What's left of Magnus Egerstedt's MOOC

    https://www.youtube.com/watch?v=aSwCMK96NOw&list=PLp8ijpvp8iCvFDYdcXqqYU5Ibl_aOqwjr

    Introduction to Autonomous Mobile Robots, Siegwart et al, 2011

    Structural properties and classification of kinematic and dynamic models of wheeled mobile robots, Campion et al, 1996

- Vehicles in general equipped with arm manipulators

    Vehicle-Manipulator Systems, Pal Johan From et al, 2014

Appendices

These appendices contain a couple of projects with detailed explanations but without code, leaving the latter as an exercise for the reader.

The robots explained here are the Zeppelin and its variants: the hovercraft, the propeller-driven car, the robotic boat, a basic submarine, a differential car, and the same differential configuration car with a manipulator arm on board.

Finally, a couple of interesting topics are addressed, one with the intention of explaining how to use more than one analog sensor on a device with few analog ports, such as the Pixhawk, and at least three ways to connect elements to the autopilot's input and output ports.

Differential Zeppelin and Variants (Additional Prototype Described Without Code As an Exercise for the Reader)

Description and applications of the Zeppelin

The zeppelin is a truly old vehicle, but beyond its age, its relevance lies in its applications on a micro scale or educational level.

In some way, we consider it the natural extension of the differential wheeled robot to aeronautical applications. The zeppelin described in this book is a differential vehicle with propellers, whose hovering is not controlled or active through actuators like servos or motors (at least not initially). Its hovering is passive and due to the use of gases lighter than air, on the other hand its planar mobility is granted by the differential combination of the propellers.

Among other things, we consider it a challenge because it is a system that only admits miniaturized and lightweight components. We also affirm that its design constitutes a step toward migrating to aquatic vehicles or more complicated active hovering/buoyancy vehicles.

Although its current use is more relegated to projecting spectacular ads at sports events, we think that due to the previous elements, it is a good platform for learning robotic design and using ArduPilot libraries.

Thus, for the purposes of this text, we will indicate that zeppelins have three basic elements that make them up: the passive hovering element, the differential planar mobility component, and an ultra-light structure. Regarding the latter, and similar to the quadcopters analyzed in previous chapters, we consider that the biggest challenge is the energy density of the batteries, which have little operational time compared to their own weight.

Regarding buoyancy/hovering, we will indicate that although the use of hot air or hydrogen is viable, given the degree of risk they represent, in this text, we opt for the use of helium gas, which is an inert and harmless gas, except for its intentional inhalation.

For more details, including its extensive mathematical models and more applications and control modes, we recommend reading the section on selected references in this book.

In the case of this appendix, we propose to the reader the realization of a differential zeppelin, which can be scaled or modified for an aquatic vehicle. To simplify the design, this zeppelin will control only its planar XY position, and the altitude will be exclusively fixed and granted by helium balloons.

The interesting thing about this project is the trade-off between weight and functionality.

Components and knowledge to build a toy-scale zeppelin
Mechanics

Materials and Tools:

- As many balloons as needed with an 11 size or superior
- Party helium tanks, as many as needed
- A lightweight structure to hold the electronics and mini Pixhawk, it can be 3D printed, cardboard, made of wooden sticks, etc.
- An element to fix the previous structure to the balloons, such as tape, glue, etc.
- If not using balloons, a toy car with low-friction wheels can be used.
- A scale capable of measuring from grams to hundreds of them, to test and reduce the weight to be lifted by the helium, including the balloons themselves
- The necessary pliers and screwdrivers

Prior Knowledge:

- Mini machining techniques

Electronics

Materials and Tools:

- Lightweight versions of motor drivers such as ESCs or H-bridges
- Two small BLDC or brushed motors with symmetrical propellers, preferably with four wide blades each propeller
- Glue, since this kind of propellers only have holes to fit onto the motors without a securing mechanism like a screw thread, they are usually adhered.

APPENDICES

- Remote control with PPM receiver, the last one as lightweight as possible
- Multimeter and oscilloscope if necessary
- Soldering iron with solder wire

Prior Knowledge:

- Basic reading of datasheets and electrical diagrams
- Wiring and soldering, given the size of the components, feasibly SMD

Programming
Materials and Tools:

- ArduPilot libraries and Mission Planner interface previously installed on a computer
- A compatible cable between the computer's USB port and the Mini Pixhawk

Prior Knowledge:

- Motor commands
- Radiocontrol commands

Control
Materials and Tools:

- Mini Pixhawk
- GPS for the Mini Pixhawk

Prior Knowledge:

- Basic logical control principles, such as those used in line followers, can be applied here, including forward, stop, and turning motions based on RC inputs.

Mechanical analysis:

For this case, mechanics is the most relevant part of the device, due to the property of helium to lift one gram per liter of volume.

The mechanics can be divided into the following sections:

- Floating mode:

Regarding helium, some guidelines for its use are the following:

1. Firstly, unlike other gases lighter than air, such as hydrogen, helium is not flammable. On the contrary, it can be found in party accessories. Its only risk is ingestion, as it displaces oxygen in the lungs.

2. It is somewhat expensive, approximately 70 dollars for a small tank.

3. Helium is the second lightest element in the periodic table, so it is also highly volatile. Once outside the tank and in the balloons, it can be used for at most 8 hours.

4. It is recommended to use it indoors with regular plastic balloons. With metalized balloons, it is viable to use it outdoors, as the sun does not pop them as easily. However, you must deal with wind and the greater weight of metalized balloons.

5. Finally, there are different qualities of helium, so it is recommended that you buy helium for balloons and not industrial helium.

APPENDICES

The next step is to recommend the type of balloons to be used. As previously mentioned, a first approach is indoor flotation due to issues like wind, dust, or direct solar incidence. Thus, latex balloons are sufficient. For reference, see Figure A-1, and remember that the weight to be lifted must include the balloon's own weight.

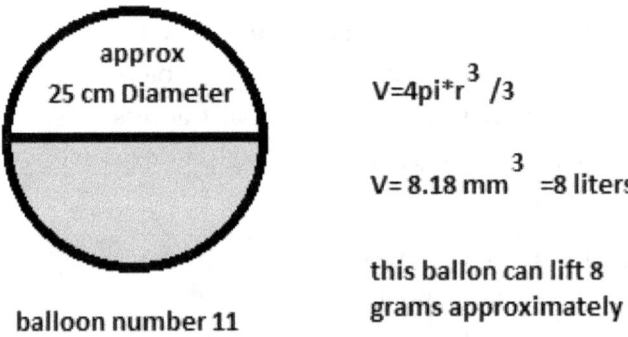

Figure A-1. *A reference for calculating the amount of liters of helium in a balloon of a given radius*

- Ultralight and strong structure

    In this case, there are several options:

    1. A single very large balloon or a pair of them from which a small basket hangs, similar to a hot air balloon.
    2. Several small balloons in a cluster.
    3. Several small balloons inside a plastic net.
    4. One or several balloons contained within a lightweight structure made of wire, cardboard, or 3D printing.

5. A lightweight structure, such as a headband, attached to the balloon using double-sided tape.

6. Components directly glued to each other and then to the balloon.

- Planar propulsion mode: This can be achieved using either BLDC (Brushless DC) or Brushed motors in combination with small propellers.

Electronic analysis:

In the electronics, there are four set of components. Given that this is a lightweight vehicle, all components must be lightweight versions of those typically used, as follows:

- Power: In this case, the driver to be used is either a brushed motor driver or a mini ESC.

- Processing and control: In this case, a MiniPix is preferred or an Arduino Nano if you want to use brushed motors.

- Control: In order to reduce the weight of a large number of connections, a PPM (Pulse Position Modulation) remote control receiver is ideal; this device contains all joystick and button signals from the transmitter into a single channel.

- Energy: Mini battery with charger.

Control analysis:

To simplify things, this project is presented introductory as a manual mode, following the logic described in Table A-1.

APPENDICES

Table A-1. *Zeppelin flight control logic*

Remote control	Motor1	Motor2	Operating Mode
Joystick or Button 1	On	On, and running at the same speed as Motor 1	Zeppelin moving forward in a straight line
Joystick or Button 2	On	Off	Turn left
Joystick or Button 3	Off	On	Turn right
Joystick or Button 4	Off	Off	Zeppelin stationary

Programming Analysis:

For the case of the extensive code, this will be left to the reader as an exercise, but it is advisable to consider at least two code blocks already explained in this book:

- The remote control reading, with the purpose of activating at least four behaviors: one where the vehicle moves exclusively forward with its motors sharing the same speed, one where the vehicle rotates to the left having one motor stopped or slower than the other, one where it turns to the right with the same behavior as before but applied to the opposite motor, and finally one for stopping.

- The writing to BLDC or DC brushed motors as explained here and in our previous book *Advanced Robotic Vehicles Programming*.

Staggered design

In this case, a staggered design of 4 or 5 stages prior to the zeppelin is proposed; see Figure A-2, these are

1. Differential hovercraft with propeller propulsion
2. Differential car with propeller propulsion
3. Differential zeppelin with car support for carrying slightly heavier objects
4. Differential zeppelin with all its components floating and following a planar control
5. Zeppelin with takeoff and landing included

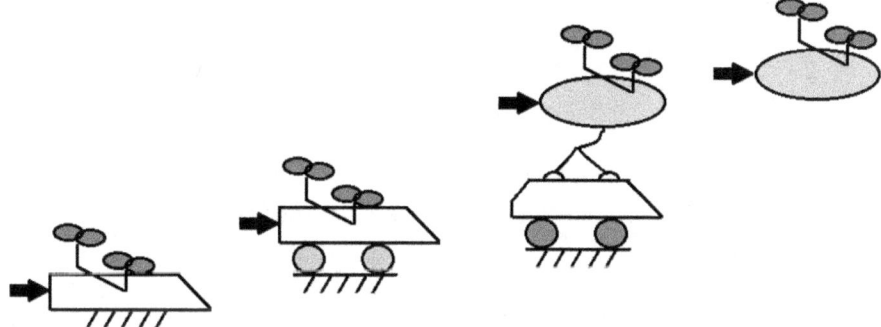

Figure A-2. *A zeppelin design seen as the staggered variant of other mobile robots*

Stages 1 and 2 are interchangeable since the hovercraft sometimes presents more difficulties than using wheels because of friction.

In the hovercraft case, a unicel structure or a previously polished surface is recommended.

For the propeller-driven car, any toy car with a van structure can serve while having low friction on their wheels.

APPENDICES

The heaviest part of the zeppelin is the battery, so a first attempt is similar to a hospital IV pole, i.e., carrying the battery in a car and everything else lifted by the helium balloons.

After that, and once enough balloons are obtained or a very light battery is available, the next process is the entire vehicle floating.

Finally, an improvement that goes beyond the basic design of this appendix is to include motorized and autonomous takeoff and landing, which can be achieved with a vectorizer, but keep in mind that this represents more dead weight.

Zeppelin's building and testing

First, here you have some possible upgrades:

1. Test with various types of metallic or plastic balloons.
2. Test with different configurations, such as clusters, lines, parallel balloons, etc.
3. Test with balloons of different sizes and shapes, including projectile-shaped ones to improve aerodynamics.
4. Attempt to add vectorizers for elevation and landing.
5. If feasible, attempt outdoor flight.
6. The heaviest part is usually the battery; look for very thin and ultralight batteries.

Regarding verifications:

1. To prevent the balloons from lifting away the lighter components, anchor them until use.
2. Preferably use helium balloons within a range of 1 to 3 hours before the test, since they start to deflate.

3. Verify that the remote control is synchronized with the autopilot.

4. Verify that the propellers do not touch the balloons.

5. Verify that the structure can be lifted by the balloons.

6. Before flight, test that the system works at least on a hovercraft or a toy-car with low friction wheels, any of the two options driven by propellers.

Finally, the assembly and testing:

A

1. Join the components to the balloons and avoid the propellers rubbing against the balloons.

2. Release the anchor once the battery or heavier components are placed, which theoretically should keep the balloons at a reasonable height.

B

1. Load the codes and remember to have a physical arming of the motors and one by code through the remote control.

2. Verify the desired operation modes.

3. Verify the adequate battery level.

4. Once the test flight is completed, re-anchor the vehicle for disassembly; if this is done several hours later, there is also a risk that the balloons will deflate and the components and motors will fall and get damaged.

APPENDICES

Related projects

We know that the limit is imagination, but the zeppelin described in this book can lead to two paths:

- The first one focused on a conventional boat whose propulsion is based on propellers.

- The second one an underwater and steerable vehicle or simply a submarine.

This is shown in Figure A-3.

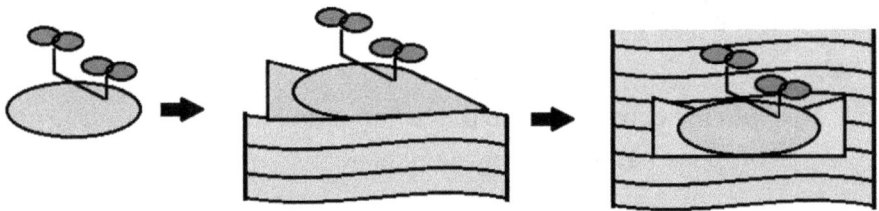

Figure A-3. *Other mobile robots seen as more complex variants of the zeppelin (a robotic boat and a submarine)*

Concerning the boat, the operation remains the same as in the zeppelin, a passive floating vehicle controlled by differential propellers but now the environment is water and keeping the vehicle afloat is not as complicated as in the zeppelin's case.

As for the submarine, the operation becomes more complex; here the floatability is not passive but adjustable, requiring a dive and ascent system. A good example is illustrated in Figure A-4.

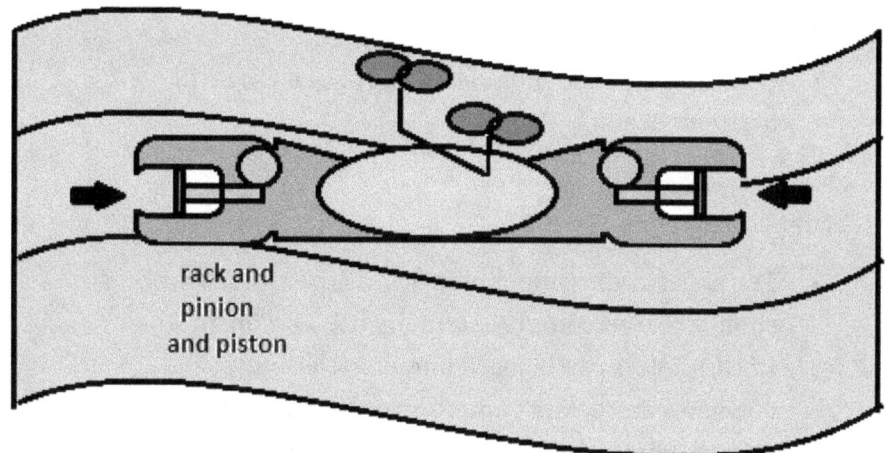

Figure A-4. *A usual mechanism for submarine immersion and emergence (based on symmetric pistons)*

In this way, the submarine inherits the problems of the zeppelin and also requires a sinking system.

In the best of cases, the proposed sinking system based on simultaneous counter-movement similar to the operation of a drawing compass also presents a differential mode that prevents autorotation in the liquid and, on the other hand, demands the synchronized action of two servos, stepper motors, or DC motors. To deal with these motors, the reader can refer to our previous book, *Advanced Robotic Vehicles Programming*.

List of materials and minimum knowledge required to operate a robotic boat

Mechanics

Materials and tools

- A pair of submersible propellers
- A floating and waterproof structure, which can be made of fiberglass or any plastic mold
- Gaskets or some hermetic sealing element to protect the electronics

APPENDICES

Prior knowledge

- Possibly fiberglass manufacturing or placement of hermetic seals

Electronics
Materials and tools

- The same as the zeppelin; in the case of motors, they should be waterproof or submersible. As a tip, most BLDC motors can be used immersed as long as the terminals are isolated and the varnish covers the internal wires, although performance may be slightly reduced. ESCs must not be submerged and must be protected from water.

- Possibly, a signal repeater to deal with water interference for long-range operations

- Motors operating in water may require more thrust

Prior knowledge

- The same as the zeppelin

Programming
Materials and tools

- The same as the zeppelin

Prior knowledge

- The same as the zeppelin

Control
Materials and tools

- The same as the zeppelin

Prior knowledge

- While working in water, it is likely that the controllers will need to be retuned

List of materials and minimum knowledge required to operate a robotic submarine

Mechanics

Materials and tools

- An active sinking system, preferably with symmetric water access such as pistons or syringes controlled by a compass-like mechanism based on anti-symmetric screws or pinions and racks
- A submersible and waterproof structure, depending on the desired depth; pressure-resistant

Prior knowledge

- Manufacturing or assembly of submersible structures
- Assembly of anti-symmetric motorized structures to prevent autorotation

Electronics

Materials and tools

- The same as the zeppelin
- Consider making or purchasing an underwater communication system for transmitting and receiving commands
- The electronic components, except possibly motors (if BLDC), must be adequately waterproofed

Prior knowledge

- Possibly, submersible data communication systems

APPENDICES

Programming
Materials and tools

- The same as the zeppelin

Prior knowledge

- At the programming level, the same as the zeppelin, and possibly data filtering and handling of signal delays due to the medium (water)

Control
Materials and tools

- The same as the zeppelin

Prior knowledge

- In this case, 6D motion control, i.e., three rotations and three translations, relatively similar to a quadcopter but in a thicker medium than air. There is already abundant literature on control of mini-submersible vehicles.

Differential Wheeled Vehicle and Variant Projects (Additional Prototype Described Without Code As an Exercise for the Reader)

Description and Components
In the case of a wheeled robot, which for our example is a car with two motors and rear wheels with independent traction and differential displacement, and front support wheels without traction.

The drawing of its structure and operation is shown in Figure A-5:

APPENDICES

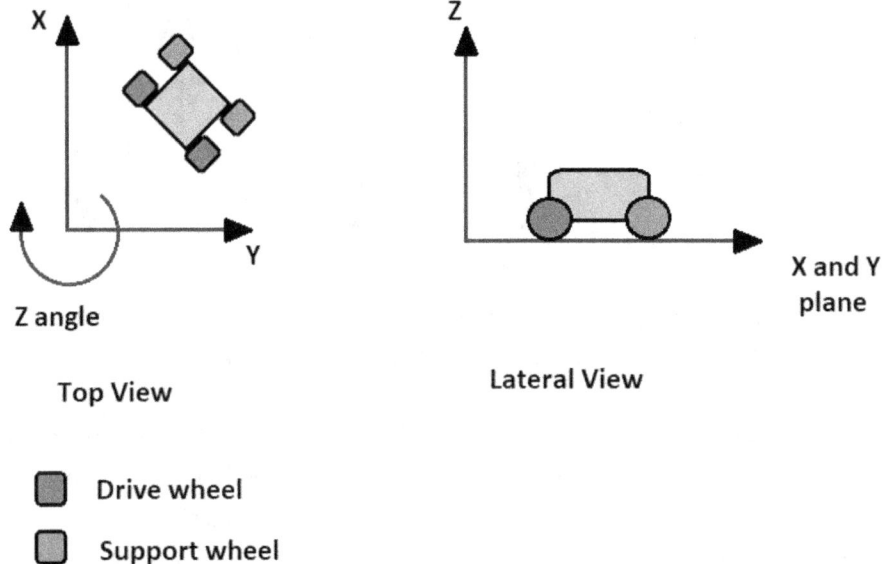

Figure A-5. *Another differential robot that, unlike the one exemplified in the initial pages of this book, has two support wheels*

To achieve this, there are two paths, see Figure A-6:

The first assumes that the vehicle's motors are BLDC type; in this case, the motors can be connected directly to the Pixhawk as if it were a quadcopter, but keep in mind that now the system obeys the allocation or propulsion matrix shown.

The second assumes that the motors are not BLDC, but standard DC; in this case, it's convenient to use Arduinos or some other means of converting PWM RC signals from the Pixhawk's motor outputs to PWM duty cycles suitable for brushed motors.

APPENDICES

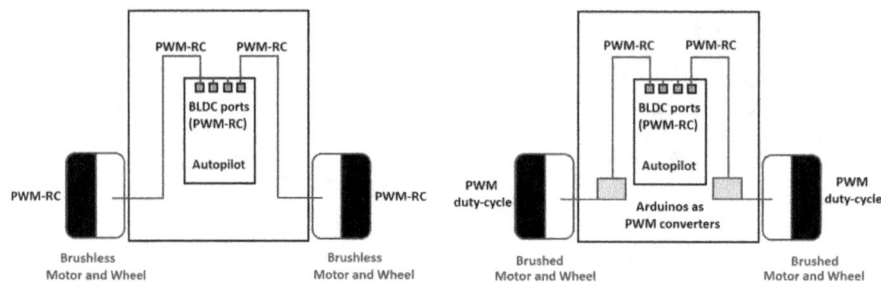

Figure A-6. *Description on how to use BLDC motors or brushed torque motors with Pixhawk for wheeled-robot applications*

In the case of Arduino, this conversion requires the pulseIn command and a mapping that normally goes from the 1000–2000 PWM-RC range to the 0–255 PWM duty cycle mode; details on this conversion and a complete example can be seen in our previous book, *Advanced Robotic Vehicles Programming*.

The biggest issue using Arduinos as PWM links is that, depending on the model, it's feasible to use one Arduino per motor given its pulse reading limitations.

For more details on this robot, including extensive mathematical models and more applications and control modes, we recommend reading the selected references section of this book.

List of materials and minimum knowledge required to operate a differential wheeled vehicle

Mechanics

Materials and Tools:

- A structure or chassis with characteristics dependent on the task to be performed, such as dustproof, splashproof, impact-resistant, etc.

APPENDICES

- Motors with wheels, preferably a gearmotor system; if encoders are used, they won't be utilized by the autopilot's position sensors or they will be used as sensor fusion. Due to the limited GPIO ports, the use or non-use of encoders must be considered.
- If using BLDCs, they must be torque-based (with gearbox) rather than speed-based.
- Depending on the application, a damping or anti-slip system may be necessary.
- A set of pliers, wrenches, and screwdrivers suitable for the vehicle's size is recommended.

Prior Knowledge:

- Mobile robo t design, at least for wheeled robots.

Electronics

Materials and Tools:

- A suitable power stage or driver for the motors used.
- A remote control with at least two DOF for forward and rotation, plus auxiliary levers or buttons (unlike quadcopters, which require one forward and three rotations).
- A power supply, which in this case can be a heavier battery, but consider that it reduces the vehicle's speed.

Prior Knowledge:

- Signal filtering.
- High-range transmission algorithms and equipment (depending on the application).
- Possibly some SLAM methodology.

APPENDICES

Programming

Materials and Tools:

- ArduPilot libraries.
- Pixhawk controller board.

Prior Knowledge:

- Object-Oriented Programming (OOP) style is highly desirable.

Control

Materials and Tools:

- Understanding of basic logical and analytical controllers.

Prior Knowledge:

- Depending on the application and wheel type, control can be kinematic or dynamic; kinematic control is more common, but dynamic control has its own set of applications. Recommended readings include Roland Siegwart's books and the article by Campion, which are listed in the references section of this book.

Mechanical analysis

The mechanical case contemplates three components:

- Chassis
- Wheels
- Terrain

In the case of the chassis, the usual approach is a symmetric, resistant, and lightweight structure. Symmetry is desired to have a homologous reference point for placing position and orientation sensors, similar to the quadcopter case at least for linear flight modes (not acrobatic or high-speed). Resistance is desired because wheeled robots are typically intended to carry loads or withstand terrain impacts (assuming it's not smooth or polished ground). Another way to address resistance without compromising the chassis weight is through a suspension system, usually based on shock absorbers. On the other hand, a lightweight structure is needed for power source durability or to avoid more weight if the vehicle is load-carrying.

Regarding the terrain, it dictates whether control is designed purely at a kinematic level or includes dynamic effects, which become noticeable and non-negligible with holes, rocks, slopes, mud, irregular distributions, etc.

Finally, the wheel represents another significant part that alters the degree and mobility capabilities of the vehicle. This includes the type of wheels (spherical, standard, mecanum, eccentric, etc.), their quantity, distribution (in-line, radial, parallel, combined, etc.), whether they are support or drive wheels, the shape of their footprint, their size in terms of radius and width relative to each other, and even whether they have vulcanization or not.

A simpler configuration can also be used, two small parallel differential wheels with a traction motor on each one and at least one front support wheel (preferably spherical), see Figure A-7.

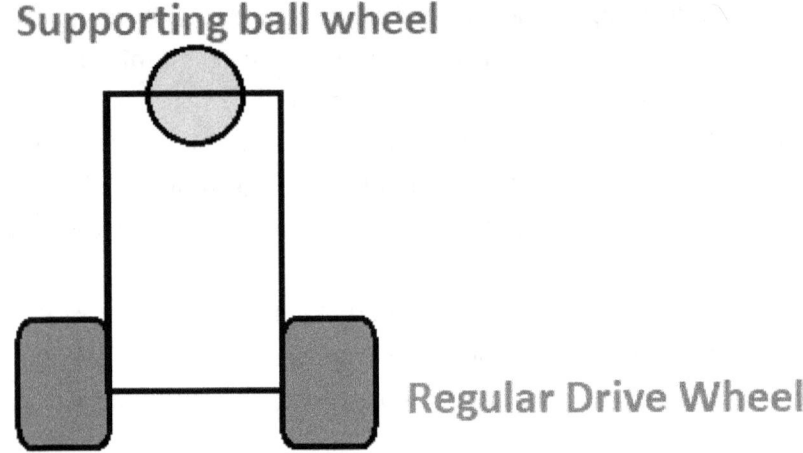

Figure A-7. *Another viable configuration of a differential robot, even available in kits*

Electronic analysis

Regarding electronics, there are many configurations for actuators, sensors, communication equipment, and power sources.

Concerning sensors, two paths are common, see Figure A-8.

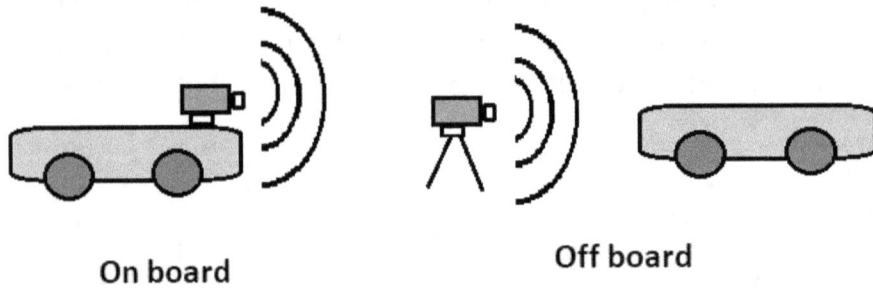

Figure A-8. *Basic configurations for mobile robot sensing (including aerial robots)*

On-board

This case can be complex, as it involves some type of SLAM or global measurement. Standard autopilots have this type of measurement but lack visual processing capabilities. Therefore, a companion computer is usually used to perform localization and visual or radar identification tasks in coordination with the autopilot.

External

This case is resolved through triangulation, either using cameras or radars and artificial vision or radio signals. Triangulation requires sending and receiving data from the autopilot to a fixed base or other mobile robots.

Regarding actuators, most robotic applications use DC motors, either brushless or brushed with a gearbox.

Concerning communication equipment:

Short- or long-range topologies are common, including Wi-Fi, Bluetooth, or LoRa, among the most well-known. However, it's convenient for the autopilot (at least for Pixhawk or others compatible with ArduPilot libraries) that these topologies have serial communication channels.

Their use is directly embedded to sending and receiving data from actuators and sensors to external bases, other mobile robots, a user, etc.

Typically, communication equipment and actuators are the components that consume the most energy in mobile robots.

Finally, the power devices:

In the case of wheeled robots, using light or heavy batteries is viable. We've already mentioned that the chassis should be lightweight, but since it doesn't fly, weight isn't a critical component as in the aerial vehicles case. Using heavier batteries assumes they'll last longer, so it's a trade-off between weight and durability. There are also versions for tunnels or mine exploration based on tethered technologies.

APPENDICES

Regarding the power stage that communicates the power source and actuators with the computer (e.g., the autopilot), drivers and controllers are available. Drivers are simple open-loop signal amplification stages, while controllers have feedback and are generally 10 to 1000 times more expensive than drivers, as they ensure a stable motor speed despite varying conditions.

Control Analysis

Depending on whether automation or automatization is desired, the designer must know the basics of both mathematical and intelligent control. The latter, as mentioned earlier, is based on action tables or truth tables or inference rules, while the arithmetic mode is an error equation that is modified by changing the desired and measured values and a set of gains.

The management of times and delays is not as critical as it is in an aircraft, so these robots can be controlled with processors of lower capabilities.

Programming analysis

This part requires the use of communication ports, especially serial transmission technologies, as well as the combined use of an autopilot and a companion computer.

If this is the case, it's common to use a Raspberry environment controlling the operation modes of the ArduPilot software.

Typically, tasks with higher processing or massive data requirements like image processing are reserved for the companion computer, while the autopilot exclusively handles vehicle control.

Given the different programming environments, it's desirable for the designer to master at least two programming languages (C++ and Python) and an interface environment (usually based on Linux).

Assembly and testing

Potential modifications

1. Depending on the terrain, it's viable to perform a vulcanization treatment on the tires.

2. Usually, wheels are attached to motor shafts with the help of set screws. However, both motor shafts and wheel hubs are cylindrical, which can lead to the wheel coming loose over time. Using retainer rings or flat-shaped connections (D-shaped wheel hubs and motor shafts) can be a solution.

3. In other variants, the wheel and shaft are coupled using a screw and thread. However, since this connection is typically made at the center of the shaft, it can come loose over time. Preferably, use multi-point eccentric connections around the main shaft, similar to those in cars. Note that points 2 and 3 can be complementary to this point for additional fixing.

4. It's common to compensate for vibrations with shock absorbers or added mass. The most common approach is the first one.

5. Depending on whether the application requires speed or load capacity, the chassis can be designed to be close to the ground or elevated. Similarly, an aerodynamic or non-aerodynamic structure can be preferred.

6. An alternative steering technique can be used, such as a steering wheel with rack-and-pinion gear, instead of the differential mode of two wheels.

APPENDICES

7. Differential mode can be purely rotational (one wheel stationary and the other rotating) or rotating-translational (one wheel moving faster than the other, both in motion).

8. In many cases, it's preferred not to connect the motor shaft directly to the wheel. Instead, a fusible mechanism like a belt or a universal joint can be used as an intermediary to protect the motor (which can be expensive) from direct impacts and shaft deformations.

Verifications

1. Check that the remote control synchronizes with the autopilot and the desired vehicle movements.

2. Activate the wheels in a floating position (without touching the ground) at their maximum speed and ensure they do not come off or detach from the motors.

3. Verify or establish the vehicle's limits or operating conditions (maximum slope, maximum curvature radius, minimum grip conditions on smooth or wet surfaces or maximum movement conditions on diverse terrain, maximum towing and payload, etc.).

4. Verify that the vehicle's center of mass is as symmetrical as possible with respect to the chassis.

5. Ensure that electrical or electronic components are at an adequate height and within the chassis, such that they are isolated from dust or water.

Assembly and testing

A

1. Assemble the chassis and distribute the weight of the components symmetrically if possible.
2. Place and tighten the tires and wheels properly.
3. Place the sensors as close as possible to the center of the vehicle.

B

1. Load the codes; here it is not necessary to physically arm the motors or test one by one with the remote control, given that in most cases the wheels, unlike propellers, are not sharp, but it's recommended to avoid any issues.
2. Verify the desired operation modes.
3. Verify the battery level.

Derivative project: Robotic arm variant of the differential terrestrial vehicle

In this case, a robotic arm mounted on the chassis of the car will be used.

Three versions are indicated below; in all of them, the robot's sensors are read by one or more Arduinos and then are sent to the autopilot.

In the first version, it is assumed that both the mobile and the arm have BLDC motors and are directly operated from the Pixhawk's outputs (a maximum of 8 plus 4 auxiliary outputs), see Figure A-9.

APPENDICES

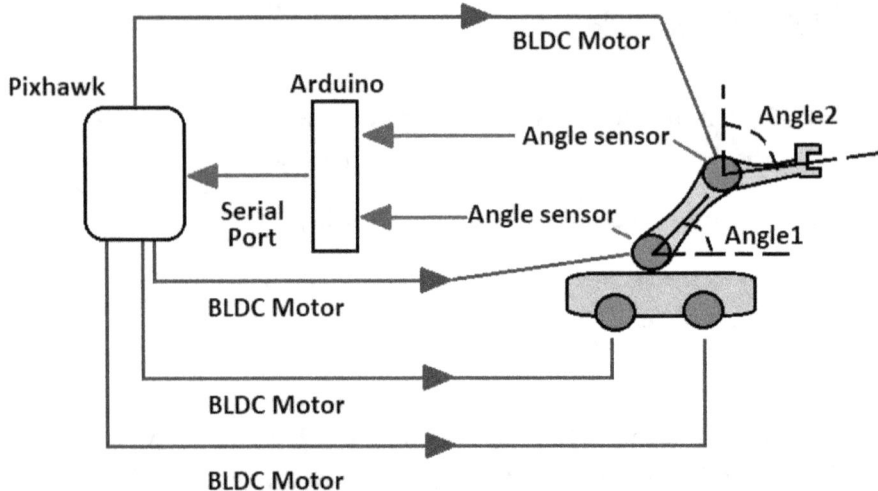

Figure A-9. *A first suggested configuration for using a manipulator on a mobile robot with Pixhawk*

In the second case, it is assumed that the mobile or the robotic manipulator have some BLDC and other kind of motors, see Figure A-10. In this case, the signals from the BLDC outputs of the autopilot are sent to one or more Arduinos to transform them from PWM RC to the type of signal used by the motors, for example, a PWM duty cycle.

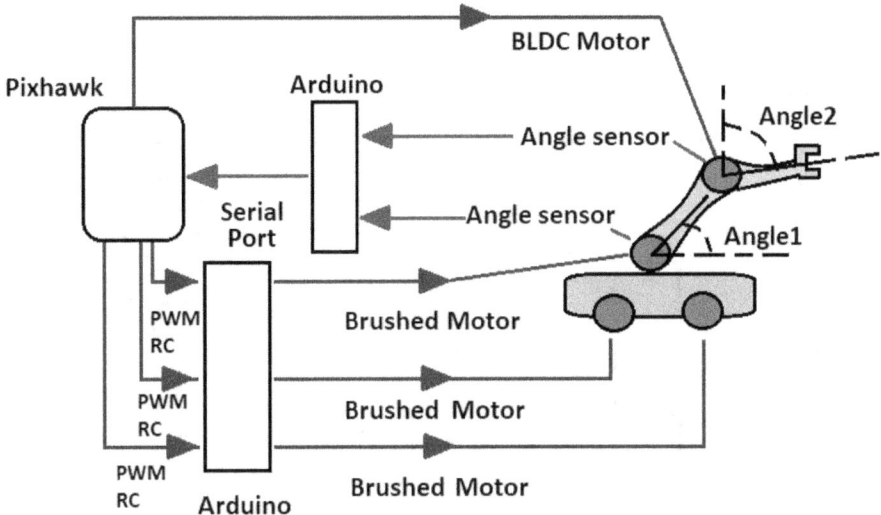

Figure A-10. *A second suggested configuration for using a manipulator on a mobile robot with Pixhawk*

Finally, it is assumed that neither the mobile nor the manipulator have a single BLDC motor, but the control signals are sent through the serial port of the autopilot to the Arduino, requiring a duplex mode of writing and reading, see Figure A-11. Considering that the serial port is already used to read the manipulator's sensors, this last mode of operation is the one that can cause a bottleneck between the different signals and make the processes slow or inefficient. However, bearing in mind that the speed of the mobile and the manipulator are generally low compared to signal processing, it is feasible that even with delays, it will work.

APPENDICES

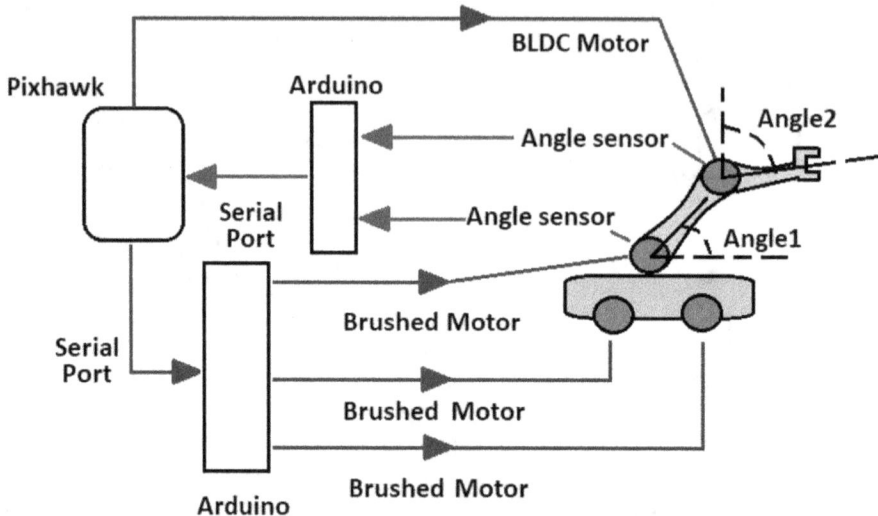

Figure A-11. *A third suggested configuration for using a manipulator on a mobile robot with Pixhawk (a two-way serial communication)*

As a further note, in addition to the UART mode described here, the Pixhawk has other more efficient serial communication modes, such as CAN. If this is the option, we recommend the web documentation.

How to Use More Than One Analog Sensor with a Single Analog Port

As an alternative to the three previous ways, if one tries to use one of the three analog ports of the Pixhawk as an input for several analog sensors, i.e., without using the serial port, a viable solution is through time-division multiplexing by using as many GPIO outputs as the Pixhawk or your favorite autopilot has available.

APPENDICES

Note This assumes that the Pixhawk allows simultaneous use of auxiliary GPIO ports with PWM motor outputs, which in some versions of ArduPilot is unstable.

To achieve this, the following connections must be made (indicated in color code to avoid crossed lines), see Figure A-12.

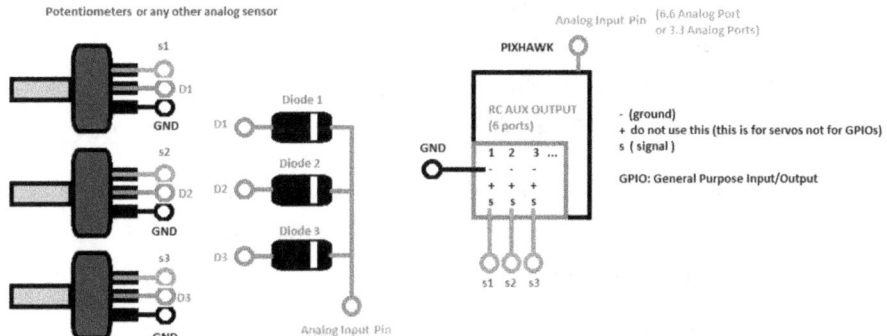

Figure A-12. *How to use more than one analog sensor through multiplexing and without other programmable devices*

The algorithm is as follows:

1. Consider a maximum of up to six digital GPIO outputs (the limit of a standard Pixhawk); in the case of the figure, they are 3. Also, design the tasks that will change the following steps of the algorithm, as well as their duration in the scheduler.

2. Each output will be activated one after the other (the logic 1 varies between autopilots from 3.3 to 5V), controlled by time or event-based, like a traffic light; those outputs that are not activated will be set to 0 (electrical value equivalent to GND).

393

APPENDICES

3. When the output is activated, it will energize the corresponding potentiometer (or analog sensor), and consequently, the internal voltage divider will send its value. This value goes to a single channel in the autopilot (the designer will determine whether it is to the input pin of the 6.6V analog port or one of the two input pins of the 3.3V analog port).

4. If the time during which the corresponding GPIO output is activated has not yet ended, then the data from the potentiometer (analog sensor) linked to that output will be stored.

5. Steps 2 to 4 are repeated until the system is de-energized or until some condition is activated to stop the analog port reading.

A more extensive explanation of this technique can be found at:

https://www.youtube.com/watch?v=QWOYcxN3pao

Note In this case, it is recommended to use the scheduler to determine how fast this "traffic light" GPIO tasks should be done, which consequently manages which analog sensor is read or not. In the case of the previous link, the author solves it with pauses (a lot of delays), which is inadequate for the autopilot.

Finally, Figure A-13 shows some of the aforementioned projects, currently being developed by our students and which will be described soon in the second part of this book which is now in preparation. Until next time!

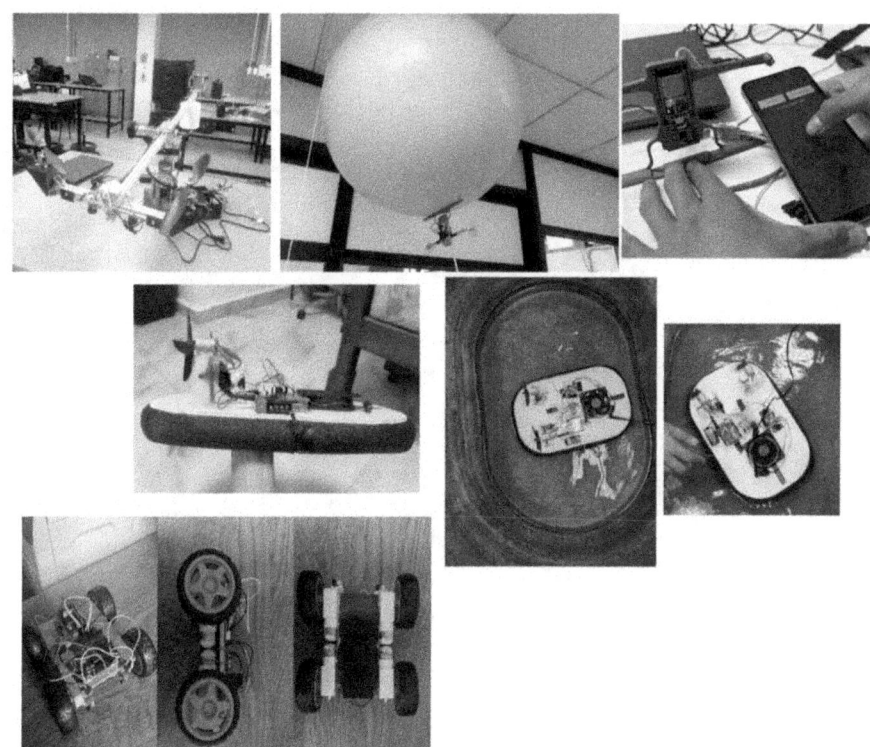

Figure A-13. *Future projects for the second part of this book*

Glossary

OOP
Object-Oriented Programming, one of several programming standards focused on arranging independent and intercommunicating code segments called modules.

IMU
Inertial Measurement Unit, an electronic sensor capable of measuring angular and translational positions.

PD
Proportional Derivative controller.

PID
Proportional Integral Derivative control.

GPS
Global Positioning System, a satellite-based system for obtaining absolute translational measurements relative to the Earth.

GUI
Graphic User Interface, a generally user-friendly and simplified graphical interface to get something started, for example, Mission Planner is a GUI for unmanned vehicles.

SDK
Software Development Kit, an environment that includes a coding interface and specialized programming libraries, for example, ArduPilot libraries.

GLOSSARY

Autopilot

A specialized processor with communication ports, sensors, inputs, and outputs usable for controlling unmanned vehicles.

ESC

Electronic Speed Control, an electronic device to control the speed of a motor, usually BLDC; simply a speed controller.

BLDC

Brushless Direct Current motor, a motor without brushes.

Index

A

Aeropendulum, 109, 124, 125, 155, 169, 279
   analog tests, 204–229
   ArduPilot libraries, 244–270
   assembly and component, 193–201
   autopilot restoring, 231–234
   code analysis, 240–244
   connections and code, 173
   connectors, 204–229
   control analysis, 238–240
   description and applications, 183–189
   electrical and electronic analysis, 200–204
   electronics, 191, 192
   ESCOM students, 188
   flowchart, 239
   mechanical analysis, 232–238
   mechanics, 190
   in operation, 265
   operational simplicity, 148
   programming, 192
   propellers, 173
   prototypes, 173
   quadcopter without propellers, 175–179
   real-time tests, 204–229
   rototypes, 172
   selected references, 354–356
   tests, 109
   two-degree-of-freedom, 185
   UserCode.cpp file, 246–248
   without propellers, 173, 174
Allen screws, 122
Allocation, 148, 150, 151, 156
Analog port test codes, 211–215, 392–395
Analytical control, 137, 138
Anchored quadcopter, 272, 273
Angular performance, 309
Angular velocity performance, 348
APM_config.h file, 93
Arduino code analysis, 240–244
Arduino libraries, programming modes, 5
Arduinos, 158, 227, 231, 379, 380
ArduPilot libraries, 33, 63, 108, 364
   activation and deactivation, 93, 94
   advantages and disadvantages, 9, 10

INDEX

ArduPilot libraries (*cont.*)
    assembly and testing, 244–270, 322–350
    code analysis, 284–292
    code compilation, 75–88
    commands, 96–104
    description, 29–32
    design and scope, 32–36
    downloading process, 66–72
    features, 96–104
    files modulation, 29–32
    GitHub folder, 78
    installing, 73–79
    Mission Planner, 41–59
    OOP features, 10, 11
    OOP work format, 12–29
    programming modes, 5
    robots, 34–36
    selected references, 353, 354
    software project, 4
    time management, 170–172
    visualization, 95
Autopilots, 41, 108, 159–162, 204
    aeropendulum, 231–234
    configuration, 266–269
    CONNECT button, 89
    description, 105
    firmware recovery, 232
    installation, 64–93
    Mission Planner, 88
    voltage verification, 211
Autorotation, 375
Axis of rotation, 232

B

Ball bearing, 115
Ball joint, 278, 285, 293–298
Battery chargers, 133, 134
Battery Eliminator Circuit (BEC), 286
Bearings, 114–116
BEC, *see* Battery Eliminator Circuit (BEC)
Bias, 154
BLDC motor, 238
Boat, 359, 360
Brushed DC motors, 134, 135
Brushless motors, 125, 126

C

Carbon fiber, 118, 119
Casings, 123
Clamping elements, 123, 124
Closed-loop control, 154
Coaxial motor, 244
Code analysis, 284–292, 320–322
Code compilation, 79–87
Commercial balancer, 319
Communication equipment, 385, 386
COM port number, 44
Connect button, 58
Connectors, 131–134, 204–229
Contrarotating brushless motors, 127–129
Controls
    analysis, 238–240

INDEX

differential robot
    concept, 148–150
    direct and indirect
        control, 155–157
    dirty derivative, 157–159
    free-flight quadcopter, 317
    gravity compensation, 154
    hierarchy, 321
    logical and analytical, 137, 138
    PD-type analytical
        control, 142–146
    quadcopter, 276, 282–284
    robustness *vs.*
        adaptability, 145–148
copter.cpp file, 218
Copter folder, 66
copter.h file, 216
Couplings, 111–114
Custom task definition, 216, 217,
    219–221, 224–229
Custom tasks, 219

D

Damped landing gear, 347
DataFlash Logs, 58
Desired values, 157
Differential wheeled robot, 361
    behavior, 149
    closed-and open-loop
        control, 154
    configuration, 151
    definitions, 148
    forward movement, 149
    logical and arithmetic
        controller, 152–154
Differential wheeled vehicle
    assembly and testing, 387–389
    control analysis, 386
    derivative project, 389–392
    electronic analysis, 384–386
    electronics, 381, 382
    manipulator, 390–392
    mechanics, 380, 381
    programming analysis, 386
    PWM duty cycles, 379
    traction, 378
    vehicle's motors, 379
Differential wheel vehicle, 148, 149
Digital GPIO outputs, 393
Dirty derivative, 158
Drone, 114, 280, 319, 323

E

Eclipse, 64, 65, 70, 77, 87, 91
    software interface 1, 91
    software interface 2, 92
    software interface 3, 92
Electronics, 107
    aeropendulum, 191, 192
    batteries/power supplies,
        132, 133
    battery chargers, 133, 134
    brushed DC motors, 134, 135
    brushless motors, 125, 126
    coaxial contrarotating brushless
        motors, 127–129

INDEX

Electronics (*cont.*)
    differential wheeled vehicle, 381, 382
    electronic speed controllers, 128, 129
    free-flight quadcopter, 316, 317
    insulation and connectors, 131–134
    motor drivers, 135, 136
    quadcopter, 275, 276
    remote control, 136, 137
    zeppelin, 365, 366, 376, 377
Electronic speed controllers (ESCs), 128, 129
EMAX PM1806, 235
ESC cables, 197, 246
ESCs, *see* Electronic speed controllers (ESCs)
Execution policy, 75

F

Filtered graph, 311
Fixed propellers, 314
Floating mode, 367, 368
Free-flight quadcopter, 313, 314, 358, 359
    applications and derivative, 314
    assembly and testing, 322–350
    code analysis, 320–322
    control, 317
    control analysis, 320
    description, 314
    electrical and electronic analysis, 318, 319
    electronics, 316, 317
    mathematical models, 316
    mechanical analysis, 318
    mechanics, 316, 317
    operation, 314
    programming, 317 *See also* Quadcopter
Free-flight tests, 109
Free-flight vehicle codes, 301
Frequently modified files, 29, 30

G

Gaskets, 375
Generic modification codes, 162–169
GitHub, 65
GPS sensor, 275
Gravity compensation, 154, 155

H

H-bridge, 136
Helium, 367
"Hello World" extension, 93–95
Hovercraft, 359, 360

I, J, K

Installation process
    ArduPilot libraries, 69–75
    configurations, 64

INDEX

downloading, 66-72
requirements, 64, 65
Install Firmware, 231
Insulation, 131-134

L

Lever arm, 190, 232, 234, 237, 238, 245
Linear flexible couplings, 111, 112
Linefollower.cpp file, 24-26
Linefollower.h file, 23, 24
Line follower robot, 139, 140
LIPO batteries, 132, 133
Lithium battery, 133
Log.cpp file modifications, 251-254, 340-343
Logical controls, 137, 138
and state machines, 138-141
LUA Scripts, 5, 8
Lugs, 122

M

Manipulator arms, 361
Mass, 234
Mathematical approximation techniques, 157
Mathematical operations, 139, 140
Matlab (R) files, 58
Matlab Simulink, 5, 6
MAVLink, 231
Maximum hanging mass, 235
Measured values, 157

Mechanics, 107
aeropendulum, 190
analysis, 232-238
bearings, 114-116
carbon fiber, 118
clamping elements, 123, 124
couplings, 111-114
differential wheeled vehicle, 380, 381
free-flight quadcopter, 316, 317
pillow blocks, 117, 118
quadcopter, 274, 275, 279-282
shafts, 110, 111
specialized fasteners, 121-123
structural profiles, 119-121
supports, 120
zeppelin, 364, 365
Mechatronic components, 39-41
Mechatronic design, 351, 352
Mechatronic design mode, 3
Mechatronic methodology, 36-39
Mission Planner (MP), 5, 7, 11, 41-59, 64, 65, 67, 89, 90, 95, 98, 225
calibrate sensors, 47-51
linkage and uses, 41-59
remote control values, 50, 51
SD card information, 53-59
serial terminal, 45-47
user-defined flight modes, 52-54
Mobile robots, 374
mode.h file modifications, 259-262, 304, 332-336

403

INDEX

mode_rolquad.cpp file, 255–259, 323–335
mode_rolquad.cpp file modifications, 302–304
Modular files, 3
modularity Follower_OOP.ino file, 27–29
modularity LED_OOP.ino file, 17, 18
modularity Leds.h file, 15–17
Molex connector, 208
Motion limiter, 235
Mounted Quadcopter, *see* Quadcopter
MP, *see* Mission Planner (MP)
Multiplexing, 393

N

Nilock, 121
Non-viable operating zone, 237
Norelem ball joint, 293

O

Object-oriented programming (OOP), 183, 270, 323–336
    selected references, 352, 353
    work format, 12–29
Onboard battery, 275, 279, 286, 287
OOP, *see* Object-oriented programming (OOP)
Open-loop control, 154

P

PD-type analytical control, 142–146
Pillow blocks, 117, 118
Pivot rotation, 186, 200, 232, 234, 245
Pixhawk, 64, 265, 353, 354, 392
    analog channel, 215
    autopilot, 314, 316
    description, 205, 207–209
    pendulum's pivot, 269, 270
    pinout, 205
    wire assembly, 208–211
Planar propulsion mode, 369
Planar trajectory, 347
Port number, 214
Potentiometers, 191, 197, 200, 214, 227, 240, 269
    analog port, 229
    analog sensor, 213
    angle measurement, 195
    autopilot, 204
    cables, 246
    counter-movement action, 187
    pivot, 244
    resistance, 201
    sensor, 200
PowerShell, 73, 75
Power sources, 202, 203
Power supply, 244, 381
Predefined cycles, 221
Prerequisites
    initialization, 15

modularity, 20–23
Previous non-functional design, 277, 278
Programming, 108
   aeropendulum, 192
   analysis, 370
   ArduPilot time management, 170–172
   differential wheeled vehicle, 382
   free-flight quadcopter, 317
   generic modification codes, 162–169
   hardware, 159–162
   PseudoSetup, 169
   quadcopter, 276
   signal filtering, 171, 172
   zeppelin, 366
Propeller balancer, 319
Propeller-driven car, 359, 360, 371
Propellers, 124, 125, 314, 316, 318, 320, 323
Propulsion matrix, 150, 151
PseudoSetup, 169

Q

Quadcopter, 99, 100, 102, 109, 172, 314, 356–358
   anchored, 272
   angular performance, 348
   ArduPilot version, 288–292
   assembly, 278, 279
   autonomous flight, 344
   ball joint, 293–298
   code analysis, 284–292
   control, 276
   control analysis, 282–284
   description, 272
   differential effect, 150
   electrical and electronic analysis, 279
   electronics, 275, 276
   materials, tools, and knowledge, 274–277
   mechanical analysis, 279–282
   mechanics, 274, 275
   mounted test stand, 272
   operational code, 271
   orientation and position, 157
   previous non-functional design, 277, 278
   programming, 276
   redesign and results, 292–312
   test stand, 124
   3D rotational structure, 271
   without propellers, 175–179
   See also Aeropendulum
Quadcopters, 364
Quanser, 184

R

RadioLink MiniPix autopilot, 159–161
Radiolink Pixhawk, 204

INDEX

Real time tasks, 217, 218, 220, 221
Real-time tests, 204–229
Redesigning the system, 292–312
Redesign process, 109
Remote control, 136, 137, 323, 381
Remote control reading, 370
Robotic arm variant, 389–392
Robotic boat, 375–378
Robotics book, 33
Robotic submarine, 377, 378
ROS, 6, 11
Rotary sensors, 200, 201

S

Safety screw, 121
SD card information, 54–60
Self-locking screw, 121
Sensors, 19, 42
Serial communication, 221–224
Shafts, 110, 111
Signal filtering, 171, 172
Single analog port, 392–395
Single-propeller
    aeropendulum, 235
Spatial misalignment, 113
Sphericity, 293
Staggered design, 371, 372
Staggered mechatronic
    design, 302
Structural profiles, 119–121
Submarine, 359, 360
Submarine immersion, 375
Symmetrical structure, 282

T

Tethered drone, 301–303
2DOF aerobot, 187
Three-dimensional rotational
    movement, 279
Three rotational mechanisms,
    280, 281
Torques, 311, 350
Trajectory tracking, 2
    63, 346, 347
Translational performance, 310
Turbulences, 185
Two-degree-of-freedom, 185

U

Ultralight and strong structure,
    368, 369
Universal joints, 112, 113
UserCode.cpp file, 94, 217, 219,
    246–248, 337–340
UserCode.cpp file modifications,
    305, 306
UserCode.cpp file second
    modification, 307, 308
User-defined flight
    modes, 53–55
USERHOOK_INIT, 212
USERHOOK_
    MEDIUMLOOP, 212
UserVariables.h file, 250
UserVariables.h file
    modifications, 305

V

Vectorizer, 372
Vortices, 185

W, X, Y

Washers, 122

Z

Zeppelin, 359, 360
    buoyancy/hovering, 364
    description, 363
    electronics, 365, 366
    flight control logic, 369
    programming, 366

GPSR Compliance
The European Union's (EU) General Product Safety Regulation (GPSR) is a set of rules that requires consumer products to be safe and our obligations to ensure this.

If you have any concerns about our products, you can contact us on

ProductSafety@springernature.com

In case Publisher is established outside the EU, the EU authorized representative is:

Springer Nature Customer Service Center GmbH
Europaplatz 3
69115 Heidelberg, Germany

www.ingramcontent.com/pod-product-compliance
Lightning Source LLC
LaVergne TN
LVHW021955060526
838201LV00048B/1577